2 Corinthians
Discipleship Lessons

and Bible Study Commentary for Personal Devotional Use, Small Groups or
Sunday School Classes, and Sermon Preparation for Pastors and Teachers

JesusWalk® Bible Study Series

by Dr. Ralph F. Wilson
Director, Joyful Heart Renewal Ministries

Additional books and reprint licenses are available at:
http://www.jesuswalk.com/books/2corinthians.htm

Free Participant Guide handout sheets are available at:
http://www.jesuswalk.com/2corinthians/2corinthians-lesson-handouts.pdf

JesusWalk® Publications
Loomis, California

Paperback
ISBN-13: 978-0-9832310-6-6
ISBN-10: 0983231060

Library of Congress Control Number: 2011914642

Library of Congress subject headings:
    Bible. N.T. Corinthians, 2nd - Commentaries.

Suggested Classifications
    Library of Congress: BS2675.3
    Dewey Decimal System: 227.3

Published by JesusWalk® Publications, P.O. Box 565, Loomis, CA 95650-0565, USA.

JesusWalk is a registered trademark and Joyful Heart is a trademark of Joyful Heart Renewal Ministries.

Unless otherwise noted, all the Bible verses quoted are from the New International Version (International Bible Society, 1973, 1978), used by permission.

110817

Preface

Paul was under overwhelming stress when he wrote 2 Corinthians about 56 AD from Macedonia.

> "We were under great pressure, far beyond our ability to endure, so that we despaired even of life.... But this happened that we might not rely on ourselves but on God, who raises the dead." (1:8-9)

He was writing to a church where his reputation had been trashed by his opponents, but that desperately needed the balance and correction that only he could give. The letter contains many nuggets of spiritual insight, such as:

- The anointing and sealing of the Spirit (1:21-22)
- Living letters written on human hearts (3:2-3)
- Unveiled faces beholding the Lord's glory (3:18)
- A treasure in jars of clay (4:7)
- Away from the body but at home with the Lord (5:6-8)
- The new creation, behold the new has come (5:16-17)
- A ministry of reconciliation, ambassadors for Christ (5:18-20)
- Christ was made to be sin for us (5:21)
- Perfecting holiness in the fear of the Lord (6:14-7:2)

Circle of Dutch painter and engraver Lucas van Leyden, "Saint Paul" (c. 1525), oil on panel, 44 x 21 cm, Museo Thyssen-Bornemisza, Madrid. The painter was also known as Lucas Hugensz or Lucas Jacobsz.

- Sowing generously, reaping generously, and the cheerful giver (9:6-7)
- Rejoicing in weakness despite a thorn in the flesh (12:7-10)

The letter is also the most intimate of Paul's epistles. In his struggle with the church at Corinth he bares his soul, and talks about how God has given him strength in spite of the horrific record of physical abuse, repeated hardship, and crushing pressure for being an apostle who moved the Kingdom forward in faith. As you read, you begin to ask:

How can Paul do this? What makes this apostle tick? What can I learn from him? And as you immerse yourself in 2 Corinthians, you'll begin to understand.

I know that over the past six months that I've been drilling down into this letter, it has brought me both insight and courage to go on when I felt worn out from the struggle. I dedicate this book to my Tuesday morning men's discipleship breakfast group at Denny's – Steve Dunlap, Steve Winther, Paul Johnson, and John Graham – who plumbed the depths of 2 Corinthians together with me. My prayer is that it will bless you as much as it has blessed me.

Yours in Christ Jesus,
Dr. Ralph F. Wilson
Loomis, California
August 15, 2011

Table of Contents

Preface   3

Table of Contents   5

Reprint Guidelines   10

References and Abbreviations   11

Introduction to 2 Corinthians   13
The City of Corinth   13
Tentative Chronology of Paul and the Corinthians (50-56 AD)   14
Literary Problems   16
Paul's Opponents in Corinth   16
Situation   17

1. The God of All Comfort (1:1-11)   18
Salutation (1:1-2)   19
The God of All Comfort (1:3-4)   19
Comfort as We Share Christ's Sufferings (1:5-7)   20
A Crushing, Hopeless Burden (1:8-10)   22
Relying on God's Deliverance (1:9-10)   23
Intercessory Prayer (1:10b-11)   24

2. Tension with the Corinthians (1:12-2:11)   27
A Legacy of Godliness and Sincerity (1:12-14)   27
Paul's Planned Visit to Corinth (1:15-18)   28
The Firm Promises of God (1:18-20)   29
Anointing, Seal, and Spirit (1:21b-22)   29
Sparing Them Another Painful Visit (1:23-2:2)   31
Paul Wrote the 'Severe' Letter Rather than Visiting (2:3-4)   32
Restoring the Disciplined Brother (2:5-9)   32
Obedience to Apostolic Authority (2:9)   33
Forgive So that Satan Doesn't Take Advantage of You (2:10-11)   35

3. The Fragrance of Christ's Ministering People   (2:12-3:6)   37
An Open Door and Peace in One's Spirit (2:12-13)   37
Marching in the Triumphal Procession (2:14)   38
The Fragrance of Knowing God (2:14-16)   38

Who Is Sufficient for This Ministry (2:16b)   40
Peddlers or Sincere Advocates (2:17)   40
Letters Written on the Heart (3:1-3)   41
Living Letters   42
Competent Servants of a New Covenant (3:4-6)   42
How Seminaries and Ordination Relate to Competency   43
The Vital Role of the Holy Spirit (3:6)   45
Ministers of a New Covenant (3:6a)   45

4. Being Changed by God's Glory (3:7-18)   **48**
The Greater Glory of the Spirit (3:7-11)   49
The Glory of God on Moses' Face (Exodus 34)   49
Boldness in Our Hope of Glory (3:12)   50
The Veil of the Old Covenant (3:13-15)   50
Spiritual Freedom from the Holy Spirit (3:16-17)   51
Beholding the Glory of God (3:18)   52
Being Changed into Christ's Likeness (3:18)   54

5. Treasures in Clay Pots (4:1-18)   **57**
Ministry by God's Mercy (4:1)   57
A Plain and Open Ministry (4:2)   57
Satan Has Blinded Unbelievers (4:3-4)   59
Christ, the Glory of God (4:5-6)   62
Treasure in Clay Jars (4:7)   62
Pressures on Every Side (4:8-9)   63
Death in Us, Life in You (4:10-12)   66
Faith in the Resurrection (4:13-14)   67
Outer Deterioration, Inner Renewal (4:15-16)   67
Focusing on Eternal Glory (4:17-18)   68
Fix Your Eyes on the Eternal (4:18)   69

6. Walking by Faith, Not by Sight (5:1-16)   **71**
Earthly Tent vs. Heavenly House (5:1)   71
Groaning and Longing (5:2-4)   73
Swallowed Up by Life (5:4b)   74
Made for Life, Guaranteed by the Spirit (5:5)   74
Longing for Home (5:6-8)   75
The Problem with the Doctrine of 'Soul Sleep'   76
Walk by Faith, Not by Sight (5:7)   77
Aiming to Please the Lord (5:9)   78
The Judgment Seat of Christ (5:10)   79

Persuading Men (5:11a)   80
Open before You and God (5:11b-12)   81
Out of Our Mind? (5:13)   81
Christ's Love Compels Us (5:13-15)   81

7. A Ministry of Reconciliation (5:17-6:2)   84
A New Creation in Christ (5:16-17)   84
Reconciliation (5:18-19)   86
Ambassadors of Reconciliation (5:18-20)   87
Substitutionary Atonement (5:21)   89
Today Is the Day of Salvation (6:1-2)   90

8. Hardships, Holiness, and Joy (6:3-7:16)   93
A No-Stumbling-Blocks Policy (6:3)   93
Commended by Hardships (6:4-5)   94
Commended by a Godly Character and Spiritual Ministry (6:6-7)   95
Commended through Paradoxical Ministry (6:8-10)   96
Open Wide Your Hearts (6:11-13)   98
Don't Yoke Yourselves to Unbelievers (6:14-16)   98
You Are the Temple of God (6:16a)   100
Old Testament Promises (6:16b-18)   100
Let Us Purify Ourselves (7:1a)   101
Perfecting Holiness (7:1b)   101
What Kind of Separation Is Required?   102
A Plea for Open Hearts (7:2)   104
Paul Is Encouraged by the Corinthians (7:3-4)   105
Fightings Without and Fears Within (7:5)   105
The Comfort of Titus' Coming (7:6-7)   106
Sorrow that Leads to Repentance (7:8-10)   106
Eagerness to Clear their Name (7:11-13a)   107
Titus' Good Report (7:13b-16)   107

9. Generosity Modeled and Encouraged (8:1-9:5)   110
The Generosity of the Macedonian Churches (8:1-5)   111
The Grace of Giving   113
Match the Macedonians' Generosity (8:6-8)   114
Christ's Generosity in Poverty Made Us Rich (8:9)   115
Jesus Was Poor Here on Earth   115
Christ Humbled Himself   116
Complete the Giving You Began (8:10-11)   117
Give According to Your Blessing (8:12-15)   117

Does the Bible Advocate Socialism or Communism?   118
Gathering Just the Amount Needed (8:14-15)   118
Representatives Who Will Carry the Offering to Jerusalem (8:16-19) 119
We Are Transparent in Financial Matters (8:20-21)   119
Show Honor to Representatives from the Churches (8:22-24)   120
Boasting to the Macedonians (9:1-4)   121
Time to Complete Your Generous Gift (9:5)   121

10. Sowing Generously (9:6-15)   **123**
The Law of Sowing and Reaping (9:6)   123
A Proverb of Generosity (Proverbs 11:24-25)   124
Principles of Blessing and Tithing (Malachi 3:10-12)   124
The Result of Failing to Put God First in Giving (Haggai 1:2-11) 125
Jesus' Teaching on Giving and Blessing (Luke 6:37-38)   126
Freedom and Joy in Giving (9:7)   126
God Can Cause You to Abound (9:8)   128
The Righteous Man   129
God's Supply, Increase, and Enlargement (9:10-11)   130
Your Giving Will Prompt Praise (9:12-15)   131

11. Paul's Defense of His Ministry (10-11)   **134**
A Change in Tone   134
Paul's Boldness (10:1-2)   134
Spiritual Warfare (10:3-6)   135
Paul's Apostolic Authority (10:7-8)   138
Forceful by Letter and in Person (10:9-12)   138
Paul's Field of Ministry (10:13-15a)   138
Led Astray from Pure Devotion to Christ (11:1-3)   139
Gullible and Easily Deceived (11:4-5)   140
Was Paul an Untrained Speaker? (11:6)   141
Paul's Refusal to Ask for Support (11:7-9)   142
Full-time Christian Ministry vs. Bi-Vocational Ministry   143
Undermining the Claims of False Apostles (11:10-14)   144
Foolish Boasting (11:16-21)   145
Paul's Jewish Heritage (11:22)   146
Paul's Sufferings (11:23-25)   146
Dangers from Travel (11:26)   147
Depravation and Stress (11:27-28)   147
Boasting in Weakness (11:29-30)   148
Paul's Escape from Damascus (11:31-33)   149

12. Paul's Vision, Thorn, and Final Words (12-13) — 150
Visions and Revelations in the New Testament (12:1) — 150
Boasting of Visions and Revelations (12:2-4) — 151
Boasting of the Truth (12:5-6) — 152
Paul's Thorn in the Flesh (12:7) — 152
Was the Thorn a Sickness? — 153
Is Sickness from Satan? — 154
My Power Is Made Perfect in Weakness (12:8-9a) — 155
God's Power in Us — 156
When I Weak, then I Am Strong (12:9b-10) — 157
The Signs of an Apostle (12:11-12) — 158
Expending His Resources for the Corinthians (12:13-15) — 160
Concern for the Corinthians' Sin and Disorder (12:20-21) — 160
The Pain of Correction (12:21a) — 163
Paul's Promise to Set Things in Order (13:1-3a) — 163
Weakness and Strength (13:3b-14) — 164
See If You Will Stand the Test (13:5-8) — 165
Authority for Building You Up (13:9-10) — 165
Concluding Words (13:11-13) — 166
Trinitarian Benediction (13:14) — 167

Appendix 1: Handouts for Group Participants — 170
Introduction to 2 Corinthians — 171
1. The God of All Comfort (1:1-11) — 173
2. Tension with the Corinthians (1:12-2:11) — 174
3. The Fragrance of Christ's Ministering People (2:12-3:6) — 176
4. Being Changed by God's Glory (3:7-18) — 178
5. Treasures in Clay Pots (4:1-18) — 179
6. Walking by Faith, Not by Sight (5:1-16) — 181
7. A Ministry of Reconciliation (5:17-6:2) — 182
8. Hardships, Holiness, and Joy (6:3-7:16) — 184
9. Generosity Modeled and Encouraged (8:1-9:5) — 186
10. Sowing Generously (9:6-15) — 187
11. Paul's Defense of His Ministry (10-11) — 189
12. Paul's Vision, Thorn, and Final Words (12-13) — 190

Appendix 2. A Brief Critique of the Prosperity Message — 192
1. Poverty — 192
2. Greed — 194
3. Pride — 195

Reprint Guidelines

Copying the Handouts. In some cases, small groups or Sunday school classes would like to use these notes to study this material. That's great. An appendix provides copies of handouts designed for classes and small groups. There is no charge whatsoever to print out as many copies of the handouts as you need for participants.

http://www.jesuswalk.com/2corinthians/2corinthians-lesson-handouts.pdf

All charts and notes are copyrighted and must bear the line:

"Copyright © 2011, Ralph F. Wilson. All rights reserved. Reprinted by permission."

You may not resell these notes to other groups or individuals outside your congregation. You may, however, charge people in your group enough to cover your copying costs.

Copying the book (or the majority of it) in your congregation or group, you are requested to purchase a reprint license for each book. A Reprint License, $2.50 for each copy is available for purchase at

www.jesuswalk.com/books/2corinthians.htm

Or you may send a check to:

Dr. Ralph F. Wilson
JesusWalk Publications
PO Box 565
Loomis, CA 95650, USA

The Scripture says,

"The laborer is worthy of his hire" (Luke 10:7) and "Anyone who receives instruction in the word must share all good things with his instructor." (Galatians 6:6)

However, if you are from a third world country or an area where it is difficult to transmit money, please make a small contribution instead to help the poor in your community.

References and Abbreviations

BDAG *A Greek-English Lexicon of the New Testament and Other Early Christian Literature*, by Walter Bauer and Frederick William Danker, (Third Edition; based on previous English editions by W.F. Arndt, F.W. Gingrich, and F.W. Danker; University of Chicago Press, 1957, 1979, 2000)

Barnett Paul Barnett, *The Second Epistle to the Corinthians* (New International Commentary on the New Testament, Eerdmans, 1997)

Barrett C.K. Barrett, *The Second Epistle to the Corinthians* (Harper New Testament Commentaries; Harper & Row, 1973)

Bruce F.F. Bruce, *1 and 2 Corinthians* (The New Century Bible Commentary; Eerdmans, 1971)

DPL Gerald F. Hawthorne, Ralph P. Martin, and Daniel Reid (editors), *Dictionary of Paul and His Letters* (InterVarsity Press, 1993)

ISBE *The International Standard Bible Encyclopedia*, Geoffrey W. Bromiley (general editor), (Eerdmans, 1979-1988; fully revised from the 1915 edition)

Kruse Colin Kruse, *2 Corinthians* (Tyndale New Testament Commentaries, 1987)

Liddell-Scott Henry George Liddell. Robert Scott, *A Greek-English Lexicon* (revised and augmented throughout by Sir Henry Stuart Jones with the assistance of. Roderick McKenzie; Oxford, Clarendon Press, 1940, Perseus Project online edition)

NIDNTT *New International Dictionary of New Testament Theology*, Colin Brown (editor; Zondervan, 1975-1978; translated with additions and revisions from Theologisches Begriffslexikon zum Neuen Testament, Coenen, Beyreuther, and Bitenhard, editors)

Robertson Archibald Thomas Robertson, *Word Pictures in the New Testament* (Sunday School Board of the Southern Baptist Convention, 1932, 1960)

Tasker R.V.G. Tasker, *2 Corinthians: An Introduction and Commentary* (Tyndale New Testament Commentaries; London: Tyndale Press, 1958)

TDNT   *Theological Dictionary of the New Testament*, Gerhard Kittel and Gerhard Friedrich (editors), Geoffrey W. Bromiley (translator and editor), (Eerdmans, 1964-1976; translated from *Theologisches Wörterbuch zum Neuen Testament*, ten volume edition). CD-ROM

Introduction to 2 Corinthians

The City of Corinth

The ancient city of Corinth showed signs of human habitation as far back as the Early Neolithic period. Its location was ideal, with an abundant water supply, only 1.5 miles south of the Isthmus of Corinth, a narrow land bridge (only 3.9 miles or 6.3 kilometers wide), which connects the Peloponnesian peninsula to the Greek mainland. Thus Corinth became prosperous from trade – both the trade moving by sea from east and west, but also north and south between Greece and the Peloponnesus. The port of Cenchreae

connected the city to the Aegean Sea to the east, while the port of Lechaeum was on the Ionian Sea. In 1893, a canal was cut across the isthmus to accommodate shipping, but in the days of the early church, there was no such luxury.

Temple of Apollo and ruins in Corinth.
Source: BiblePlaces.com

Ruins of the Temple of Apollo, dating to the sixth century BC, can still be seen. Shops and monuments lining the Agora, larger than the Forum in Rome, also persist. The Temple of Asclepius, the god of healing, was built on the north edge of the city. To the south, the Acro-Corinthian fortress at the height of 1,886 feet could control all the trade routes.

At its peak stood the Temple of Aphrodite, goddess of love and beauty, where 1,000 female prostitutes served, contributing to the city's reputation for immorality. In fact, the coined Greek word "to Corinthianize" meant to practice immorality and the phrase "Corinthian girl" designated a prostitute.

The Romans conquered and destroyed Corinth in 146 BC. In 46 BC, Julius Caesar re-founded it as a Roman colony. In 27 AD, it became the seat of government for the Roman province of Achaia.[1] As a Roman colony, its citizens were primarily Romans, perhaps freedmen from Italy, but its population also included Greeks and a considerable

---

[1] Donald H. Madvig, "Corinth," ISBE 1:772-774.

Jewish community. As a chief trade center, it would become a strategic base of operations for Paul, since he would meet and minister to many people travelling through, causing the gospel to spread even farther.

Tentative Chronology of Paul and the Corinthians (50-56 AD)

Below, I've tried to outline in order what we can piece together of Paul's contacts with the Corinthian church.

1. **First Visit** (50-52 AD). Paul first visited Corinth about 50 AD, during the last phase of his second missionary journey, after starting churches in Macedonia – Philippi, Thessalonica, and Berea (Acts 16-17). He came to Corinth after visiting Athens and stayed with a couple of Jewish tentmakers, Aquila and Priscilla, who had recently been forced to leave Rome due to an edict by Emperor Claudius (about 49 AD; Acts 18:2-3). Paul was joined in Corinth by Silas and Timothy. Under their ministry the church grew. Paul seems to have been in danger during this time, because the Lord spoke to him in a night vision:

   "Do not be afraid, but speak and do not be silent; for I am with you, and no one will lay a hand on you to harm you, for there are many in this city who are my people" (Acts 18:9-10).

   When the Jews appealed to the Roman proconsul Gallio (in office 51 to 52 AD) to force Paul to leave, they were rebuffed (Acts 18:12-17). Paul left Corinth probably in the spring of 52 AD, giving him two years in Corinth. After leaving Corinth, Paul stops at Ephesus and then returns to Antioch, and from there he goes to Jerusalem (Acts 20:18-22).

2. **"Previous Letter" from Paul** is no longer extant. Paul, who is now in Ephesus (52 to 55 AD), writes to Corinth rebuking vice and fornication by church members (mentioned in 1 Corinthians 5:9-11). This letter is referred to by scholars as Corinthians A.

3. **Report to Paul:** Chloe's people report to Paul about the party spirit and quarrels at Corinth.

4. **Letter to Paul:** Stephanas, Fortunatas, and Achaicus probably bring Paul the letter that reports on problems at Corinth with marriage, divorce, food sacrificed to idols, spiritual gifts, and the collection he was organizing for the Jerusalem believers (1 Corinthians 16:17).

5. **Timothy is dispatched** to Corinth to deal with some of the problems (1 Corinthians 4:17; 16:10-11).

6. **1 Corinthians Letter**: In the Spring of 55 AD, Paul writes during his final year at Ephesus the letter we know as 1 Corinthians concerning problems reported to him. Perhaps this letter was carried to Corinth by Stephanas. This is sometimes called Corinthians B. At this point Paul is planning a soon visit to Macedonia with a stop in Corinth. (1 Corinthians 4:18-21).

7. **Second visit, the "painful visit,"** is a quick trip to deal with troubles in Corinth that were serious enough to require direct personal confrontation (2:1; 13:2). During this visit Paul was personally attacked by one of the members (2:5; 7:12). This visit was difficult for both Paul and his converts in Corinth.

8. **"Tearful letter" or "severe letter"** from Paul (2:3-4), no longer extant, is written from Ephesus, probably carried by Titus in lieu of Paul going himself. In it, Paul apparently professed his love for the Corinthians and required them to discipline the man who had led in defying his apostolic authority on his second visit. This is sometimes referred to as Corinthians C. Apparently, this letter was quite effective in producing repentance (7:8-12).

9. **Proposed visits** don't come to pass (1 Corinthians 16:1-8) due to intervening circumstances, such as severe danger in Asia and Paul's depression (1:8-10), as well as Paul's desire not to make another "painful visit" (2:1).

10. **Paul travels to Troas and Macedonia** amidst various afflictions, but meets Titus there and is encouraged by his good report about the Corinthian church (7:5-7).

11. **"Super-Apostles" challenge Paul's authority**, apparently Jewish Christians from Judea, perhaps seeking to impose the authority of the mother church over the Gentile churches. The "superlative apostles" (11:5; 12:11) seemed to bring another take on the gospel. Some believe that possibly Paul sent another letter (called Corinthians E, consisting of chapters 10-13) to counter these "super-apostles," but this is just speculation (see below under "Literary Problems").[2]

12. **2 Corinthians Letter:** Paul sends our 2 Corinthians letter from Macedonia about 56 AD, sometimes called Corinthians D (at least chapters 1-9).

13. **Third Visit to Corinth** occurs about 57 AD, when Paul gathers with those who are preparing to send the gift collected to relieve the Jerusalem saints (Acts 19:21-22). Apparently, matters have been resolved to some extent, since

---

[2] This section draws heavily on Bruce, *1 and 2 Corinthians*, pp. 23-25, 164-166; and F.F. Bruce, *Paul: Apostle of the Heart Set Free* (Eerdmans, 1977), chapter 24, pp. 264-279.

from Corinth Paul wrote to the Roman church:

> "Macedonia and Achaia have been pleased to share their resources with the poor among the saints at Jerusalem" (Romans 15:26).

> Paul stays in Corinth three months, then escapes to Macedonia to avoid a Jewish plot, meets his companions in Troas (Acts 20:1-5), and leaves for Jerusalem where he is arrested.[3]

We don't hear anything more about the Corinthian church after this until about 95 AD when Clement of Rome writes *1 Clement* to address the disharmony at Corinth.

To summarize, Paul's letters to the Corinthian church seem to have been written during Paul's three-year ministry in Ephesus. First Corinthians was probably written from Ephesus about 55 AD. Second Corinthians was probably written from Macedonia in 56 AD, but the date is "complicated." Let me explain.

Literary Problems

The date isn't clear because of a problem understanding the seeming discontinuity between chapters 1-9 and chapters 10-13. Why does the mood change so abruptly to Paul's defense of his apostolic authority and denunciation of those who came to Corinth and tried to replace his authority among the converts? There have been several explanations:

1. **Prior letter**. Chapters 10-13 preserve part of the "tearful letter" that Paul refers to in 2:3-4. In other words, some hold that chapters 10-13 (Corinthians C) was written *prior* to chapters 1-9 (Corinthians B). However, Bruce sees the reference to Titus visiting Corinth in 12:18 as the conclusive argument against dating chapters 10-13 before chapters 1-9.[4]
2. **Later letter**. Chapters 10-13 belong to a later letter (Corinthians E).[5]
3. **Same letter**. Chapters 10-13 are part of the same letter as 1-9, but were written after receiving some fresh news from Corinth. (This makes the most sense to me.)

Paul's Opponents in Corinth

Who are the visitors to Corinth who try to undermine Paul's authority there? Some

---

[3] Bruce, *Paul*, pp. 339-340.
[4] Bruce, *1 and 2 Corinthians*, pp. 168-169.
[5] Seeing chapters 10-13 as preserving a later correspondence (Corinthians E) is how Bruce tentatively resolves the issue (p. 169-170).

have supposed them to be "Gnostics of ecstatic temperament and libertine ethics." Others see them as Judaizers. But most likely they are Palestinian Jews, not Judaizers in the Galatian sense, but perhaps men who tried to impose the authority of the mother church over the Christian world.[6] We'll discuss this further when we come to it in the text.

Situation

To summarize the situation, Paul is writing to a six-year-old church that he founded in 50-51 AD. Since he moved on, the church has encountered problems, particularly some Jewish Christian leaders who have worked to undermine Paul's influence so they could substitute their own. So in 2 Corinthians, Paul writes about 56 AD to restore his relationship with the church and regain his influence, so he can help them with the problems they are having with holiness and hardship, generosity and church order, and their testimony to the non-Christians around them.

---

[6] Bruce, p. 174.

1. The God of All Comfort (1:1-11)

Starting a new congregation in America is difficult, with only a modest chance of long-term success. But planting a church in a pagan city, known for its immorality and swirl of cults and religions was especially challenging. And the Church at Corinth, now about six years old, was in the midst of struggles.

Paul had founded the church about 50 AD on his second missionary journey. It had been a struggle from the beginning. But in the midst of threats to his life, the Lord had encouraged him in a vision:

> "Do not be afraid, but speak and do not be silent; for I am with you, and no one will lay a hand on you to harm you, for there are many in this city who are my people." (Acts 18:9-10)

All in all, Paul had remained in Corinth for two years, leaving in 52 AD. But in his absence, the church had

Saint Paul writing. From an early 9th century manuscript version of Saint Paul's letters now in Stuttgart, ascribed to the Monastery of St. Gall, Switzerland, scribe Wolfcoz.

experienced rampant immorality and deep divisions. Paul's reputation as a faithful apostle had been trashed by enemies trying to destroy his authority so they could garner power for themselves.

As mentioned in the Introduction, Paul, engaged in ministry in Ephesus, had written a letter and then dispatched Timothy to deal with the church's problems. In 55 AD, he wrote a longer letter that we know as 1 Corinthians, followed by a short, painful visit when he had tried to put things in order, only to have his authority challenged by one of the members. It was followed by a severe letter. Two planned visits were cancelled, as Paul could see that the timing was wrong.

In the meantime, Paul has been going through one of the most difficult periods of his life, trying to deal with physical threats, a severe depression, as well as his deep concern for the troubled Corinthian Church.

It is now 56 AD, and Paul is with Timothy in Mesopotamia, having just received encouraging news about the church in Corinth from his co-worker Titus. He now sits down to write yet another letter, seeking to repair this rift between the founding apostle and this rancorous church that has broken his heart.

Salutation (1:1-2)

Greek letters in Paul's time began with a kind of formula: first the name of the sender, then the name of the recipient, and finally a greeting.

> "¹ Paul, an apostle of Christ Jesus by the will of God, and Timothy our brother, To the church of God in Corinth, together with all the saints throughout Achaia: ² Grace and peace to you from God our Father and the Lord Jesus Christ." (1:1-2)

In his first sentence he asserts that his apostolic authority comes directly from God himself. Then he addresses the "church of God in Corinth." Though it no doubt met in numerous house churches rather than in a single building, Paul addresses it as a single church. Then he extends his address to the other believers throughout Achaia (that is, Greece), calling them "saints," that is, people who are dedicated or consecrated to God.[1]

He greets them with "grace and peace" from the Father and the Son. "Grace" was the typical greeting in the Greek-speaking world; "peace" (*shalom*) was the customary greeting among Jews. Paul combines them.

The God of All Comfort (1:3-4)

We usually get conversations started with small talk, and this was the pattern with Greek epistles also. They would typically begin with best wishes for the recipients' health or praise for an answer to prayer. To begin this letter, Paul offers praise to God who comforts them. Both the church and Paul had gone through severe trials since they had seen each other. So Paul begins by praising God on this common ground of comfort.

> "³ Praise be to the God and Father of our Lord Jesus Christ, the Father of compassion and the God of all comfort, ⁴ who comforts us in all our troubles, so that we can comfort those in any trouble with the comfort we ourselves have received from God." (1:3-4)

It's amazing how a traumatic experience can get us in touch with our emotions and produce deep thankfulness in us! Paul speaks of God's compassion and comfort because

---

[1] "Saints" is *hagios*, originally an adjective, "pertaining to being dedicated or consecrated to the service of God," but here used as a noun, "believers, loyal followers, saints," of Christians, as "consecrated to God" (BDAG 11, 2dβ).

he has just been through horrendous difficulties and found God faithful.

"Father of compassion" (NIV), "Father of mercies" (NRSV, KJV), couples the word "Father" with *oiktirmos*, "display of concern over another's misfortune, pity, mercy, compassion."[2] God is not some distant deity out of touch with his creatures. Rather, he feels their pain and is full of mercy towards them. Jesus was our prime example of compassionate love in action as he reflected the character of "the Father of compassion."

"God of all comfort" uses the noun *paraklēsis*, literally, "the calling alongside." It can refer to exhortation as well as strong appeal. But here it means, "lifting of another's spirits, comfort, consolation."[3] Notice that this word is modified by the extremely common adjective *pas*, "all." He is the God of every kind of comfort imaginable![4] He is the one who comes alongside through his Spirit to encourage and console us in every struggle we go through.[5] He is there for us!

If you haven't experienced God's comfort, then you will have little to say to someone crushed by life's difficulties. But if you have gone through hard times with God's help, you can point people to his faithfulness. You become an evangelist for what God can do.

"It is no secret what God can do!
What he's done for others, he can do for you...."[6]

Dear friend, is there any redeeming value in the struggles and losses you've experienced in your life? Yes! They enable you to experience the Father of compassion and God of all grace and to share him with those around you who are suffering:

"... Who comforts us in all our troubles, so that we can comfort those in any trouble with the comfort we ourselves have received from God." (1:4)

Comfort as We Share Christ's Sufferings (1:5-7)

"For just as the sufferings[7] of Christ flow over[8] into our lives, so also through Christ our

---

[2] *Oiktirmos*, BDAG 700.

[3] *Paraklēsis*, BDAG 766, 3.

[4] Depending on the context, *pas* can refer to: (1) Pertaining to totality with focus on its individual components, "each, every, any," (2) any entity out of a totality, "any and every, every," (3) a marker of the highest degree of something, "all," (4) pertaining to a high degree of completeness or wholeness, "whole," and (5) everything belonging, in kind, to the class designated by the noun, "every kind of, all sorts of" (BDAG 784).

[5] "Troubles" (NIV), "affliction" (NRSV), "tribulation" (KJV) is *thlipsis*, literally, "pressing, pressure," used twice in verse 4 as well as in verse 8. Here is refers to "trouble that inflicts distress, oppression, affliction, tribulation" (BDAG 457, 1).

[6] Stuart Hamblen, "It Is No Secret" (© 1950, Duchess Music Corp).

[7] "Sufferings" is *pathēma*, from which we get our English word "pathos." It means "that which is suffered or endured, suffering, misfortune," in the New Testament almost always in plural: "sufferings" (BDAG 747,

comfort overflows." (1:5)

Notice how Paul links our sufferings with the "sufferings of Christ." Often, we suffer the same heartache and trouble that is common to all humankind. But sometimes, we suffer for our stand for Christ and our commitment to a lifestyle congruent with his.

As we'll see later in this letter, Paul is aware that his sufferings – and his response to them – serve as a blessing to others.

"So then, death is at work in us, but life is at work in you." (4:12)

He is saying something similar here: that the common experience of suffering and God's comfort unites God's people.

"[6] If we are distressed,[9] it is for your comfort and salvation; if we are comforted, it is for your comfort, which produces in you patient endurance[10] of the same sufferings we suffer. [7] And our hope for you is firm, because we know that just as you share in our sufferings, so also you share in our comfort." (1:6-7)

As hard as life is, the Christian can lay hold on the resources of God himself. Think of the struggles and pain of your non-Christian friends who face life without God and his ultimate hope. Friends, we have a comfort and hope worth passing on.

Look again at verse 7:

"We know that just as you share in our sufferings, so also you share in our comfort." (1:7)

"Share" (NIV, NRSV), "are partakers" (KJV) is koinōnos, "one who takes part in something with someone, companion, partner, sharer in something."[11]   Even though people may be hundreds or thousands of miles away from us, there is a spiritual sense in which we are one with them and can feel both their pain and their comfort.

---

1). The related verb (verse 6b) is paschō, "suffer, endure," from which we get our word "Paschal," as in "Paschal Lamb."

[8] "Flow over" (NIV) "are abundant" (NRSV), "abound" (KJV) is perisseuō, "be in abundance, abound," with the connotation of "to be more than enough, be left over," hence the NIV translation of "overflow," or "be present in abundance" (BDAG 805, 1aα,β).

[9] "Distressed" (NIV), "be/being afflicted" (NRSV, KJV) in verse 6 is the related verb, thlibō, here in the passive sense, "be afflicted, distressed" (BDAG 457, 3).

[10] "Patience endurance" (NIV), "patiently endure" (NRSV), "enduring" (KJV) is hypomonē, "the capacity to hold out or bear up in the face of difficulty, patience, endurance, fortitude, steadfastness, perseverance" (BDAG 1039, 1).

[11] Koinōnos, BDAG 553, 1bα.

Q1. (2 Corinthians 1:3-7) What kind of comfort do you receive from your faith in God? From your personal daily relationship with God? How might you share the blessing of this kind of comfort with a friend or relative who is currently suffering? What words of comfort can you bring to others?

http://www.joyfulheart.com/forums/index.php?showtopic=1071

A Crushing, Hopeless Burden (1:8-10)

Now Paul begins to share with this church he loves some of his own pain. Since the goal of this letter is to effect a reconciliation with the Corinthian church and reestablish his authority as founder and apostle, his strategy is to open up to them personally and with transparency so they can begin to understand what he's been going through. Indeed, 2 Corinthians is by far the most revealing of any of Paul's letters about the depth of his suffering for the gospel.

> "We do not want you to be uninformed, brothers, about the **hardships**[12] we suffered in the province of Asia. We were under **great pressure**, far beyond our **ability to endure**, so that we **despaired** even of life." (1:8)

The phrase, "we were **under ... pressure**" (NIV), "we were ... **crushed**" (NRSV), "we were pressed" (KJV) employs the verb *bareō*, "to press down as if with a weight, weigh down, burden," so the clause would read, "we were burdened altogether beyond our strength."[13] But the extent of this pressure is accentuated by two prepositional phrases:

1. **Beyond measure.** The noun *hyperbolē* (from which we get the English word "hyperbole") describes a "state of exceeding to an extraordinary degree a point on a scale of extent." With the preposition *kata*, it carries the meaning, "to an extraordinary degree, beyond measure, utterly."[14]

2. **Beyond our power.** The noun is *dynamis* (from which we get our word "dynamic"), "power." It is preceded by the preposition *hyper*, here connoting "over and above, beyond, more than," in the sense of excelling, surpassing.[15]

"Despair" is *exaporeō*, "to be at a loss psychologically, be in great difficulty, doubt, embarrassment," used here and at 4:8.[16]

---

[12] "Hardships" (NIV), "affliction" (NRSV), "trouble" (KJV) in verse 8 is *thlipsis*, which we saw in verse 4 above.

[13] *Bareō*, BDAG 166, b.

[14] *Hyperbolē*, BDAG 1032).

[15] *Hyper*, BDAG 1030, B).

[16] *Exaporeō*, BDAG 345. This is a compound verb from *aporeō*, "to be in a confused state of mind," the extent

This sentence in Greek powerfully expresses Paul's desperate situation. Here is how some translations render it:

> "We were under great pressure, far beyond our ability to endure, so that we despaired even of life." (NIV)

> "We were so utterly, unbearably crushed that we despaired of life itself." (NRSV)

> "We were pressed out of measure, above strength, insomuch that we despaired even of life." (KJV)

> "It was so bad we didn't think we were going to make it." (The Message)[17]

> "The burdens laid on us were so great and so heavy, that we gave up all hope of living" (TEV)[18]

> "At that time we were completely overwhelmed; the burden was more than we could bear; in fact, we told ourselves that this was the end." (Phillips)[19]

We're not told the exact situations that Paul was facing. But twice more in this letter he alludes to the types of sufferings he has experienced (4:8; 11:23-29).

Relying on God's Deliverance (1:9-10)

His most recent situation involved the threat of death.

> "[9] Indeed, in our hearts we felt the sentence of death. But this happened that we might not rely on ourselves but on God, who raises the dead. [10] He has delivered us from such a deadly peril, and he will deliver us. On him we have set our hope that he will continue to deliver us." (1:9-10)

It could have been a fatal illness, perhaps. But it seems more likely to be some kind of external threat.

"Sentence" in verse 9 is *apokrima*, "official report, decision,"[20] but in this case the "sentence of death" seems to be Paul's own assessment.[21] He thought he was a "gonner." He calls it a "deadly peril," literally "so great a death,"[22] that he believes God rescued him from certain death.[23] Was Paul afraid of death? I don't think so, since later

---

of which is heightened by the appended preposition *ek-*, which carries the idea here of "utterly, entirely" (Thayer 192, *ek*, VI-6).

[17] Eugene H. Peterson (translator), *The Message: The Bible in Contemporary Language* (NavPress, 2002).

[18] *Today's English Version* (Third edition; American Bible Society, 1966, 1971).

[19] J. B. Phillips, *The New Testament in Modern English* (Macmillan, 1947, 1958).

[20] *Apokrima*, BDAG 113. "An official resolution that decides a matter" (Friedrich Büchsel, *krinō, ktl.,* TDNT 3:933-954).

[21] Paul describes the judgment as literally "in ourselves" (KJV), rather than from some magistrate or court.

[22] "Deadly peril" (NIV, NRSV), "death" (KJV) is *thanatos*, "death," here, "danger of death" (BDAG 443, 1c).

[23] "Delivered" (NIV) is *rhyomai*, "to rescue from danger, save, rescue, deliver, preserve someone" (BDAG

in this letter he talks about his desire to be "at home with the Lord" (5:8). But when we are threatened with bodily harm, especially a threat that continues for a period of time, it takes its toll on our emotional and physical well-being. Though we are believers in Jesus, we are still human. We are not immune to stress. Jesus wasn't immune to stress either (Luke 22:44).

This traumatic experience had a profound effect on Paul:

> "This happened that we might not **rely on**[24] ourselves but on God, who raises the dead.... On him we have **set our hope**[25] that he will continue to deliver us." (1:9)

When things are going well we are prone to trust in our own resources. This event caused Paul to rely on God in a new way and to refocus his hope on God's deliverance, rather than his own ingenuity and survival skills.

Q2. (2 Corinthians 1:9-10) How does facing a harrowing crisis help us grow in the Lord? How has a crisis helped your spiritual life? What is the value of learning not to rely on ourselves? What does this do to our pride? How does this improve our effectiveness as God's servants?
http://www.joyfulheart.com/forums/index.php?showtopic=1072

Intercessory Prayer (1:10b-11)

Notice how Paul is eager for the prayers of the saints as they call out to God on his behalf:

> "[10b]... He will continue to deliver us, [11] as you **help us by your prayers**.[26] Then many will give thanks on our behalf for the gracious favor[27] granted us in **answer to the prayers of many**." (1:10b-11)

How prayer works is a mystery to us. It's natural, of course, to call out to God for help

---

907).

[24] "Rely on" (NIV, NRSV), "trust in" (KJV) is *peithō*, "depend on, trust in." (BDAG 792, 2a).

[25] "Set our hope" (NIV, NRSV), "trust" (KJV) is *elpizō*, "to look forward to something, with implication of confidence about something coming to pass, hope, hope for," here, specifically, "put one's confidence in someone or something" (BDAG 319, 1c).

[26] "Help" (NIV), "join in helping" (NRSV), "helping together" (KJV) is *synypourgeō*, "join in helping, co-operate with by means of something" (BDAG 977). This is a triple compound verb *syn-*, "along with" + *hypo*, "under" + *ergō*, "to work, toil." "Prayers" is *deēsis*, "entreaty," in the New Testament, "urgent request to meet a need, exclusively addressed to God, prayer" (BDAG 213).

[27] "Gracious favor" (NIV), "blessing" (NRSV), "gift" (KJV) is *charisma*, "that which is freely and graciously given, favor bestowed, gift" (BDAG 1081, a).

when we're in trouble, just like a child would call for a parent. But since he is both omnipresent and omniscient, why doesn't he just help us without us having to ask? And why should the prayers of many influence God more than the prayers of one person? The Bible doesn't really answer these philosophical questions.

But we see again and again in Paul's writings a reliance on the prayers of others to call on God for him. For example:

> "**Pray** in the Spirit on all occasions with all kinds of **prayers** and requests. With this in mind, be alert and always **keep on praying** for all the saints. **Pray** also for me, that whenever I open my mouth, words may be given me so that I will fearlessly make known the mystery of the gospel, for which I am an ambassador in chains. **Pray** that I may declare it fearlessly, as I should." (Ephesians 6:18-20)[28]

Jesus taught his disciples to pray by his own example of personal prayer and intercession (Luke 22:31-32; John 17:9-11). The united prayer that the early church practiced surely resulted from Jesus' teaching while he was with them (Acts 1:14; 2:42; 4:31; 6:4; etc.). One of Jesus' keys to prayer was praying with one mind, in one accord.[29]

> "Again, I tell you that if two of you on earth agree[30] about anything you ask for, it will be done for you by my Father in heaven. For where two or three come together in my name, there am I with them." (Matthew 18:19-20)

Q3. (2 Corinthians 1:10-11) Why does Paul ask people to pray for him? How do the prayers of others have an effect? What happened in your life that has helped you enter into a ministry of intercessory prayer?

http://www.joyfulheart.com/forums/index.php?showtopic=1073

We've spent quite a bit of time on the first few verses. It's amazing how much we learn from hardship. It's also such a comfort to have brothers and sisters around us who will comfort us and pray for us when we are going through difficulties! What a blessing!

Prayer

Father, thank you for your for us, even when we are stretched beyond our own resources and find ourselves far out of our comfort zone. Thank you for teaching us.

---

[28] Also Romans 15:30-32; Colossians 4:2-4; Philippians 1:19; 2 Thessalonians 3:1-2; James 5:16-18.

[29] Acts 1:14. "Together" (NIV, NRSV), "one accord" (KJV) is *homothymadon*, "with one mind / purpose / impulse" (BDAG 706), from *homos*, "one and the same, common" + *thymos*, "passion."

[30] *Symphōneō*, "to have come to an agreement about something, be of one mind, agree" (BDAG 963, 3).

Thank you for your patience. Thank you for your comfort. Now teach us to comfort others as you have comforted us. In Jesus' name, we pray. Amen.

Key Verses

"Praise be to the God and Father of our Lord Jesus Christ, the Father of compassion and the God of all comfort, who comforts us in all our troubles, so that we can comfort those in any trouble with the comfort we ourselves have received from God." (2 Corinthians 1:3-4)

"We were under great pressure, far beyond our ability to endure, so that we despaired even of life. Indeed, in our hearts we felt the sentence of death. But this happened that we might not rely on ourselves but on God, who raises the dead." (2 Corinthians 1:8b-9)

2. Tension with the Corinthians (1:12-2:11)

Paul has struggled with how to help the Corinthian church in its difficulty. He has written letters, he has made a short painful visit (see Introduction), but still the problems persist. In this lesson, he explains his change of plans to them and the reasons for the change. While we're not too interested now, two millennia later, in changes of plans, we do learn much from Paul's incidental teaching as he makes his explanation.

A Legacy of Godliness and Sincerity (1:12-14)

First, Paul affirms his sincerity in his relations with the Corinthians. Their current leaders manipulated and exploited them (11:20), but Paul reminds them that he didn't do this.

Andrei Rublev, "Apostle Paul" (1420s), tempera on wood, 160 x 109 cm, The Tretyakov Gallery, Moscow

> "Now this is our boast: Our conscience testifies that we have conducted ourselves[1] in the world, and especially in our relations with you, in the holiness and sincerity that are from God. We have done so not according to worldly wisdom but according to God's grace." (1:12)

Paul's demeanor towards the Corinthians has been characterized by openness and selflessness. He employs two words to indicate this. The first conveys the idea of singleness of motive, the second of being unmixed with other motives.

    1. **Simple love.** James warns against double-mindedness (James 1:8; 4:8). Paul emphasizes his singleness of motive with the word *haplotēs*, from a root mean-

---

[1] "Conducted ourselves" (NIV), "behaved" (NRSV), "had our conversation" (KJV) is *anastrephō*, "to conduct oneself in terms of certain principles, act, behave, conduct oneself, live" (BDAG 72, 3).

ing "single" as opposed to "two-fold."[2]

2. **Sincerity**. "Sincerity" is *eilikrineia*, which has the basic meaning of "unmixed, without alloy." Here it is used in a moral sense, "pertaining to being sincere, without hidden motives or pretense, pure."[3]

Even his letters are clear and understandable.

"[13] For we do not write you anything you cannot read or understand. And I hope that, [14] as you have understood us in part, you will come to understand fully that you can boast[4] of us just as we will boast of you in the day of the Lord Jesus." (1:13-14)

Paul is seeking restoration of a relationship to the point where both he and the Corinthians admire each other so much that they are proud of each other.

Paul's Planned Visit to Corinth (1:15-18)

Now Paul tells them of his previous plans to visit them, not because of some selfish motive, but to benefit them.

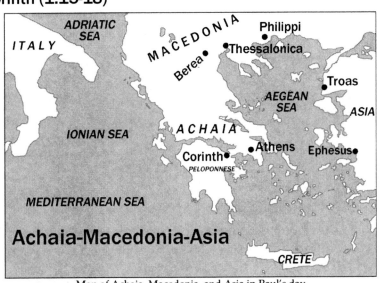

Map of Achaia, Macedonia, and Asia in Paul's day

"[15] Because I was confident of this, I planned to visit you first so that you might benefit[5] twice. [16] I planned to visit you on my way to Macedonia and to come back to you from Macedonia, and then to have you send me on my way to Judea." (1:15-16)

Paul planned to sail from Ephesus across the Aegean Sea to Corinth and stay with

---

[2] "Holiness" (NIV), "frankness" (NRSV), "simplicity" (KJV) is *haplotēs*, of personal integrity expressed in word or action (like our colloquial expression, "what you see is what you get") "simplicity, sincerity, uprightness, frankness" (BDAG 104).

[3] *Eilikrineia*, BDAG 282.

[4] "Boast" (NIV, NRSV), "rejoicing" (KJV) is *kauchēma*, "act of taking pride in something or that which constitutes a source of pride, boast." (BDAG 536).

[5] "Benefit" (NIV, KJV), "favor" (NRSV) is *charis*, "grace," here, "practical application of goodwill, (a sign of) favor, gracious deed/gift, benefaction." (BDAG 1079, 3).

them for a while. Then travel by land north to Macedonia (Philippi, Thessalonica, Berea). Then after his time in Macedonia, return to Corinth for another visit. Then sail from Corinth (actually, from the nearby port of Cenchreae just east of Corinth) to Jerusalem, bearing a monetary gift to aid the poverty-stricken believers there.

His motive was pure, but now he feels he has to defend even his change of plans to his opponents in Corinth, who might take this as a pretext to criticize him for being indecisive and vacillating. So he explains:

> "When I planned this, did I do it lightly?[6] Or do I make my plans in a worldly manner so that in the same breath I say, 'Yes, yes' and 'No, no'?"(1:17)

The Firm Promises of God (1:18-20)

Then Paul reinforces his sincerity and clarity of purpose by pointing to the clear, unequivocal message of Christ that he had brought to them.

> "18 But as surely as God is faithful, our message to you is not 'Yes' and 'No.' 19 For the Son of God, Jesus Christ, who was preached among you by me and Silas and Timothy, was not 'Yes' and 'No,' but in him it has always been 'Yes.' 20 For no matter how many promises God has made, they are 'Yes' in Christ. And so through him the 'Amen' is spoken by us to the glory of God. 21 Now it is God who makes both us and you stand firm in Christ." (1:18-21)

Christ is the fulfillment of all of God's promises for Israel in the Old Testament. To which we respond: "Amen," a word transliterated from the Hebrew as a strong affirmation of something that has been stated, an expression of faith: "let it be so, truly, amen."[7]

Anointing, Seal, and Spirit (1:21b-22)

Not only is Christ the fulfillment of God's promises. Through Christ, God also acts on our behalf by the Holy Spirit.

> "21b Now it is God who makes both us and you stand firm in Christ. He anointed us, 22 set his seal of ownership on us, and put his Spirit in our hearts as a deposit, guaranteeing what is to come." (1:21b-22)

Look at some of the blessings to us from the Holy Spirit:

---

[6] "Lightly" (NIV), "vacillating" (NRSV), "lightness" (KJV) is *elaphria*, "condition of treating a matter frivolously, as by irresponsible change of mind, vacillation, levity" (BDAG 314).

[7] *Amēn*, BDAG 53, 1a. A liturgical formula at the end of the liturgy, spoken by the congregation.

1. **Established**. Through the Spirit we are firmly founded in Christ.[8]
2. **Anointed**. The idea of anointing by the Spirit is at least as old as Samuel anointing Saul and David with oil to be king, after which the Holy Spirit came upon them. In the New Testament, the term "anointing," putting oil on a person, is sometimes nearly synonymous with the Holy Spirit's presence in a Christian's life (1 John 2:20, 27). Here, the anointing of the Holy Spirit sets us apart for his service.[9]
3. **Marked as God's property**. In ancient times a seal marked a document, or item, or shipment as authentic and the property of the owner of the seal.[10] The Holy Spirit is the identifier that we belong to God. Indeed, Paul writes: "If anyone does not have the Spirit of Christ, he does not belong to Christ" (Romans 8:9).
4. **Guaranteed eternal life**. "A deposit, guaranteeing what is to come" (NIV), "a first installment" (NRSV), "earnest" (KJV) is *arrabōn*, "payment of part of a purchase price in advance, first installment, deposit, down payment, pledge." This either secures a legal claim to the article in question, or makes a contract valid; in any case, *arrabōn* is a payment that obligates the contracting party to make further payments.[11]

Dear friends, so often we take the Spirit for granted. We believe in the Father and the Son, but seem to know little about the Spirit. He is the member of the Trinity who enjoys our own personal interface with the Godhead. Meditate on verses 21b-22 again. What does it mean to you to be established, anointed, belong to God, and have a built-in guarantee of eternity? It's awesome!

Q1. (2 Corinthians 1:21b-22) According to this verse, what does the presence of the Holy Spirit in our lives signify? How does the Spirit unite us with God? What is the promise of future blessing inherent in the Spirit's presence?
http://www.joyfulheart.com/forums/index.php?showtopic=1074

---

[8] "Makes … stand firm" (NIV), "establishes" (NRSV), "stablisheth" (KJV) is *bebaioō*, which is used in two ways, (1) "to put something beyond doubt, confirm, establish," and (2) as here, "to make a person firm in commitment, establish, strengthen" (BDAG 173).

[9] "Anointed" is *chriō*, "anoint," in our literature only in a figurative sense of an anointing by God setting a person apart for special service under divine direction (BDAG 1091, d).

[10] "Set his seal of ownership" (NIV), "put his seal" (NRSV), "sealed" (KJV) is *sphragizō*, "to mark with a seal as a means of identification, mark, seal," so that the mark denoting ownership also carries with it the protection of the owner (BDAG 980, 3). Also in Revelation 7:3; Ezekiel 9:4; Ephesians 1:13; 4:30; John 6:27.

[11] *Arrabōn*, BDAG 134.

Sparing Them Another Painful Visit (1:23-2:2)

After this wonderful passage, Paul continues his explanation of why he didn't visit the Corinthians as planned.

> "²³ I call God as my witness that it was in order to spare you that I did not return to Corinth. ²⁴ Not that we lord it over your faith, but we work with you for your joy, because it is by faith you stand firm.

> ¹ So I made up my mind that I would not make another painful visit to you. ² For if I grieve you, who is left to make me glad but you whom I have grieved?" (1:23-2:2)

Sometimes in a family, there are issues that aren't wise to raise – yet. You wait for the opportune moment. To force the issue may be your right, but may be extremely unwise for the health of the family.

So Paul seeks to spare[12] the Corinthians from one more battle that will hurt more than it will help; it will cause grief.[13] So instead of another "painful visit,"[14] he sends Titus to learn how things are and finds that conditions have improved in response to a previous letter from Paul. (See "Tentative Chronology of Paul and the Corinthians" in the Introduction.)

He deflects the criticism that he is too authoritative, that he "lords it over" them[15] – though later in this letter he warns that when he comes he will set thing in order without sparing the guilty (13:1-2). Paul's goal isn't accruing personal power, however. He leads with humility in accord with Jesus' teaching to his disciples (Mark 10:42-44). Rather, Paul works to develop their faith, which results in joy and stability.[16]

Q2. (2 Corinthians 1:24) What does it mean to "lord it over" someone? What is the balance between (1) good, strong leadership, (2) micromanaging, and (3) a complete *laissez-faire* approach to leadership? What are the dangers of an authoritative leadership style? What are the dangers of a weak leadership style?
http://www.joyfulheart.com/forums/index.php?showtopic=1075

---

[12] "Spare" is *pheidomai*, "to save from loss or discomfort, spare" (BDAG 105, 1).

[13] The verb *lypeō* is found in verses 2 and 4, active, "to cause severe mental or emotional distress, vex, irritate, offend, insult," passive, "become sad, sorrowful, distressed" (BDAG 604, 1 and 2b).

[14] "Painful visit" (NIV, NRSV), literally "come in heaviness" (KJV) in verse 1 and "be distressed" (NIV), "suffer pain" (NRSV), "have sorrow" (KJV) both use the noun *lypē*, "pain of mind or spirit, grief, sorrow, affliction" (BDAG 605).

[15] "Lord it over" (NIV, NRSV), "have dominion" (KJV) is *kyrieuō*, "to exercise authority or have control, rule" (BDAG 576, 1).

[16] "Stand firm" (NIV, NRSV), "stand" (KJV) is *histēmi*, "stand," here in the sense of, "stand firm so as to remain stable, stand firm, hold one's ground" (BDAG 483, B4).

Paul Wrote the 'Severe' Letter Rather than Visiting (2:3-4)

Now Paul explains a bit about why he had written them a "severe" letter sometime in the previous couple of years. Unfortunately, we have no copy of this letter.

> "I wrote as I did so that when I came I should not be distressed by those who ought to make me rejoice. I had confidence in all of you, that you would all share my joy." (2:3)

During Paul's brief "painful visit" to Corinth, his apostolic authority had been openly resisted by a member of the church – and the other members did nothing to defend Paul. In the "severe" letter, Paul had insisted that this offending brother be disciplined (which we'll consider in 2:5-11 below).

So in verse 3, he explains that he wrote a letter instead of visiting so that this offending brother would be dealt with by the congregation and he wouldn't have to endure more distress. "I have confidence in all of you," he says, and his confidence was well-placed, because the church *did* discipline the brother.

Now Paul opens up a bit about his own emotions that lay behind that letter.

> "For I wrote you out of great distress[17] and anguish[18] of heart and with many tears, not to grieve you but to let you know the depth of my love for you." (2:4)

Restoring the Disciplined Brother (2:5-9)

The offending brother had indeed been disciplined. The Corinthians have been rigorous in following through on Paul's letter – perhaps too rigorous. So Paul seeks to end the period of discipline. First, he points out that the man's offence was primarily against Paul, but has affected all of them.

> "If anyone has caused grief,[19] he has not so much grieved me as he has grieved all of you, to some extent – not to put it too severely."[20] (2:5)

Now it's time to bring him back into your fellowship, says Paul.

> " [6] The punishment[21] inflicted on him by the majority is sufficient[22] for him. [7] Now

---

[17] "Distress" (NIV, NRSV), "affliction" (KJV) is *thlipsis*, literally, "pressing, pressure," here, "inward experience of distress, affliction, trouble" (BDAG 457, 2).

[18] "Anguish" is *synochē*, literally, "a holding together, narrowing," here metaphorically, "a state of distress that involves a high degree of anxiety, distress, dismay, anguish" (BDAG 974, 2 ; Thayer 606).

[19] "Caused grief/grieve" (NIV, KJV) is *lypeō*, first in active causative sense, "to cause severe mental or emotional distress, vex, irritate, offend, insult someone," then in the emotional sense, "to experience sadness or distress" (BDAG 604, 1, 2a,b).

[20] "Put too severely" (NIV), "to exaggerate" (NRSV), "overcharge" (KJV) is *epibareō*, "to be a burden to, weigh down, burden.""2 Corinthians 2:5 seems to have the meaning 'in order not to heap up too great a burden of words' = in order not to say too much" (BDAG 368).

[21] "Punishment" is *epitimia*, here as a technical term in congregational discipline for the church's

instead, you ought to forgive[23] and comfort[24] him, so that he will not be overwhelmed[25] by excessive sorrow. [8] I urge you, therefore, to reaffirm[26] your love for him." (2:6-8)

In our day, few churches seem to exercise the kind of discipline described in the New Testament (Matthew 18:15-18; 1 Corinthians 5:1-5; 2 Corinthians 13:1-10; 1 Timothy 5:20). As a result, too often we have members who are allowed to hurt and bully others, to gossip, to backbite, to quench the Holy Spirit, to block the church from moving forward, and to destroy the peace and unity of the body. Our lack of discipline keeps our churches sick. Rightly, lovingly, and sensitively exercised, church discipline makes the congregation stronger and puts would-be offenders on notice that they will be held accountable for their words and actions. Church discipline is designed to help congregations become healthy social and spiritual organisms.

Obedience to Apostolic Authority (2:9)

Now we come upon a curious verse about obedience.

"The reason I wrote you was to see if you would stand the test[27] and be obedient in everything." (2:9)

Most Americans have an independent streak and don't like the idea of obedience to a spiritual superior (with the exception of Catholic clergy and those in religious orders). But clearly, Paul uses the word to remind the Corinthians of his apostolic authority.

The word *hypēkoos* refers to "one who is in subjection, obedient."[28] This idea of obedience occurs five times in 2 Corinthians, in addition to this verse:

"punishment" or "censure" (E. Stauffer, *epitimáō, epitimía*, TDNT 2:623-27).

[22] "Sufficient" (NIV, KJV), "enough" (NRSV) is *hikanos*, which can mean "sufficient in degree, sufficient, adequate, large enough," but more likely here, "pertaining to meeting a standard, fit, appropriate, competent, qualified, able," with the connotation "worthy, good enough for something" (BDAG 472, 2).

[23] "Forgive" is *charizomai*, "give graciously," here, "to show oneself gracious by forgiving wrongdoing, forgive, pardon" (BDAG 1078, 3). *Charizomai* is used three times in verse 10.

[24] "Comfort" "console" is *parakaleō*, literally, "call to one's side," here with the connotation, "to instill someone with courage or cheer, comfort, encourage, cheer up" (BDAG 764, 4).

[25] "Overwhelmed" (NIV, NRSV), "swallowed up" (KJV) is *katapinō*, literally "swallow up," here with the idea of being destroyed (BDAG 524, 2b).

[26] "Reaffirm" (NIV, NRSV), "confirm" (KJV) is *kyroō*, originally, "ratify, make legally binding," here, perhaps "to come to a decision in a cognitive process, conclude, decide in favor of" or "reaffirm" (BDAG 579).

[27] "Test" (NIV, NRSV), "proof" (KJV) is *dokimē*, "a testing process, test, ordeal" (BDAG 256, 1). "A proving" (Thayer 154, 1). Also at 8:2 and 9:13.

[28] *Hypēkoos*, BDAG 103. *Hypēkoos* the substantive of *hypakouo*, "to listen attentively," that is, "heed," thus, it differs a bit from a related word, *hypotassomai*, "to voluntarily submit to or place oneself under another" (though *hypotassomai* can also indicate obedience as well). For greater depth on these and similar words, see Lesson 13 of my book *Ephesians: Discipleship Lessons* (JesusWalk, 2011).

"And [Titus'] affection for you is all the greater when he remembers that you were all **obedient**, receiving him with fear and trembling." (7:15)

"Men will praise God for the **obedience** that accompanies your confession of the gospel of Christ, and for your generosity in sharing." (9:13)

"We take captive every thought to make it **obedient** to Christ. And we will be ready to punish every act of **disobedience**, once your **obedience** is complete." (10:5-6)

I think that we've been so aware of the dangers of the tyranny of leaders who seek to control their followers, that we have backed off from the idea of obedience entirely. However, the Scriptures clearly call us to obedience, not just to apostles, but to our spiritual leaders.

"But we appeal to you, brothers and sisters, to **respect**[29] those who labor among you, and **have charge**[30] of you in the Lord and **admonish**[31] you; esteem them very highly in love because of their work." (1 Thessalonians 5:12-13, NRSV)

"**Obey**[32] your leaders and submit to [their authority]. They keep watch over you as men who must give an account. [Obey them] so that their work will be a joy, not a burden, for that would be of no advantage to you." (Hebrews 13:17, NIV)

Of course, the only basis that a spiritual leader has to expect obedience is that he or she is, in turn, listening to and passing on the word and direction of God. If we exercise authority with humility we can follow Christ's teachings concerning servant leadership (Mark 10:35-45; 1 Peter 5:1-6).

Q3. (2 Corinthians 2:9) How does obedience to servant leaders help the church of Jesus Christ? How does obedience to self-serving leaders hurt the church? Are you obedient to those whom God has placed over you in the Lord? Why or why not? What is the relationship between obedience and church unity?
http://www.joyfulheart.com/forums/index.php?showtopic=1076

---

[29] "Respect" (NIV, NRSV), "know" (KJV) is *eidō*, "to know," here, "to recognize merit, respect, honor" (BDAG 694, 6).

[30] "Over you" (NIV, KJV), "have charge over" (NRSV) is *proistēmi*, "to exercise a position of leadership, rule, direct, be at the head (of)" (BDAG 870, 1).

[31] "Admonish" is *noutheteō*, "to counsel about avoidance or cessation of an improper course of conduct, admonish, warn, instruct" (BDAG 679).

[32] *Peithō*, in the passive voice means "be persuaded," which sometimes moves over to "listen to, obey, follow" (BDAG 792, 3b; Liddell-Scott, B2).

Forgive So that Satan Doesn't Take Advantage of You (2:10-11)

Now Paul mentions the central importance of forgiveness in the Christian faith.

"[10] If you forgive[33] anyone, I also forgive him. And what I have forgiven – if there was anything to forgive – I have forgiven in the sight of Christ for your sake, [11] in order that Satan might not outwit us. For we are not unaware of his schemes." (2:10-11)

To forgive is to refuse to hold something against a person any longer, but to let it go. Paul says that since he was the main person sinned against, that he forgives. Note clearly, the reason:

"… in order that Satan might not outwit us. For we are not unaware of his schemes." (2:11)

If we don't forgive, we provide a foothold that Satan can use to defeat us. In a similar way, Paul wrote to the Ephesian church:

"'In your anger do not sin': Do not let the sun go down while you are still angry, and **do not give the devil a foothold**." (Ephesians 4:26-27)

Nursing an offence from one day to the next allows it to turn into bitterness, which gives the devil a "foothold" (literally, a "place") in our spirits from which to attack and undermine us further. Jesus told his disciples:

"I will not speak with you much longer, for the prince of this world is coming. He has **no hold on me**" (NIV) – literally "**nothing in me**." (KJV, John 14:30)

If we want to be free of Satan's power over us, we must give him no opportunity to work, such as holding onto bitterness and unforgiveness. Notice that unforgiveness can give Satan an opportunity to deceive us.

"… in order that Satan might not **outwit** us. For we are not unaware of his **schemes**." (2:11)

The deception is that we think we are being righteous to hold a person responsible for their sin, while Satan outwits (NIV, NRSV) or "takes advantage" (KJV) of us in doing so. The word is *pleonekteō*, "to take advantage of, exploit, outwit, defraud, cheat,"[34] from the adjective *pleonektēs*, "greedy, eager for gain."

Paul has learned that unforgiveness is one of Satan's most common traps that catches Christians everywhere.[35] We cannot afford to be "unaware" (NIV) or "ignorant" (NRSV,

---

[33] "Forgive" here is *charizomai*, "to show oneself gracious by forgiving wrongdoing, forgive, pardon," from *charis*, "grace, gift" (BDAG 1079, 3).

[34] *Pleonekteō*, BDAG 824, 1b. *Pleonekteō*, is used five times in the New Testament (here as well as 2 Corinthians 12:17-18; 2 Thessalonians 4:6).

[35] "Scheme" (NIV), "design" (NRSV), "device" (KJV) is *noēma*, "that which one has in mind as product of

KJV)[36] of how he works.

Dear friend, do you hold unforgiveness for some past wrong? Has Satan used this to make you an angry, bitter person without God's peace. It's time to let it go, to give it to God. Your anger and "righteous" unforgiveness aren't succeeding in hurting the person who has sinned against you – but it is destroying you!

Q4. (2 Corinthians 2:10-11) How does Satan take advantage of our unforgiveness? What are the symptoms in our own heart of unforgiveness? According to Matthew 6:14-15, how does holding unforgiveness hurt our spiritual lives? What would you have to do to really let go of your resentment and give it to God?
http://www.joyfulheart.com/forums/index.php?showtopic=1077

Paul's letter to the Corinthians began with the theme of comfort – being comforted by the God of all comfort and then learning to comfort others. Dear friend, in the place of the open, festering wound of anger and unforgiveness, receive God's comfort by obeying Christ's command to forgive.

Prayer

Father, thank you for Paul's example of offering love and forgiveness in the face of false accusations and tension. Help us – help me – to do the same. Relax the knotted muscles of our tension and unforgiveness with your grace. In Jesus' name, we pray. Amen.

Key Verses

"Now it is God who makes both us and you stand firm in Christ. He anointed us, set his seal of ownership on us, and put his Spirit in our hearts as a deposit, guaranteeing what is to come." (2 Corinthians 1:21-22)

"I have forgiven in the sight of Christ for your sake, in order that Satan might not outwit us. For we are not unaware of his schemes." (2 Corinthians 2:10b-11)

---

intellectual process," here "design, purpose, intention," from *noeō*, "to perceive with the mind, think upon, ponder" (BDAG 675, 1b; Thayer 426).

[36] The verb is *agnoeō*, "to be uninformed about, not to know, be ignorant (of)" (BDAG 13, 1a).

3. The Fragrance of Christ's Ministering People (2:12-3:6)

Now Paul turns from asking the Corinthians to forgive and restore a disciplined member to describing his longing to hear from them and give them a report concerning a recent missionary trip.

An Open Door and Peace in One's Spirit (2:12-13)

Paul's ministry center was Ephesus during this time, but from there he made various trips to strengthen the churches.

The remains of several ancient vaulted chambers at the Baths of Herodes Atticus, near Troas.

"Now when I went to Troas to preach the gospel of Christ and found that the Lord had opened a door for me...." (2:12)

He travelled north in the province of Asia by road to Troas, an important seaport and commercial center, and gateway from Asia to Macedonia and Thrace.

Paul had passed through Troas on his second missionary journey (Acts 16:7-12), but did not stay to preach there. He received his "Macedonian call" in a dream and sailed to Macedonia to begin the church in Philippi. But now Paul finds "an open door," an expression that Paul uses to indicate receptiveness to the gospel, an opportunity for "effective work" (1 Corinthians 16:9), "something made possible or feasible."[1] And so he begins to preach in Troas, establishing a church.[2] But he doesn't stay very long.

"[13] I still had no peace of mind,[3] because I did not find my brother Titus there. So I said

---

[1] *Thyra*, BDAG 462, 1bγ. The expression is also found in 1 Corinthians 16:9; Colossians 4:3; Acts 14:27.

[2] Paul returned to preach in the Troas church (and put Eutychus to sleep during a late-night meeting) at the conclusion of his Third Missionary Journey (Acts 20:5-12).

[3] "Peace" (NIV), "rest" (NRSV, KJV) is *anesis*, literally, "relaxing, loosening," here, "relief from something onerous or troublesome, rest, relaxation, relief" (BDAG 77, 2). It is used twice more in this letter (7:5; 8:13). Here, it is used along with *pneuma*, "spirit," as "as the source and seat of insight, feeling, and will,

good-by to them and went on to Macedonia." (2:12-13)

He has hoped to find Titus at this possible meeting place. However, still concerned about the report that Titus will bring regarding the situation in Corinth, he sails from Troas to Macedonia where he finds Titus at last (7:5-7).

Marching in the Triumphal Procession (2:14)

Now he pauses to reflect on the amazing experience of seeing God open people to the gospel as he had at Troas. So many are closed to God, but some have been prepared to receive the Word.

> "But thanks be to God, who always leads us in triumphal procession in Christ and through us spreads everywhere the fragrance of the knowledge of him." (2:14)

Paul's image of a triumphal expression is a graphic – and controversial – one. "Triumphal procession" (NIV, NRSV), "triumph" (KJV) is *thriambeuō*, used here and in Colossians 2:15. It has four possible meanings:

1. To cause someone to triumph (KJV), but this has been abandoned by modern interpreters.
2. To put someone on show or display.
3. To lead captives in a triumphal procession. Though this use has the best lexical support, being led as a captive suggests shame, which isn't Paul's point here.
4. To lead someone as a soldier in a triumphal procession. This fits the context best and has been adopted by the NIV, NRSV, NASB, New Jerusalem Bible. This makes the most sense to me.[4]

The image is striking: a victorious general leading his army in a triumphant procession through a conquered city – or even into the capital city of the empire. During such a parade, incense would be burned to the gods and its fragrance would be carried to the crowds lining the streets. The aroma would be unforgettable.

Up until now, Paul has talked about the trials and struggles that have accompanied his ministry. This reference to a triumphal procession doesn't reflect triumphalism, but a balanced view of ministry effectiveness that God brings in spite of difficulties.

The Fragrance of Knowing God (2:14-16)

It is this idea of fragrance that Paul carries forward to describe his ministry of salvation.

---

generally as the representative part of human inner life" (BDAG 833, 3b).
[4] Kruse, pp. 88-89; *thriambeuō*, BDAG 459.

"¹⁴ But thanks be to God, who always leads us in triumphal procession in Christ and through us spreads everywhere the **fragrance** of the knowledge of him. ¹⁵ For we are to God the **aroma** of Christ among those who are being saved and those who are perishing. ¹⁶ To the one we are the **smell** of death; to the other, the **fragrance** of life. And who is equal to such a task?" (2:14-16)

Two Greek nouns are used to describe this scent:

1. "**Fragrance**" (NIV, NRSV), "savor" (KJV) in verses 14 and 16 is *osmē*, generally, "odor, smell," of a pleasant odor or a bad odor, then figuratively, the quality of something that affects the mind as with an odor."[5] The word in verse 14 is in a positive sense. Then the word occurs twice in verse 16, first of the smell of death and then of the fragrance of life.

2. "**Aroma**" (NIV, NRSV), "sweet savor" (KJV) in verse 15 is *euōdia*, "aroma, fragrance," used elsewhere of the fragrance from a sacrifice, pleasing to God.[6]

The fragrance of the gospel – and of the carriers of this gospel – is "the knowledge of God." Wherever Paul went, he told people about Jesus, spread the knowledge that there is a Savior – and he reflected in his life the intimate knowledge of a personal relationship with Jesus, the fragrance of a pleasant, winsome character.

Paul contrasts two types of smells in verse 16:

1. **Smell of death** is the odor of the putrefying flesh of a corpse. Even when masked by funeral spices, the smell is still present. No one is fooled. It is the smell of people who are "perishing," *apollymi*, "to cause or experience destruction," here in the middle voice, "perish, be ruined."[7] Many Christians don't really believe that people are lost, dying, and being destroyed forever to end up in a hell eternally separated from God. But that is the pungent odor of eternal death that Paul is trying to contrast with the fragrant smell of life and victory.

2. **Fragrance of life** is the pleasant smell of perfumed incense that fills the nostrils with the stimulating scent of safety and joy, signified by a victory parade. It is the fragrance of people being saved and rescued from their lives of sin.

Dear friend, do you have any strong spiritual "scent" when you are around people, or have you given up on it so as not to offend those who are allergic to Christian perfume? Jesus said that it's possible for disciples to lose their "saltiness" (to employ a different analogy, Matthew 5:12). We must be authentic – be who we really are in Christ

---

[5] *Osmē*, BDAG 728, 2.

[6] *Euōdia*, BDAG 417. Also Philippians 4:18 and Ephesians 5:2. This is different from the name Euodia (Philippians 4:2), since her name is spelled differently in Greek and means "fine travelling."

[7] *Apollymi*, BDAG 115, 1bα, present participle.

– realizing that to some (those whom the Holy Spirit has prepared) we will be welcome messengers of eternal life, and to others (who resist the Holy Spirit), we will be seen as bearers of a restrictive message that would hobble a person's licentious lifestyle. The gospel has a way of clarifying the issue, leading some to eternal life and confirming others in their destination of eternal death.

Q1. (2 Corinthians 2:14-16a) In what sense is knowing God fragrant to people who are open to God? In what way is this fragrance repugnant to people who are closed to God? Have you suppressed your "fragrance" because some people are allergic to Christian perfume? If so, how can you regain the fragrance of Christ's gospel?
http://www.joyfulheart.com/forums/index.php?showtopic=1078

Who Is Sufficient for This Ministry (2:16b)

Paul closes this brief section with a question:

"And who is equal to such a task?" (NIV)
"Who is sufficient for these things?" (NRSV, KJV)

Who is really able to spread the fragrance of Christ around him or her to draw people to the gospel of love? The answer to this question is found later in this lesson in 3:4-6, where the questions of sufficiency and competency[8] is explored. But with his next sentence, Paul implies that though he and his associates are equipped for the task of the gospel ministry, his opponents are not – those who are mere peddlers of the word.

Peddlers or Sincere Advocates (2:17)

Now Paul turns to motives for ministry, since his motives have been called into question by his opponents in Corinth.

"Unlike so many, we do not peddle the word of God for profit. On the contrary, in Christ we speak before God with sincerity, like men sent from God." (2:17)

He contrasts two motives:

1. **Selfish**. "Peddle for profit / peddlers" (NIV, NRSV), "corrupt" (KJV) is the verb *kapēleuō*, "trade in, peddle, huckster," in the context of retail trade, often used of tavern-keepers in secular Greek. Because of the tricks of small trades-men of using false weights, or thinning the wine with water, the word almost

---

[8] "Equal" (NIV), "sufficient" (NRSV, KJV) is *hikanos*, which we see several times in 3:5-6.

comes to mean, "adulterate."[9] The motive of self-appointed false apostles is always self-seeking, self-aggrandizing, sometimes with a financial incentive. Too often we've seen preachers abuse money! But this verse also applies to those who will water down the requirements of the gospel in order to get followers. We've seen a lot of people promoting "easy believe-ism" in our day, since to get people to embrace the concept of discipleship might result in them walking sadly away from Jesus – and from us.

2. **Unselfish.** "Sincerity" (NIV) is *eilikrineia*, "the quality or state of being free of dissimulation, sincerity, purity of motive."[10] The motive of "men sent from God" is to bear the truth without any selfish motive or trickery, but with sincerity. We have been sent to people to please God our Sender, not to please ourselves. It is not about us! We are bearers of God's word, not reinterpreters of it in order to suit the hearers' fancies.

Letters Written on the Heart (3:1-3)

Paul's opponents question and undermine his apostolic authority. Does he have credentials that prove he is an apostle? Or is he just promoting himself? Paul answers these innuendoes head on.

> "Are we beginning to commend ourselves again? Or do we need, like some people, letters of recommendation to you or from you?" (3:1)

The verb "commend" is *synistēmi*, from *syn-*, "together" + *istēmi*, "place, set," that is, "to bring together." Here it has the specialized meaning, "to bring together as friends or in a trusting relationship by commending or recommending, present, introduce/recommend someone to someone else."[11] This theme of commending or recommending is mentioned a number of places in 2 Corinthians.[12]

Letters of introduction or recommendation were widespread in the ancient world. Often the bearer of the letter would be the one commended and would receive appropriate hospitality and welcome upon arrival.[13] Paul himself sent such letters, for example, to the Roman church, he says:

> "I commend to you our sister Phoebe, a servant of the church in Cenchrea. [2] I ask you to

---

[9] *Kapēleuō*, BDAG 508.

[10] *Eilikrineia*, BDAG 282. Also used at 1:12.

[11] *Synistēmi*, BDAG 972, 2. "Recommendation" (NIV, NRSV), "commendation" (KJV) is the adjective *systatikos*, "introducing, commendatory" (BDAG 978).

[12] 2 Corinthians 3:1-3; 4:2; 5:12; 6:4; 10:12-18; and 12:11.

[13] Barnett, p. 161, fn. 12.

receive her in the Lord in a way worthy of the saints and to give her any help she may need from you, for she has been a great help to many people, including me." (Romans 16:1-2)

Some of the Corinthians seem to be agitating for Paul to produce a letter stating his apostolic credentials. His answer is to the point:

"² You yourselves are our letter,¹⁴ written on our hearts, known and read by everybody. ³ You show that you are a letter from Christ, the result of our ministry, written not with ink but with the Spirit of the living God, not on tablets of stone but on tablets of human hearts." (3:2-3)

Do you want proof that I am an apostle? You're it! You are the fruit of my apostolic ministry. I founded your church. I brought many of you to faith in Christ. Rather than someone else's recommendation of us, you yourselves are the evidence.

Living Letters

Paul's insight is quite remarkable. People can read you like a book. They can sense if you're genuine or not. That's why outward piety is so disgusting. What convinces people of Christian authenticity is the unmistakable inner spirit. Peter told women who were tempted to dress to impress:

"Instead, it should be that of your inner self, the unfading beauty of a gentle and quiet spirit, which is of great worth in God's sight." (1 Peter 3:4)

You, dear friend, are a letter from Christ to your neighbor, to your son or daughter, to your co-worker. Let the Spirit of God have his full way with you so that the letter doesn't get distorted or become unreadable because of your smudges!

Q2. (2 Corinthians 3:2-3) In what sense are we "living letters"? In what way can people "read us"? Why is it so important to be authentic, not phony, in our lives? What happens when people "read" something in you that they admire and mention it to you? How might you respond appropriately?
http://www.joyfulheart.com/forums/index.php?showtopic=1079

Competent Servants of a New Covenant (3:4-6)

Because he knows the fruit of his ministry, Paul is confident – but he doesn't take personal credit for this fruit. Back in 2:16, Paul asked the rhetorical question: "Who is

---

¹⁴ "Letter" is *epistolē*, (from which we get our word, "epistle"), "letter, epistle" (BDAG 383).

sufficient (*hikanos*) for these things?" (NRSV, KJV). Now he answers the question.

> "[4] Such confidence[15] as this is ours through Christ before God. [5] Not that we are **competent** (*hikanos*) in ourselves to claim anything for ourselves, but our **competence** (*hikanotēs*) comes from God. [6] He has **made us competent** (*hikanoō*) as ministers of a new covenant – not of the letter but of the Spirit; for the letter kills, but the Spirit gives life." (3:4-6)

"Competent" (NIV, NRSV), "sufficient" (KJV) is the adjective *hikanos*, which has the basic sense of "sufficient, enough, large enough."[16] We saw it first in 2:16 above. Here it means "pertaining to meeting a standard, fit, appropriate, competent, qualified, able," with the connotation, "worthy, good enough."[17] The word group also appears in this verse as a verb *hikanoō*[18] and a noun *hikanotēs*.[19]

How Seminaries and Ordination Relate to Competency

The question Paul is addressing is: What makes a minister competent? Is it a letter of recommendation – which is the ancient equivalent of a certificate of ordination, which is an organizational recommendation? Or is it a diploma of graduation from a Bible course or a theological seminary? What makes a minister competent?

Paul's answer is that God makes us competent by his Spirit – pure and simple. With the gifts and calling of God, a minister is competent to nurture and give birth to spiritual life in people who don't know the Lord. This is from God!

So if our competence for ministry is from the Spirit, then does theological training and ordination have any meaning? Yes! Let me explain.

First, let's discuss the value of theological training. I grant that many seminaries offer inadequate training. They deal with the intellectual questions of the faith and equip pastors to lead existing churches. Too often, however, they don't offer enough in the areas of character development and practical topics such as leadership, church planting, and evangelism that are necessary to grow the church. But in my experience, seminaries, and to some extent Bible colleges, provide excellent help in (1) training pastors to

---

[15] "Confidence" (NIV, NRSV), "trust" (KJV) is *pepoithēsis*, "a state of certainty about something to the extent of placing reliance on, trust, confidence," found four times in 2 Corinthians (here and in 1:15; 8:22; 10:2) (BDAG 796, 1b).

[16] Karl H. Rengstorf, *hikanós, ktl.*, TDNT 3:293-296.

[17] *Hikanos*, BDAG 472, 2.

[18] "Made competent" (NIV, NRSV), "made able" (KJV) is *hikanoō*, "to cause to be adequate, make sufficient, qualify," perhaps shading into the sense "empower, authorize" someone for something (BDAG 473).

[19] *Hikanotēs*, "state of being qualified or adequate for something, fitness, capability, qualification" (BDAG 473).

interpret scripture and (2) background to be able to think critically, to ask the important questions.

Next, let's talk about the role of the local church. Frankly, an indispensible place for ministers to be prepared is through experience in the local church under the mentoring of a wise pastor. Here is where character formation happens along with leadership development and experience with evangelism and growth.

Finally, let's examine the place of licensing (for pastors-in-training working in the local church) and ordination (for those who have been trained and are ready to go out on their own). Licensing says: We believe this person is called by God and is qualified to work in ministry under supervision. Ordination is essentially a letter of recommendation to people who come across the path of the minister that he or she has gone through an adequate training program, possesses gifts of the Holy Spirit, is of strong Christian character, and has placed himself or herself in an ongoing relationship of accountability to other leaders in the Church.

I've met some "self-made" pastors who seem to be functioning well in ministry – and many who aren't. I've heard seminaries called "cemeteries" by groups that have an anti-intellectual bias. (And some seminaries probably are!) I've heard people say dismissively, "I don't need *man's* ordination; it is *God* who ordains people." But often these kinds of statements are made out of a combination of ignorance, pride, arrogance, and rebelliousness.

To have a healthy ministry, the Church (usually a denomination or association of like-minded churches) needs to make sure that those in ministry leadership roles:

1. Know the Scriptures and can interpret them soundly and wisely,
2. Have spiritual gifts for ministry and exercise them with care and wisdom,
3. Are of tested moral character and live a holy life,
4. Have a healthy and growing devotional life,
5. Act properly in terms of money, sex, and power (areas that have derailed many promising ministries), and
6. Continue in accountability to their elders and peers in the larger Church, so that they don't get off track doctrinally, morally, or spiritually.

There are always mavericks in ministry – some of whom bring a real corrective to the Church. But it is valuable to local churches when seeking a pastor to have a letter of recommendation from other trusted Christian leaders that this candidate meets important criteria as a spiritual leader. I believe that training and ordination have an important place.

The Vital Role of the Holy Spirit (3:6)

Having said that, Paul is absolutely correct in stating that our competency – that is, our ability to do effective ministry – comes from God working through the Spirit.

> "He has made us competent as ministers of a new covenant – not of the letter but of the Spirit; for the letter kills, but the Spirit gives life." (3:6)

We can have the best training that seminaries can provide, we can have powerful spiritual gifts, we can have great personal charisma, we can have a dynamic work ethic. But none of this by itself will produce spiritual fruit that remains. Only coupled with submission to the dynamic Spirit of God will we see fruit that remains – and that is the purpose of ministry, whether ordained or lay ministry.

Q3. (2 Corinthians 3:4-6) What is the balance between the need for training in ministry (either in the local church or in schools) and personal submission to the Spirit of God? Are you able to "listen to the Spirit's voice" in your own life? Why would this ability be so important in being a competent minister?
http://www.joyfulheart.com/forums/index.php?showtopic=1080

Ministers of a New Covenant (3:6a)

> "He has made us competent as ministers of a new covenant" (3:6a)

I've spent quite a bit of time discussing theological training and ordination, as if it were necessary for ministry within the local church. It's not! For church members who aspire to lead *other* congregations, however, these elements are very important.

Each Christian, each member, has been given spiritual gifts and has a ministry – no matter how seemingly insignificant – within the local church. After all, the word "minister" in 3:6 is the word *diakonos* (from which we get our word "deacon"), which means simply, "one who serves," "generally, one who is busy with something in a manner that is of assistance to someone."[20] People who serve according to their gifts make any local church effective. Without them, the church doesn't work. In this sense, think of yourself as a "minister" who is serving Christ and Christ's body, the church.

One of the serious consequences of not attending church regularly is that you probably aren't exercising your spiritual gifts in ministry, and you may not be giving of your finances to support Christ's mission in your community. Every church has flaws, since it

[20] *Diacanos*, BDAG 232.

is made up of flawed people, but you must be part of a church because it an integral part of Jesus' strategy to minister to his people and to the world. If you're out of regular fellowship with a church – unless you're physically unable to attend – it's time to reconsider!

Q4. (2 Corinthians 3:6a) Why is a Christian's spiritual health so closely related to his or her involvement in ministry? What are the consequences of dropping out of church – for the believer? For Christ's Kingdom?
http://www.joyfulheart.com/forums/index.php?showtopic=1081

The other important phrase in this verse is "new covenant." The Old Covenant brought through Moses and spelled out in the Mosaic Law, has now been fulfilled and is therefore obsolete. We are under the New Covenant, promised by the Prophet Jeremiah (Jeremiah 31:31) and ushered in by Jesus through his own blood – a Kingdom that operates not on the basis of a written law or code, but on the basis of the Holy Spirit now living in each believer. The old has passed, behold the new has come!

> "In the same way, after the supper he took the cup, saying, "This cup is the new covenant in my blood, which is poured out for you." (Luke 22:20; cf. 1 Corinthians 11:25)

> "... To Jesus the mediator of a new covenant...." (Hebrews 12:24; also see Hebrews 8:8; 9:15)

Because of the New Covenant in Jesus' blood and the life of the Holy Spirit within you, you have eternal life – now and an unfading hope of life with Christ – forever! You have a fragrance around you that attracts people to salvation in Jesus. You have the ability to serve by the Spirit. And you are a competent minister of the Messiah. Hallelujah!

Prayer

Thank you, Father, for all the blessings you bestow upon me through the Spirit. Keep me humble before you and before my brothers and sisters, so that your Spirit may flow unimpeded and uncontaminated through me to touch others. In Jesus' name, I pray. Amen.

Key Verses

> "But thanks be to God, who always leads us in triumphal procession in Christ and through us spreads everywhere the fragrance of the knowledge of him. [15] For we are to

God the aroma of Christ among those who are being saved and those who are perishing." (2 Corinthians 2:14-15)

"You yourselves are our letter, written on our hearts, known and read by everybody. You show that you are a letter from Christ, the result of our ministry, written not with ink but with the Spirit of the living God, not on tablets of stone but on tablets of human hearts." (2 Corinthians 3:2-3)

"He has made us competent as ministers of a new covenant – not of the letter but of the Spirit; for the letter kills, but the Spirit gives life." (2 Corinthians 3:6)

4. Being Changed by God's Glory (3:7-18)

Paul has just introduced a contrast between the Old Covenant and the New Covenant, between the letter of the Mosaic law and the leadership of the dynamic Spirit of God.

> "He has made us competent as ministers of a new covenant – not of the letter but of the Spirit; for the letter kills, but the Spirit gives life." (3:6)

Now Paul continues this contrast in 3:7-18 by showing the basis of the Old Covenant as the work of the Spirit through Moses, the Spirit that – under the New Covenant – works through all believers.

But why is Paul explaining such things to an overwhelming-

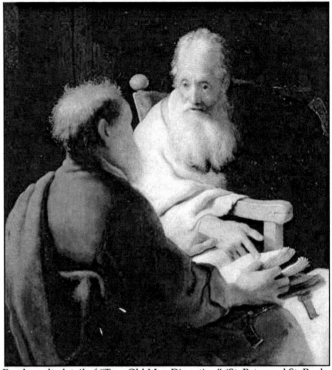

Rembrandt, detail of "Two Old Men Disputing" (St. Peter and St. Paul in Conversation) (1628), oil on wood, 72.4 x 59.7 cm, National Gallery of Victoria, Melbourne.

ly Gentile church? Probably because his opponents in Corinth had Jewish connections and were trying to "out-Hebrew" Paul himself. Later in this letter, Paul argues against these false apostles:

> "Are they Hebrews? So am I. Are they Israelites? So am I. Are they Abraham's descendants? So am I." (11:22)

In his letter to the Philippians, Paul offers a similar defense, for the same reason – to counteract the Jewish or Jewish-Christian opponents there:

> "... Circumcised on the eighth day, a member of the people of Israel, of the tribe of Benjamin, a Hebrew born of Hebrews; as to the law, a Pharisee...." (Philippians 3:5)

The Greater Glory of the Spirit (3:7-11)

Paul, the trained Pharisee, corrects these Jewish-Christian opponents with a typical Rabbinic argument from the lesser to the greater.

1. Ministry of Spirit is more splendid than ministry of death (3:7-8)
2. Ministry of righteousness is more splendid than the ministry of condemnation (3:9-10)
3. Permanent ministry is more splendid than that which passes away (3:11).[1]

You'll see these themes in the text:

> "[7] Now if the ministry that brought death, which was engraved in letters on stone, came with glory, so that the Israelites could not look steadily[2] at the face of Moses because of its glory, fading[3] though it was, [8] will not the ministry of the Spirit be even more glorious? [9] If the ministry that condemns men is glorious, how much more glorious is the ministry that brings righteousness! [10] For what was glorious has no glory now in comparison with the surpassing[4] glory. [11] And if what was fading away came with glory, how much greater is the glory of that which lasts![5]" (3:7-11)

The Glory of God on Moses' Face (Exodus 34)

Paul agrees that the Old Covenant, characterized by the Ten Commandments ("engraved with letters on stone") was glorious. He refers to Moses' experience of encountering God on Mount Sinai and his practice of talking to God in his tent of meeting and then emerging with the glow of God's glory on his face.

> "[29] When Moses came down from Mount Sinai with the two tablets of the Testimony in his hands, he was not aware that his **face was radiant** because he had spoken with the LORD. [30] When Aaron and all the Israelites saw Moses, his **face was radiant**, and they were afraid to come near him....

> "[33] When Moses finished speaking to them, he put a **veil over his face**. [34] But whenever he entered the LORD's presence to speak with him, he removed the veil until he came

---

[1] Following Kruse, p. 94.

[2] "Look steadily" (NIV), "steadfastly behold" (KJV), "gaze" (NRSV) is *atenizō*, "look intently at, stare at something or someone" (BDAG 148), also found in verse 13.

[3] "Fading" (NIV), "set aside" (NRSV), "done away" (KJV) is *katargeō*, "to cause something to come to an end or to be no longer in existence, abolish, wipe out, set aside." (BDAG 526, 3). This word is used twice more in verses 11 and 13 to refer to the fading of the glory on Moses' face. In verse 14 it is used in the sense "take a way, remove," of the removal of the veil.

[4] "Surpassing" (NIV), "greater" (NRSV), "that excelleth" (KJV) is *hyperballō*, "to attain a degree that extraordinarily exceeds a point on a scale of extent, go beyond, surpass, outdo" (BDAG 1032).

[5] "That which lasts" (NIV), "the permanent" (NRSV), "that which remaineth" (KJV) is the common verb *menō*, "abide, continue," here, "to continue to exist, remain, last, persist, continue to live" (BDAG 632, 2b).

out. And when he came out and told the Israelites what he had been commanded, [35] they saw that his **face was radiant**. Then Moses would put the veil back over his face until he went in to speak with the LORD." (Exodus 34:29-30, 33-35)

I envy Moses! He had prayed, "Show me your glory," and God had answered in this unique expression of God's glory on Moses' face. That's how the law was given. That's how Israel was led through the desert – by a man who sought God and spoke with him face to face.

But, Paul argues, that however glorious its origins, the law didn't bring life to God's people as the Spirit does. In Paul's analogy, the glory of the law fades or passes away, while the Spirit of God continues with us to this day.

Q1. (2 Corinthians 3:7-11) Why did Moses' face glow? Why did he cover it when he was out with the people? Why didn't more people's face glow in Moses' time? What's the difference between the spread of God's glory in Moses' time when compared to our own time?
http://www.joyfulheart.com/forums/index.php?showtopic=1082

Boldness in Our Hope of Glory (3:12)

Having such great promises and expectation in the Spirit encourage us. Paul says,

"Therefore, since we have such a[6] hope,[7] we are very bold.[8]" (3:12)

Moses' ministry in bringing the Old Covenant was indeed glorious. But the era of the Spirit and the New Covenant is even more glorious, and because of it we have a great expectation for the future.

The Veil of the Old Covenant (3:13-15)

Paul has made his main point, that the New Covenant was more glorious than the Old. Now he takes this concept of the veil over Moses' face to symbolize the darkness of the Jews who can't grasp the New Covenant.

"[13] We are not like Moses, who would put a **veil**[9] over his face to keep the Israelites from

---

[6] "Such/such a" is *toioutos*, a correlative adjective "pertaining to being like some person or thing mentioned in a context, of such a kind, such as this, like such" (BDAG 1012, bα bet).

[7] "Hope" is *elpis*, "the looking forward to something with some reason for confidence respecting fulfillment, hope, expectation" (BDAG 319, 1bβ).

[8] "Be very bold" (NIV), "plainness of speech" (KJV) is *parrēsia*, "a use of speech that conceals nothing and passes over nothing, outspokenness, frankness, plainness" (BDAG 783, 1).

> gazing at it while the radiance was fading away. [14] But their minds were made **dull**[10], for to this day the same **veil** remains when the old covenant is read. It has not been removed, because only in Christ is it taken away.[11] [15] Even to this day when Moses is read, a **veil** covers their hearts." (3:13-15)

How sad! The Israelites are dull to the truth. Who has made their minds dull? God? No. Read what Paul says a bit later in this letter – still with the imagery of the veil:

> "[3] And even if our gospel is **veiled**, it is veiled to those who are perishing. [4] The god of this age has **blinded** the minds of unbelievers, so that they cannot see the light of the gospel of the glory of Christ, who is the image of God." (4:3-4)

Satan has blinded the eyes of the Israelites.

Spiritual Freedom from the Holy Spirit (3:16-17)

> The Spirit of God is the One who takes away this blindness.

> "[16] But whenever anyone turns to[12] the Lord, the veil is taken away.[13] [17] Now the Lord is the Spirit, and where the Spirit of the Lord is, there is freedom." (3:16-17)

It is clear that the Holy Spirit is the bringer of spiritual light, revelation, and freedom from the Law. But verse 16 confuses us.

We're used to a stricter differentiation between the Father, Son, and Holy Spirit. So Paul, at least verbally, offends our Trinitarian doctrine here. What does Paul mean, "Now the Lord is the Spirit"?

This gets a little confusing, but the clearest answer seems to come from the passage quoted above about Moses' radiant face and the veil he used to wear.

> "But whenever he entered the LORD's presence to speak with him, he removed the veil until he came out." (Exodus 34:34a)

Paul seems to be saying: Now the Lord *in this passage* refers to or corresponds to the

---

[9] "Veil" in verses 13, 14, 15, and 16 is *kalymma*, "head-covering, veil," literally, of the veil with which Moses covered his face, then, figuratively, "veil, covering that prevents right understanding" (BDAG 505).

[10] "Made dull" (NIV), "hardened" (NRSV), "blinded" (KJV) is *pōroō*, primarily, "harden, petrify," in the New Testament only figuratively, "to cause someone to have difficulty in understanding or comprehending ... make dull, obtuse, blind, close the mind" (BDAG 900).

[11] "Taken away" (NIV), "set aside" (NRSV), "done away" (KJV) is *katargeō*, which we saw with reference to "fading" in verses 7, 11, and 13.

[12] "Turn to" is *epistrephō*, "return," here, "to change one's mind or course of action," for better or worse, "turn, return" (BDAG 382, 4a).

[13] In verse 16, "taken away" (NIV, KJV), "removed" (NRSV) is *periaireō*, "take away from around something, take away, remove" (BDAG 799, 1), from *peri-*, "around" + *aireō*, "take."

Spirit of God.[14] Bruce comments that usually Paul is careful to distinguish between the Lord (Christ) and the Spirit, "but dynamically they are one, since it is by the Spirit that the life of the risen Christ is imparted to believers and maintained within them."[15] Kruze has it right when he says:

> "So when under the new covenant they turn to the Lord, they experience him as the Spirit. The expression 'the Lord is the Spirit,' is not a one-to-one identification, but rather a way of saying that under the new covenant the Lord is to us the Spirit."[16]

Today's English Version captures the idea well:

> "But [the veil] is removed, as the Scripture says, 'Moses' veil was removed when he turned to the Lord.' Now 'the Lord' in this passage is the Spirit; and where the Spirit of the Lord is present, there is freedom.[17]" (3:16-17, TEV)

What kind of freedom is this? It is freedom from the letter of the law that comes when a person begins to follow the guidance of the Holy Spirit. In his discussion of flesh vs. Spirit in Galatians 5, Paul observes:

> "It is for freedom that Christ has set us free. Stand firm, then, and do not let yourselves be burdened again by a yoke of slavery." (Galatians 5:1)

> "But if you are led by the Spirit, you are not under law." (Galatians 5:18)

Q2. (2 Corinthians 3:16-17) Why is the Holy Spirit essential to help people see truth clearly and be able to grasp it? What enables people to come to Christ at all? What kind of freedom does the Spirit give us when we become Christians?
http://www.joyfulheart.com/forums/index.php?showtopic=1083

Beholding the Glory of God (3:18)

Paul concludes this section with a wonderful verse that describes Christian sanctification, the process of Christ's character being formed in us.

---

[14] Barnett (pp. 200-201) notes that verse 17 has been understood in two ways: (1) the "pneumatological," which neatly identifies "Lord" = "Spirit" or (2) the "associational," in which "the Spirit" identifies the "Lord," to whom one turns under the New Covenant, as "Spirit" or "spiritual."

[15] Bruce, p. 193.

[16] Kruze, p. 99. Similarly, Barrett, pp. 122-123.

[17] "Freedom" (NIV, NRSV), "liberty" (KJV) is *eleutheria*, "the state of being free, freedom, liberty." It is used especially of freedom that stands in contrast to constraint of the Mosaic law, looked upon as slavery (Gal 2:4; 5:1) (BDAG 316).

"[18] But we all, with unveiled[18] face **beholding as in a mirror** the glory of the Lord, are being transformed into the same image from glory to glory, just as from the Lord, the Spirit." (3:18, NASB)

The Greek verb is *katoptrizō*, formed from the noun *katoptron*, "mirror." Three possible renderings have been suggested:

1. "to behold as in a mirror" (NRSV, NASB, KJV),
2. "to reflect like a mirror" (NIV, NJB), or
3. "to behold or gaze," with no association with a mirror (RSV). [19]

Of these three, "look at something as in a mirror, contemplate something,"[20] seems to fit both the derivation of the word and the understanding of early translations of the Bible. The idea of *reflecting* God's glory doesn't appear before Chrysostom.[21]

So how do we behold God's glory? We might ask: How did Moses behold God's glory? Yes, he had some experiences of great glory on the mountain when he saw God's form while sheltered in the cleft of the rock (Exodus 33:18-23). But as we saw above, Moses' practice of speaking to the Lord both in the pre-tabernacle tent of meeting and later in the tabernacle left a mark on both his face and his character.

"[Moses'] face was radiant because he had spoken with the LORD." (Exodus 34:29b)

"But whenever he entered the LORD's presence to speak with him, he removed the veil until he came out. And when he came out and told the Israelites what he had been commanded, [35] they saw that his face was radiant. Then Moses would put the veil back over his face until he went in to speak with the LORD." (Exodus 34:34-35)

Why did Moses face glow? I guess because it absorbed just a little bit of God during these times of speaking with him.

Q3. (2 Corinthians 3:18) Moses glowed by spending time with God on Mt. Sinai, in his tent of meeting, and in the Tabernacle. How can we get a similar glow of the Spirit in our lives? In what way is meditating on Scripture beholding God? Is the low plane of Christianity in our day related to the time we spend in communion with the Lord? What is God leading you to do to increase your glow?

http://www.joyfulheart.com/forums/index.php?showtopic=1084

---

[18] "Unveiled faces" (NIV, NRSV), "open faces" (KJV) is *anakalyptō*, above. In verse 18 we see the opposite to veiling: "unveiled" (NIV, NRSV), "with open face" (KJV) is *anakalyptō*, "uncover, unveil" (BDAG 65), from *ana-*, "back, backward" (in the sense of reversal) + *kalyptō*, "cover."

[19] Barnett, p. 205, fn 38.

[20] *Katoptrizō*, BDAG 535. So Barrett, p. 125, and Barnett, pp. 204-206. Barnett sees Philo's phrase (*Allegorical Interpretation* 3.101), "see ... as in a looking glass," as an apt parallel.

[21] Tasker, p. 68.

Being Changed into Christ's Likeness (3:18)

Yes, Moses' glow had to be renewed by repeated sessions, but it had the effect of altering him. This is the idea that Paul is focusing on here.

I like the simple way the Revised Standard Version puts it:

> "And we all, with unveiled face, beholding the glory of the Lord, **are being changed into his likeness** from one degree of glory to another; for this comes from the Lord who is the Spirit." (3:18, RSV)

As a result of beholding God in communing with him, we are "being transformed" (NIV, NRSV), "being changed" (KJV, RSV). The verb is *metamorphoō*, "to change inwardly in fundamental character or condition, be changed, be transformed."[22] It is a compound verb, formed from *meta-*, "exchange, transfer, transmutation" + *morphoō*, "to form, shape." From this we get our English word "metamorphosis."

This process of change morphs us into God's "likeness" (NIV, RSV), "image" (NRSV, KJV). The noun *eikōn* here means "that which represents something else in terms of basic form and features, form, appearance."[23]

For our character to be changed into God's image is our destiny. Paul taught,

> "For those God foreknew he also predestined to be conformed to the likeness (*eikōn*) of his Son, that he might be the firstborn among many brothers." (Romans 8:29)

The word "conformed" in this verse is the adjective *symmorphos*, "pertaining to having a similar form, nature, or style, similar in form,"[24] from *syn-*, "participation, together, completely" + *morphē*, "form."

This is sanctification, the gradual process of becoming holy and godly in our character to match our holy standing, which was brought about instantly through Christ's gift of salvation on the cross.

> "Live by the Spirit, I say, and do not gratify the desires of the flesh.... The fruit of the Spirit is love, joy, peace, patience, kindness, goodness, faithfulness, gentleness, self-control." (Galatians 5:16, 22-23)

> "If you sow to your own flesh, you will reap corruption from the flesh; but if you sow to the Spirit, you will reap eternal life from the Spirit. So let us not grow weary in doing what is right, for we will reap at harvest time, if we do not give up." (Galatians 6:8-9, NRSV)

My dear friend, going to church will not transform you. What changes you is worship

---

[22] *Metamorphoō*, BDAG 639, 2.
[23] *Eikōn*, BDAG 282, 3.
[24] *Symmorphos*, BDAG 958.

before the Lord, meditating on him, singing to him, speaking to him, drinking him in through the Word and the Spirit. Just like Moses spent time before the Lord and was transformed by it, so as you spend time with the Lord it will change you.

This transformation is a gradual process, literally "from glory to glory" (KJV). This means, as the NRSV puts it, "from one degree of glory to another."[25]

The agent of change, according to our verse, "comes from the Lord, who is the Spirit" (3:18). In other words, this is the sanctifying work of the Holy Spirit of God, the fruit of the Holy Spirit gradually filling our character, replacing the common and unclean with the holiness and glory of the Lord.

Decades ago when I was in college, I attended a small gospel church in the MacArthur Park area of downtown Los Angeles. There I learned a song, based on the King James Version of this verse, that indelibly impressed the meaning of this verse on my soul.

> "From glory to glory He's changing me,
> Changing me, changing me.
> His likeness and image to perfect in me,
> The love of God shown to the world.
> For He's changing, changing me,
> From earthly things to the heavenly.
> His likeness and image to perfect in me,
> The love of God shown to the world."[26]

Q4. (2 Corinthians 3:18) Why is character change directly related to time deliberately spent in God's presence? What is the theological word for the process of maturing in Christ? Have you noticed a change in the "degree of glory" you're experiencing now compared to a few years ago? Why or why not?

http://www.joyfulheart.com/forums/index.php?showtopic=1085

Dear friend, my prayer for you is that you will indeed so live your life in his presence that his Spirit of Holiness will transform your life. That when people see you, they will

---

[25] There's a similar construction in 4:17, literally "from excess to (*eis*) excess." *Eis* can carry the idea of a marker of degree, "up to," as well as marker of goals involving affective / abstract / suitability aspects, "into, to," here, of change from one state to another with verbs of changing (*Eis*, BDAG 289, 3 and 4b).

[26] I found reference to a 1978 song with this title by Evelyn Marie Montgomery (1926-) and Eddie Montgomery (1926-), but I first heard the song about 1966.

not see your imperfections, but the glow of Jesus, so that people might recognize that "these men had been with Jesus." (Acts 4:13)

Prayer

O Lord, grant in me and in my brothers and sisters the acquired glow of your glory. Let us bask in your presence that we might know you, learn to love you more, and become like you! In the name of the Father, and of the Son, and of the Holy Spirit, we pray. Amen!

Key Verses

"Now the Lord is the Spirit, and where the Spirit of the Lord is, there is freedom." (2 Corinthians 3:17, NIV)

"And all of us, with unveiled faces, seeing the glory of the Lord as though reflected in a mirror, are being transformed into the same image from one degree of glory to another; for this comes from the Lord, the Spirit." (2 Corinthians 3:18, NRSV)

5. Treasures in Clay Pots (4:1-18)

In earlier chapters, Paul has been reflecting on his ministry – fragrance of Christ, sincerity, and a reliance on the Holy Spirit. In this passage, Paul continues to lay out his own personal philosophy of ministry in the face of troubles and difficulties, unbelief and struggle.

Ministry by God's Mercy (4:1)

He begins by identifying the source of his ministry: God's mercy.

> "Therefore, since through God's mercy we have this ministry, we do not lose heart." (4:1)

It is possible for God's servants to "lose heart" (NIV) or "faint" (KJV). The word is *ekkakeō*, "to be utterly spiritless, to be wearied out, exhausted, lose heart."[1] I've been there, and perhaps you have too. Paul himself had experienced those feelings, as we'll see later in this lesson (4:7-12). One reason he can recover from hurt and discouragement, however, is

Adamo Tadolini, "St. Paul" (1838) statue in front of St. Peter's Basilica, Vatican, Rome, 18.2 feet high.

his sincerity of motive. He is doing what God called him to do and knows it – "through God's mercy we have this ministry!"

A Plain and Open Ministry (4:2)

There's a saying in sports, "Winning isn't everything. It's the only thing."[2] People

---

[1] *Ekkakeō*, BDAG 303, Thayer 195.

[2] The saying is attributed to UCLA Bruins football coach Henry Russell ("Red") Sanders about 1950, according to Wikipedia.

who play only to win will do *anything* to win – especially if they don't think they'll get caught. The end, however, doesn't justify the means. Paul is clear about his ministry ethics:

> "We have renounced secret and shameful ways; we do not use deception, nor do we distort the word of God. On the contrary, by setting forth the truth plainly we commend ourselves to every man's conscience in the sight of God." (4:2)

I was once in a congregation where I sometimes served the "catcher" when people were "slain in the Spirit," that is, they collapsed to the floor under the presence of God. I often saw the real power of God, but once I observed a guest speaker who was giving people a gentle push to help them fall so that his ministry might appear more effective.[3] I've seen pastors and evangelists manipulate people. I've seen leaders say the most misleading, ingenuous, vicious, and utterly false things – all to achieve their goals, to win. No! This is not what we're called to do!

Paul sets the example for us. He has "renounced" (NIV, KJV), that is, "refused to practice" (NRSV)[4] various kinds of behavior that characterize his opponents:

1. **"Shameful"** (NIV, NRSV), "dishonest," (KJV) is *aischynē,* "a sensitivity respecting possibility of dishonor, modesty, shame," here, "what one conceals from a feeling of shame."[5]

2. **"Deception"** (NIV), "cunning" (NRSV), "craftiness" (KJV) is *panourgia,* "rascally, evil" ... "cunning, craftiness, trickery," literally, "readiness to do anything."[6]

3. **"Distort"** (NIV), "falsify" (NRSV), "handle deceitfully" (KJV) is *doloō,* generally, "to beguile by craft," then, "to make false through deception or distortion, falsify, adulterate."[7]

In contrast, Paul ministers by clear, open, honest communication.[8] He doesn't have to trick people into a response. He trusts the Holy Spirit to speak to their consciences. After all, to convict and convince is the Holy Spirit's ministry, not ours (John 16:8-11).

Dear friend, if you've been sleazy in your ministry, repent now! You serve a God who is far bigger than your smallness! If you've been hurt by a leader's sins, don't let it

---

[3] Some of my thoughts on spiritual phenomena are found in my essay, "Spirit Baptism, the New Birth, and Speaking in Tongues" (www.joyfulheart.com/scholar/spirit-baptism.htm).

[4] *Apeipon,* "disown, renounce" (BDAG 100).

[5] *Aischynē,* BDAG 29, 1.

[6] *Panourgia,* BDAG 754.

[7] *Doloō,* BDAG 256.

[8] "Setting forth plainly" (NIV), "open statement" (NRSV), "manifestation" (KJV) is *phanerōsis,* "disclosure, announcement" (BDAG 1048).

fester any longer. Put it into God's hands and move on. Life is too short to let Satan immobilize you by someone else's shameful example. God has plans for you!

Q1. (2 Corinthians 4:1-2) How do questionable ethics and ministry practices hurt the work of Christ? What is Paul's alternative in verse 2b?
http://www.joyfulheart.com/forums/index.php?showtopic=1086

Satan Has Blinded Unbelievers (4:3-4)

After all, our ministry is not about human manipulation. Rather, it is a spiritual ministry by the Holy Spirit that appeals to the inner person. That doesn't mean, however, that all respond. Paul picks up on his previous comments about the veil over Moses' face and over the unbelieving Jews' eyes (3:13-18):

> "3 And even if our gospel is veiled,[9] it is veiled to those who are perishing. 4 The god of this age has blinded the minds of unbelievers, so that they cannot see the light of the gospel of the glory of Christ, who is the image of God." (3:3-4)

For the past year and a half, verse 4 has burned in my heart. Currently, I'm serving as interim pastor in a small town known for its rampant New Age inclusiveness – occult practices, Tarot readings held in a coffee shop across the street from a church, open marijuana use, statues of the Hindu god Shiva displayed in many shop windows, worship of ancient gods and goddesses, and an annual psychic festival! For our congregation to bear spiritual fruit in this community, the answer isn't to just shout louder. Victory will come only through learning to pray more powerfully. This is the spiritual warfare that Paul talked about in the great, but demon-ridden, cities where he ministered:

> "For our struggle is not against flesh and blood, but against the rulers, against the authorities, against the powers of this dark world and against the spiritual forces of evil in the heavenly realms." (Ephesians 6:12)

Spiritual struggle isn't limited to my city – it just seems concentrated there. It exists in cities and towns around the world – and even where you live. But it has certainly got my attention.

Look at these verses with me.

The subject is lost people, "unbelievers" (verse 4), "those who are perishing" (verse

---

[9] "Veiled" (NIV, NRSV), "hid" (KJV) is *kalyptō*, "to cause something not to be known, hide, conceal, keep secret" (BDAG 505, 2b).

3). "Perishing" (NIV, NRSV), "lost" (KJV) is *apollymi*, a present middle/passive participle, indicating an ongoing condition. The verb means, "perish, be ruined, die," especially of eternal death.[10] Perishing / lost means that men and women, boys and girls are in the process of spiritual death – forever and ever. This is a life and death struggle we're engaged in for the souls of mankind. The stakes couldn't be higher!

The culprit is "the god of this age," that is, the false god worshipped by the world around us – Satan. Jesus called him "the prince of this world" (John 14:30; 16:11). Paul called him, "the ruler of the kingdom of the air, the spirit who is now at work in those who are disobedient" (Ephesians 2:2). He currently exercises his power is this world (1 John 5:19; Revelation 12:12-13). He is a deceiver, "a liar and the father of lies" (John 8:44). People don't realize that they are obeying Satan and worshipping him (Ephesians 2:2); they're just going with the flow of society. A true Satanist is rare, even in California where I live. But even though people are *deceived* by Satan, that doesn't mean that they won't *reap the bitter fruits* of their deception. This is no game; this is real life.

It is important, however, to realize that Satan does not have a right to this world! He is a usurper, seeking to encroach on God's property.

> "The earth is the LORD's, and everything in it,
> the world, and all who live in it." (Psalm 24:1)

> "The thief comes only to steal and kill and destroy;
> I have come that they may have life, and have it to the full" (John 10:10).

Satan's strategy is deception, blinding man's mind. Blinding means "to deprive of sight."[11] People think they see clearly, but "they **cannot see** the light of the gospel of the glory of Christ, who is the image of God" (3:3-4). They don't get it. Their minds[12] seem veiled.[13] They can't comprehend the gospel. It doesn't make sense to them. Instead of seeing in the gospel "the glory of Christ," it seems to them like a mere fairy tale. They have no sense of the awfulness of sin, of the judgment upon their lives, or of their own desperate situation. They have no sense of holiness, of God's love, or of Christ's humbling himself to take upon himself the sin of the world. They parody the gospel. They make fun of people who fear God.

They can't see it. Why? Two factors, I believe:

---

[10] *Apollymi*, BDAG 116, 1bα. I explore this word and concept rather thoroughly in an article, "People Aren't Really 'Lost' ... Are They?" (www.joyfulheart.com/evang/lost.htm).

[11] "Blinded" is *typhloō*, "to deprive of sight, to blind" (BDAG 1021).

[12] "Minds" is *noēma*, "the faculty of processing thought, mind, understanding" (BDAG 675, 2).

[13] "Veiled" (NIV, NRSV), "hid" (KJV) is *kalyptō*, "to cause something not to be known, hide, conceal, keep secret" (BDAG 505, 2b).

1. Blinding by Satan and
2. Deliberate refusal to believe."

People aren't just dupes of Satan. They bear responsibility for their guilt. Paul says of the end time:

> "The coming of the lawless one will be in accordance with the work of Satan displayed in all kinds of counterfeit miracles, signs and wonders, and in every sort of evil that **deceives** those who are perishing. They perish because they **refused to love the truth** and so be saved." (2 Thessalonians 2:9-10)

They refused to grasp, receive, take hold of[14] the truth they *do* have. As a result, they are dead meat. They are not innocent unbelievers, but culpable and responsible for the truth they have heard.

The counterinsurgency strategy. What should we do in the face of this deceptive, spiritual blindness that is maintained over lost mankind by the evil one? We do what Paul did:

1. **We fight with prayer and spiritual weapons** (Ephesians 6:10-20). We under-gird a ministry of evangelism with earnest prayer and intercession.
2. **We are open and honest** in our own communication (4:2), not deceptive or manipulative. We're not going to "save" people, even if we can "get" them to pray the sinner's prayer. This is God's work.
3. **We declare the good news of Jesus Christ with clarity** and his death for our sins – even if it is met with disdain (1 Corinthians 1:17-18). We fight falsehood with truth: the "belt of truth" and "the sword of the Spirit, which is the Word of God" (Ephesians 6:14, 17). There is spiritual power in the gospel for those who are being saved! Paul said,

   > "I am not ashamed of the **gospel**, because **it is the power of God** for the salvation of everyone who believes: first for the Jew, then for the Gentile." (Romans 1:16)

4. **We love our unsaved friends** with the degree of intensity that "God so loved the world that he gave his one and only Son...." (John 3:16). I've heard hateful, blaming street-corner sermons that only serve to turn people away, rather than communicate "the light of the gospel of the glory of Christ, who is the image of God." (4:4)

Nobody said ministry is easy, friends. To minister to the lost is to engage in the spiritual battle as a determined participant, rather than a bystander – or worse, a

---

[14] *Dechomai* in 2 Thessalonians 2:10 means, "receive, grasp," here, "to indicate approval or conviction by accepting, be receptive of, be open to, approve, accept" (BDAG 222, 5).

spiritually blinded and neutralized believer.

We've spent a lot of time on verse 3 and 4, but they contain an important key to understanding the lay of the spiritual land.

Q2. (2 Corinthians 4:3-4) Since Satan has blinded people's eyes to the truth, is there any hope for them? What strategies must we use to overcome spiritual blindness? How many people are likely to find Christ without intercessory prayer?
http://www.joyfulheart.com/forums/index.php?showtopic=1087

Christ, the Glory of God (4:5-6)

Paul continues,

"⁵ For we do not preach ourselves, but Jesus Christ as Lord, and ourselves as your servants for Jesus' sake. ⁶ For God, who said, 'Let light shine out of darkness,' made his light shine in our hearts to give us the light of the knowledge of the glory of God in the face of Christ." (4:5-6)

This isn't about us, says Paul. We point to Christ. We are only your servants for Jesus' sake, that is, out of our love for Jesus and his mission. It is God's sovereign work to bring spiritual enlightenment, to make the message clear to people's blinded minds. It is an act of creation of the God who spoke his creative word: "Let light shine out of darkness" (Genesis 1:3, 14). But it is our job to declare it.

Treasure in Clay Jars (4:7)

Now Paul talks about the reality of ministry. We bear the precious and awesome "light of the knowledge of the glory of God in the face of Christ" (4:6), but we are just weak, human vessels, subject to imperfection and breakage. It's a paradox. Paul says,

"But we have this treasure in jars of clay to show that this all-surpassing power is from God and not from us." (4:7)

Again – this is not about us! "Jars of clay" (NIV, cf. NRSV) or "earthen vessels" (KJV, RSV) are pottery containers. The verse contains four key words that I'd like to highlight.

The first word is *ostrakinos*, "made of earth/clay."[15] You probably have a few kiln-fired flower pots at your house. The least expensive ones are made of red clay, formed and fired. The best have a colorful glaze on the surface that bring beauty. But when you look at the bottom of a glazed pot you can see that it is still just clay – nothing exotic.

---

[15] *Ostrakinos*, BDAG 430.

Archaeological digs have found many, many thousands of pieces of broken pottery. Pottery vessels are useful for a while, but have a limited working life. Then they fail, crack, break, and ultimately dissolve.

The second word is *skeuos*, **"vessel**, jar, dish, a container of any kind," then figuratively, "a human being exercising a function, instrument, vessel."[16] Again: The focus shouldn't be on about. We're just the container. The focus should be on the contents: "the light of the knowledge of the glory of God in the face of Christ" (4:6), the "all-surpassing power" of God at work within us (Ephesians 3:20).

A third word describes the contents, *hyperbolē*, **"all-surpassing"** (NIV), "extraordinary" (NRSV), "excellency" (KJV), which we see also in 1:18; 12:17; and will examine later in this lesson at 4:17. It means, "a state of exceeding to an extraordinary degree a point on a scale of extent, excess, extraordinary quality/character."[17]

A fourth word names the contents, *dynamis*, **"power."**

No, it's not about us.

> "We have this treasure in jars of clay to show that this all-surpassing power is from God and **not from us**." (4:7)

This is about Christ, his love, and his power! Have you ever felt weak, powerless in yourself. I'm sure that Paul did, too. But the One who indwelt Paul – and now, you – is not weak and powerless. You are a limited vessel. He is the unlimited contents of that vessel poured out to quench the spiritual thirst of lost humankind. It's not about you! It's about him!

Q3. (2 Corinthians 4:7) What truth is Paul seeking to communicate by this analogy of a treasure in a pottery jar? What does the clay jar represent? What does the treasure represent? What's the paradox here?
http://www.joyfulheart.com/forums/index.php?showtopic=1088

Pressures on Every Side (4:8-9)

Now Paul talks about some of the pressures of the Christian life and ministry. He has alluded to them before (1:8-9) and will speak more about them later (11:22-28). He says,

> "8 We are hard pressed on every side, but not crushed; perplexed, but not in despair; 9 persecuted, but not abandoned; struck down, but not destroyed." (4:8-9)

[16] *Skeuos,* BDAG 928, 2 and 3.
[17] *Hyperbolē,* BDAG 1032.

In this sentence, Paul lays out four pairs of words – first, the difficulty the "clay" faces, then second, the hope the "treasure" affords.

Word Pair 1. Pressure

"Hard pressed" (NIV), "afflicted" (NRSV), "troubled" (KJV), not just in one area at a time but "on every side." There are multiple pressures. The verb is *thlibō*, which has the basic idea of "to press, compress, make narrow." Here it is used figuratively, "to cause to be troubled, oppress, afflict."[18] Have you ever had a sinus headache, when your head seemed to be in a vise? This is a spiritual headache – from multiple sources!

"But not crushed" (NIV, NRSV), "not distressed" (KJV) is the negative particle plus *stenochōreō*. The verb means basically, "to confine or restrict to a narrow space, crowd, cramp, confine, restrict." Figuratively, it means, "to be in a circumstance that seems to offer no way out, be distressed."[19] Yes, you are under pressure, says Paul, but you have a way out – you aren't restricted to only that narrow space. You find freedom in God!

Word Pair 2. Confusion

"Perplexed" is *aporeō*. It has the basic meaning, especially found in ancient Greek papyrus documents, of "to be without resources." From this evolved the meaning, "to be in a confused state of mind, be at a loss, be in doubt, be uncertain."[20] You can identify with that! You wonder: What in the world is going on?

"Not in despair" (NIV, KJV), "not driven to despair" (NRSV). The verb is *exaporeō*, a compound word from the root of *aporeō*, the first word in the pair. The preposition *ex-* compounded to this verb adds the idea of "entirely, utterly"[21] to the original verb: "to be utterly at a loss, be utterly destitute of measures or resources, to renounce all hope, be in despair."[22]

Yes, Paul was confused at times – perplexed, at a loss for what to do. But he found God's help in it so that he wasn't without someone to turn to.

Word Pair 3. Persecuted

"Persecuted" is *diōkō*. Literally, it means, "to make to run or flee, put to flight, drive away." But most of the time in the New Testament, it means, "to harass someone,"

---

[18] *Thlibō* is used three times in 2 Corinthians: here and at 1:6 and 7:5 (BDAG 457, 3).

[19] *Stenochōreō*, BDAG 492, 2.

[20] *Aporeō*, BDAG 119.

[21] *Ex*, Thayer 192, VI, 6.

[22] *Exaporeō*, Thayer 222; "to be at a loss psychologically, be in great difficulty, doubt, embarrassment" (BDAG 345).

especially because of beliefs, "trouble, molest, persecute."[23] In ancient Greek papyrus documents it sometimes means, "to accuse."[24]

"Abandoned" (NIV), "forsaken" (NRSV, KJV) is *enkataleipō,* "to separate connection with someone or something, forsake, abandon, desert."[25] We have God's promise: "I will never leave you or forsake (*enkataleipō*) you" (Hebrews 13:5, NRSV, quoting Deuteronomy 31:6).

Sometimes we feel alone, but we are not. Jesus said to us disciples, "surely I am with you always, to the very end of the age" (Matthew 28:20).

Word Pair 4. Struck Down

"Struck down" (NIV, NRSV), "cast down" (KJV) is *kataballō,* "to strike with sufficient force so as to knock down, throw down, strike down."[26] It probably happened to Paul literally, considering all the physical violence directed his way (11:23-25). But in its figurative sense, this happens to us a lot. We "get the wind knocked out of our sails." We "take a hit" that "throws us for a loop." We have devastating circumstances that we don't bounce back from right away. We think that we can never endure this! Paul felt that way:

> "We were under great pressure, far beyond our ability to endure, so that we despaired even of life. Indeed, in our hearts we felt the sentence of death. But this happened that we might not rely on ourselves but on God, who raises the dead." (1:8-9)

"Not destroyed" is *apollymi,* "destroyed," here in the passive voice, "perish, be ruined." We saw this same word in 2:15 and earlier in this lesson at 4:3 in the sense of eternal destruction. But here, Paul is probably talking more in physical and psychological terms.

The Message paraphrase renders these word pairs in the vernacular:

> "We've been surrounded and battered by troubles, but we're not demoralized;
> we're not sure what to do, [9] but we know that God knows what to do;
> we've been spiritually terrorized, but God hasn't left our side;
> we've been thrown down, but we haven't broken."

In the natural order, we'd be wiped out by all this conflict and pressure, threat and blows. But we are not to be incapacitated. Jesus said:

> "I have told you these things, so that in me you may have peace. In this world you will

---

[23] *Diōkō,* BDAG 254, 2; Thayer 153, 2.
[24] A. Oepke, *diōkō,* TDNT 2:229-230.
[25] *Enkataleipō,* BDAG 273, 2.
[26] *Kataballō,* BDAG 514, 2.

have trouble. But take heart! I have overcome the world." (John 16:33)

Death in Us, Life in You (4:10-12)

Everyone in the world is seeking to be happy. It's natural to avoid pain and suffering at all costs. But paradoxically, that can be a deceptive path. The saying, "No pain, no gain," applies to physical exercise, but also to spiritual growth and to serving God. In the verses that follow, Paul shares this unique – and unpopular – insight.

> "We always carry around in our body the death of Jesus, so that the life of Jesus may also be revealed in our body." (4:10)

Everyone – even sinners – experiences problems. Christians too. But they also share in Christ's sufferings, especially when we take righteous actions that expose others' sin and selfishness. Paul told Timothy:

> "Everyone who wants to live a godly life in Christ Jesus will be persecuted." (2 Timothy 3:12)

Jesus told his disciples:

> "No servant is greater than his master. If they persecuted me, they will persecute you also. If they obeyed my teaching, they will obey yours also." (John 15:20)

Given the fact of suffering, it's instructive to see how Christ can use it to work out his purposes.

> "¹⁰ We always carry around in our body the death of Jesus, so that the life of Jesus may also be revealed in our body. ¹¹ For we who are alive are always being given over to death for Jesus' sake, so that his life may be revealed in our mortal body. ¹² So then, death is at work in us, but life is at work in you." (4:10-12)

When we are exposed to struggle, stress, and pain, our inner self is exposed. People can see us for what we are. If we're sniveling cowards, that will become obvious. If we exhibit God's grace under pressure, people will see that as well. When we suffer, people can see Jesus' work within us and will be attracted to the authenticity they see. That's why Paul talks about his weaknesses and sufferings so much. His opponents at Corinth, the so-called "super-apostles" (11:5; 12:1), boasted without cause and had never suffered for Christ.

Paul knew that his sufferings revealed Christ's reality to others. So he was able to be transparent and real. Christ's life "may be revealed in our mortal body," if we are surrendered to him. We experience problems, but others are blessed by seeing God's grace in action in our lives.

Trouble has a way of cracking the earthenware pot, but that just allows others to see the glory of the treasure that lies within (4:7).

Q4. (2 Corinthians 4:8-12) How does it encourage you to know that Paul went through tremendous stress and pressure? What effect did these sufferings have on the way people could see Christ in Paul? Why is pain necessary to spiritual growth? How does our pain allow others to assess our authenticity as Christians?
http://www.joyfulheart.com/forums/index.php?showtopic=1089

Faith in the Resurrection (4:13-14)

Now Paul refers to a passage that recounts the words of a suffering psalmist:

"It is written: 'I believed; therefore I have spoken.'" (4:13a)[27]

Paul claims the same kind of wisdom that arises from faith that has suffered yet prevailed:

"13b With that same spirit of faith we also believe and therefore speak, 14 because we know that the one who raised the Lord Jesus from the dead will also raise us with Jesus and present us with you in his presence." (4:13b-14)

Faith considers the long view. Life is more than present happiness. A life well-lived in Christ, no matter how much pain has been endured, will be rewarded in resurrection at Christ's coming. Pain is only temporary. Christ wins!

Outer Deterioration, Inner Renewal (4:15-16)

Pain can tempt us to get discouraged, to lose heart – the words with which Paul began this chapter (4:1). Perspective helps:

"15 All this is for your benefit, so that the grace that is reaching more and more people may cause thanksgiving to overflow to the glory of God. 16 Therefore we do not lose heart. Though outwardly we are wasting away, yet inwardly we are being renewed day by day." (4:15-16)

Paul outlines two reasons not to lose heart in suffering:

1. **Others benefit from our suffering**. Selfish people don't care if others benefit from their suffering. They're just plain miserable. But Paul looks to what will benefit[28]

---

[27] The full reference is as follows: "I believed; therefore I said, 'I am greatly afflicted'" (Psalm 116:10).

[28] Your benefit" (NIV) is more literally, "for your sake" (NRSV, KJV), using the preposition *dia*, here a "marker of something constituting cause, the reason why something happens, results, exists; because of, for the sake of" (BDAG 225, 2a).

the Corinthians the most. As a result of seeing others benefit, Paul doesn't lose heart.

2. **We benefit from our own suffering.** Look at verse 16 once more.

> "Though outwardly we are wasting away, yet inwardly we are being renewed day by day." (4:16b)

Wasting Away. If we live long enough – or go through enough persecution – our bodies gradually develop chronic problems. Our joints and organs begin to wear out. Our eyesight and hearing dim. "Outwardly" (literally, in "our outer man") we're breaking down. "Wasting away" (NIV, NRSV), "perish" (KJV) is the verb *diaphtheirō* in the present tense, which indicates continuous ongoing action. The word means, "to cause the destruction of something, spoil, destroy," and is used to describe the action of rust and of food spoiling, as well as the ongoing physical deterioration suggested in this passage.[29]

Being Renewed. At the same time, "inwardly" (literally, in "our inner man") we are being "renewed." *Anakainoō*, properly means, "to cause to grow up (*ana-*) new, to make new."[30] We see the same word in Colossians:

> "[You] have put on the new self, which is being renewed in knowledge in the image of its Creator." (Colossians 3:10)

This is an ongoing process. It happens "day by day," a little bit at a time. Your body gradually loses vigor, but at the same time, in Christ, you gain in vigor and power and faith. This, dear friends, is simply another way of describing the process of sanctification.

Focusing on Eternal Glory (4:17-18)

Paul concludes this section with a pair of marvelous promises and insights.

> "For our light and momentary troubles are achieving for us an eternal glory that far outweighs them all." (4:17, NIV)

If you've just gone through some terrible experience and the pain is fresh, you may be offended by Paul's description of "light and momentary troubles." That may seem too callous. But Paul is speaking in comparative terms. The NRSV is a bit more literal so you can see the contrasts:

> "For this slight momentary affliction is preparing us for an eternal weight of glory beyond all measure." (4:17, NRSV)

---

[29] *Diaphtheirō*, BDAG 239, 1.
[30] *Anakainoō*, Thayer, p. 38. This Greek word is unique to Paul.

    1. Light/slight[31] affliction[32] vs. weight[33] of glory

    2. Momentary[34] vs. eternal.

Nor are these just equal pairs. The long-term glory exceeds the momentary light trouble by so much that the comparison is trivial – beyond all measure![35]

Fix Your Eyes on the Eternal (4:18)

If we just look at our present troubles, we fall into despair. We must see our current problems in the light of our glorious inheritance in heaven. This is the secret of ever-increasing faith!

> "So we fix our eyes not on what is seen, but on what is unseen. For what is seen is temporary, but what is unseen is eternal." (4:18)

This phrase "fix our eyes" (NIV), "look at" (NRSV, KJV) is *skopeō* (from which we get our English word "scope"), "to pay careful attention to, look (out) for, notice someone or something."[36] Paul is recommending thought control, selective attention. Don't be discouraged by the problems you can see in this physical world. They are "temporary" (NIV, NRSV) or "temporal" (KJV), lasting only for a time.[37]

The world usually operates on a very time-bound point-of-view, a human perspective that can be skewed and mistaken (5:18). Its philosophy: Live every moment to the fullest now. Grab the gusto now; you only pass this way once. You don't have tomorrow; you only have today. *Carpe diem* ("seize the day"). But though this may get you to take some action, since it lacks perspective, the action you choose may be the wrong one. Paul suggests, rather, live your lives now with an awareness of eternity. View your troubles with an awareness of heaven to come.

Dear friend, even if you have been enduring a very heavy burden for what seems to be a very long time, in view of eternity this will be just a split second and light as a feather when compared to the weightiness of the riches God will bestow upon you in his Presence.

---

[31] *Elaphros*, "having little weight, light" in weight, "insignificant" (BDAG 314, 1).

[32] *Thlipsis*, "trouble that inflicts distress, oppression, affliction, tribulation" (BDAG 457, 1).

[33] *Baros*, "weight, burden," here "fullness" (BDAG 167, 3). In Hebrew "glory" carries the idea of heaviness, substance, so "weight of glory" to a Hebrew speaker doubles the idea of weightiness.

[34] "Momentary" is *parautika*, "pertaining to a point of time immediately subsequent to another point of time, on the spot, immediately, for the present" (BDAG 772).

[35] The Greek uses the idiom "from excess to excess," which we also see in 3:18, "from one degree of glory to another." *Eis*, "marker of degree, up to" (BDAG 289, 3).

[36] *Skopeō*, BDAG 932.

[37] *Proskairos*, "lasting only for a time, temporary, transitory" (BDAG 880), from *pros-*, "to, for," of a thing adjusted to some standard + *kairos*, "time" (*pros*, Thayer, 543, IV, 5).

Q5. (2 Corinthians 4:15-18) In what way do problems and physical deterioration help us toward "an eternal weight of glory"? Why is it so easy to focus on temporal matters to the exclusion of eternal things? Why is a focus on eternal things so important to our spiritual growth? What can we do to help shift our focus?

http://www.joyfulheart.com/forums/index.php?showtopic=1090

Prayer

Father, so often I see things from a human point of view. I don't see the big picture, so I'm overwhelmed by today's gritty details. Please broaden my faith and my perspective. Teach me to fix my eyes on what is important and lasting, not on what is trivial and fleeting. Help me, O God, to see things as you see them, and so transcend my time-bound world to live in Christ in heavenly places. In Jesus' name, I plead. Amen.

Key Verses

This week's lesson has a number of memorable verses!

"The god of this age has blinded the minds of unbelievers, so that they cannot see the light of the gospel of the glory of Christ, who is the image of God." (2 Corinthians 4:18)

"But we have this treasure in jars of clay to show that this all-surpassing power is from God and not from us." (2 Corinthians 4:7)

"We are hard pressed on every side, but not crushed; perplexed, but not in despair; persecuted, but not abandoned; struck down, but not destroyed." (2 Corinthians 4:8-9)

"We always carry around in our body the death of Jesus, so that the life of Jesus may also be revealed in our body." (2 Corinthians 4:10)

"Therefore we do not lose heart. Though outwardly we are wasting away, yet inwardly we are being renewed day by day." (2 Corinthians 4:16)

"For our light and momentary troubles are achieving for us an eternal glory that far outweighs them all." (2 Corinthians 4:17)

"So we fix our eyes not on what is seen, but on what is unseen. For what is seen is temporary, but what is unseen is eternal." (2 Corinthians 4:18)

6. Walking by Faith, Not by Sight (5:1-16)

Pompeo Giralamo Batoni (1708-1787), "St. Paul," oil on canvas, Basildon Park, The National Trust, UK.

Paul has been talking about the wasting away of the outer person, the body, and preparation for an "eternal weight of glory" in heaven, the contrast between the temporary and the eternal. This passage continues this theme by examining what things will be like in God's presence, our eternal home – and the faith walk that we are engaged in.

Earthly Tent vs. Heavenly House (5:1)

Paul begins by using the analogy that compares a tent, the most impermanent of structures, with a house, designed to last indefinitely.

"Now we know that if the earthly[1] tent[2] we live in is destroyed, we have a building[3] from God, an eternal[4] house[5] in heaven,[6] not built by human hands."[7] (5:1)

The "earthly tent" Paul is talking about is, of course, our human body. If you've been

---

[1] "Earthly" is *epigeios*, "pertaining to what is characteristic of the earth as opposed to heavenly, earthly" (BDAG 369, 1a).

[2] Literally, "house of our tabernacle" (KJV). Uses *oikia*, "house" and *skēnos*, "a temporary abode as opposed to a permanent structure, tent, lodging" (BDAG 929).

[3] "Building" is *oikodomē*, "a building as the result of a construction process, building, edifice" (BDAG 697, 2b).

[4] "Eternal" is *aiōnios*, "pertaining to a period of unending duration, without end"(BDAG 33, 3).

[5] "House" is *oikia*, "a structure used as a dwelling, house" (BDAG 695, 1b).

[6] "Heavens" is the plural of *ouranos*, "transcendent abode, heaven" (BDAG 739, 2d).

[7] "Not built by human hands" (NIV), "not made with hands" (NRSV, KJV) is *acheiropoiētos*, "not made by (human) hand," here and Colossians 2:11 (of circumcision) and Mark 14:58 (of a transcendent temple) (BDAG 159).

tent-camping you know that when it comes time to "break camp" or "strike the tent," the poles are taken down, the stakes are pulled, and the tent collapses, finally to be rolled into a relatively small bundle. The word Paul uses is "destroyed" (NIV, NRSV), "dissolved" (KJV).[8] A tent is temporary and portable, never intended to be thought of as permanent. The tent in this analogy is our human body.

But what does our "eternal house in heaven" represent? Here you'll find a number of interpretations, some of them pretty obscure:

1. The Body of Christ, the Church,
2. The New Jerusalem,
3. The heavenly temple of the Lord's presence,
4. The mansion-like abode to which the Lord's people go after death, and
5. Our resurrection body.

Option 4 was adopted by a number of older Bible interpreters, including St. Thomas Aquinas. It imports into this passage Jesus' analogy of death – a large house with individual rooms.

> "**In my Father's house are many rooms**; if it were not so, I would have told you. I am going there to prepare a **place** for you. And if I go and prepare a **place** for you, I will come back and take you to be with me that you also may be where I am. You know the way to the **place** where I am going." (John 14:2-4)

The problem with the mansion interpretation is that it breaks Paul's own analogy:

- Single Tent to House
- Temporary to Eternal

The mansion interpretation would require an analogy of single tent to many-roomed mansion, an idea which isn't found anywhere in the context. It would also require *oika*, "house," to be used two very different ways in the same sentence.[9] Not very likely.

I believe that the best way to understand "eternal house in heaven" is as a resurrection body. I reach this conclusion for a number of reasons:

1. Paul has already introduced resurrection a few verses previously at 4:14.
2. Paul taught the Corinthians about resurrection bodies extensively in a previous letter, especially:

> "For the perishable must clothe itself with the imperishable, and the mortal with immortality. When the perishable has been clothed with the imperishable, and the mor-

---

[8] *Katalyō*, "to cause the ruin of something, destroy, demolish, dismantle," here, figuratively, "tear down, demolish" (BDAG 523, 2b).

[9] Barnett, p. 258, fn. 15.

tal with immortality, then the saying that is written will come true: 'Death has been swallowed up in victory.'" (1 Corinthians 15:53-54)

3.   The vocabulary of "groaning" (5:2) is found in conjunction with resurrection, "the redemption of our bodies" in Romans 8:18-24, written about the same time as 2 Corinthians.

4.   The vocabulary of "being clothed" (5:2, 4) is found in conjunction with resurrection bodies in the passage quoted above (1 Corinthians 15:53).[10]

It seems likely that here Paul is comparing our impermanent physical bodies with our permanent resurrection bodies.

Groaning and Longing (5:2-4)

Now Paul continues as he contemplates our present state:

"[2] Meanwhile we groan,[11] longing[12] to be clothed[13] with our heavenly dwelling,[14] [3] because when we are clothed,[15] we will not be found naked.[16] [4] For while we are in this tent, we groan and are burdened,[17] because we do not wish to be unclothed[18] but to be clothed with our heavenly dwelling, so that what is mortal may be swallowed up by life." (5:2-4)

Here Paul mixes his metaphors, adding to the idea of a heavenly dwelling the idea of being clothed.

The strong dualism of the Greeks saw death as an opportunity to be freed from the "evil" physical body so that the "good" spirit might be free at last. But Paul teaches that death is not the freeing of the spirit (resulting in being found naked, unclothed), but the putting on of another kind of clothing, a teaching similar to what he had taught this church about resurrection in 1 Corinthians 15:53-54.

---

[10] For this interpretation see Kruse, pp. 112-114; Barnett, pp. 256-260; Bruce, pp. 200-202; Barrett, pp. 149-157.

[11] "Groan" is *stenazō*, "to express oneself involuntarily in the face of an undesirable circumstance, sigh, groan" (BDAG 942, 1).

[12] "Longing" is *epipotheō*, "to have a strong desire for something, with implication of need, long for, desire" (BDAG 373).

[13] "Clothed" is *ependyomai*, "to put a garment on over an existing garment, put on (in addition)" (BDAG 363).

[14] "Dwelling" is *oikētērion*, "a place for living, dwelling, habitation" (BDAG 695).

[15] *Endyō*, middle voice, "to put any kind of thing on oneself, clothe oneself in, put on, wear something" (BDAG 333, 2a).

[16] "Naked" is *gymnos*, "naked," here figuratively, "uncovered, bare" (BDAG 208, 1b).

[17] "Burdened" is *bareō*, "to press down as if with a weight, weigh down, burden," here, "oppressed" (BDAG 166, b).

[18] "Unclothed" is *ekdyō*, "to remove clothing from the body, strip, take off" (BDAG 303, 1).

Swallowed Up by Life (5:4b)

In our physical bodies we groan now and are burdened with physical aches and pains, as well as the other hardships of life, but death brings us into a whole new existence.

> "We … wish … to be clothed with our heavenly dwelling, so that what is mortal[19] may be swallowed up by life."[20] (5:4b)

"Swallowed up" is *katapinō*, literally, "drink down, swallow," here figuratively, with the idea of "to destroy completely … to cause the end of something, swallow up."[21] The mortal existence will be fully replaced by Life with a capital L.

Made for Life, Guaranteed by the Spirit (5:5)

Indeed, this resurrection body was God's intention all along.

> "Now it is God who has made[22] us for this very purpose[23] and has given us the Spirit as a deposit, guaranteeing what is to come." (5:5)

Sometimes we act as if this physical world is all there is. Oh, we believe in heaven, but don't give it a lot of thought. But notice what this verse says.

> "He who has prepared us for this very thing is God." (5:5a, NRSV)

God has not only prepared us for life in this world, but also for life forever in heavenly places. And the Holy Spirit he has given us is our bridge to this heavenly world.

> "... who has given us the Spirit as a guarantee." (5:5b)

Guarantee of what? This phrase "a deposit, guaranteeing what is to come" (NIV), "as a guarantee" (NRSV), "earnest" (KJV) is *arrabōn*, "payment of part of a purchase price in advance, first installment, deposit, down payment, pledge."[24] We saw this word already in 1:22. The Holy Spirit serves as a reminder that there is more to come. As you get to know the Holy Spirit, you begin to find out that nothing is impossible. You discover that he opens the door to a great adventure in God. (Sadly, many Christians have never got to know him.)

Is the Holy Spirit only a pledge? Of course not. He is God himself living within us.

---

[19] "What is mortal" (NIV, NRSV), "mortality" (KJV) is *thnētos*, "mortal" in contrast to immortal. (BDAG 458), literally, "subject to death," from *thanō*, "to die."

[20] "Life" is *zōē*, "life, existence," here, "transcendent life" (BDAG 433, 2bβ).

[21] *Katapinō*, BDAG 524, 3.

[22] "Made" (NIV), "prepared" (NRSV), "wrought" (KJV) is *katergazomai*, "to cause to be well prepared, prepare someone" (BDAG 532, 3).

[23] "Purpose" (NIV) is actually "thing."

[24] *Arrabōn*, BDAG 134. *Arrabōn* also appears in Ephesians 1:14.

But he expands our field of view to see what lies beyond us in the heavenly world to come and he abides in us to remind us that more is coming.

Q1. (2 Corinthians 5:1-5) In what sense are our bodies like tents? If we were to truly look forward to our "house not made with hands," how would it affect our daily lives here?
http://www.joyfulheart.com/forums/index.php?showtopic=1091

Longing for Home (5:6-8)

"6 Therefore we are always confident and know that as long as we are at home in the body we are away from the Lord. 7 We live by faith, not by sight. 8 We are confident, I say, and would prefer to be away from the body and at home with the Lord." (5:6-8)

The presence of the Holy Spirit in us increases our confidence,[25] so that our fear of death is decreased and we are confident of life beyond this life, confident enough that we will live our lives accordingly.

Now Paul sets up a dichotomy between life in our bodies here on earth, and life in God's immediate presence in heaven.

In verse 6-9, Paul uses two compound words built around a single root: *dēmos*, "a country district, people of a country."[26]

1. *Endēmeō*, "to be in a familiar place, to be at home."[27]
2. *Ekdēmeō*, "leave one's country, take a long journey," here, "leave, get away from."[28]

"6 Therefore we are always confident and know that as long as we are **at home** (*endēmeō*) in the body we are **away from** (*ekdēmeō*) the Lord. 7 We live by faith, not by sight. 8 We are confident, I say, and would prefer[29] to be **away from** (*ekdēmeō*) the body and **at home** (*endēmeō*) with the Lord." (5:6-8)

You can't be both places at once. For a believer, it's either one or the other.

We see a similar teaching in Paul's letter to the Philippians on whether or not he will

---

[25] "Confident" is *tharreō*, "to have certainty in a matter, be confident, be courageous" (BDAG 444). The word occurs here in verses 6 and 8, and 7:16; 10:1-2.

[26] *Dēmos*, Henry George Liddell and Robert Scott, *An Intermediate Greek-English Lexicon* (Oxford: Clarendon Press, 1889).

[27] *Endēmeō*, BDAG 332.

[28] *Ekdēmeō*, BDAG 300, 1.

[29] "Prefer" (NIV), "rather be" (NRSV, KJV) is *eudokeō*, "wish rather, prefer" (BDAG 404, 1).

be executed in prison:

> "²²If I am to go on living in the body, this will mean fruitful labor for me. Yet what shall I choose? I do not know! ²³ I am torn between the two: **I desire to depart**[30] **and be with Christ, which is better by far**; ²⁴ but it is more necessary for you that I remain in the body." (Philippians 1:22-24)

The Problem with the Doctrine of 'Soul Sleep'

The reason we're spending time on this is because our Seventh Day Adventist brothers and sisters have a doctrine known as "soul sleep."[31] Essentially, it teaches that when a believer dies, he isn't immediately with Christ, but his soul sleeps or is unconscious until the resurrection of the dead when Christ returns. Then suddenly he awakes, unaware that any time has passed.

The confusion comes from a common euphemism of death as sleeping (for example, John 11:11-14) and a lack of understanding by some Old Testament authors of eternal life (Psalm 146:4; Ecclesiastes 9:5-6), a truth that was fully revealed in the New Testament. But Paul's teaching here in 5:6-8 makes it pretty clear that "soul sleep" is an inadequate explanation. There is no intermediate "sleeping" state. We're either in the body or with the Lord! As Jesus said to the dying thief on the cross:

> "I tell you the truth, today you will be with me in paradise." (Luke 23:43)

Dear friend, when you die, your spirit immediately goes to be with God. It is with him that you will enjoy the time between your death and the resurrection. Note carefully Paul's teaching to the church in Thessalonica concerning Christ's return and the resurrection:

> "¹⁴ᵇ **Through Jesus, God will bring with him those who have fallen asleep**. ¹⁵ For this we declare to you by the word of the Lord, that we who are alive, who are left until the coming of the Lord, **shall not precede those who have fallen asleep**. ¹⁶ For the Lord himself will descend from heaven with a cry of command, with the archangel's call, and with the sound of the trumpet of God. And **the dead in Christ will rise first**; ¹⁷ then we who are alive, who are left, shall be caught up together with them in the clouds to meet the Lord in the air; and so we shall always be with the Lord." (1 Thessalonians 4:14-17, RSV)

We see a similar teaching in 1 Corinthians:

> "Listen, I tell you a mystery: We will not all sleep, but we will all be changed – in a flash,

---

[30] "Depart" is *analyō*, originally, "loose, untie," here, "depart, return." (BDAG 67, 2).

[31] The doctrine is also known by Seventh Day Adventists as "conditional immortality" and is part of their belief on the "state of the dead."

in the twinkling of an eye, at the last trumpet. For the trumpet will sound, the dead will be raised imperishable, and we will be changed." (1 Corinthians 15:51-52)

Revelation also gives us a glimpse of Christian martyrs in heaven prior to the resurrection:

> "When he opened the fifth seal, I saw under the altar **the souls** of those who had been slain because of the word of God and the testimony they had maintained.... Each of them was **given a white robe**, and they were told to wait a little longer, until the number of their fellow servants and brothers who were to be killed as they had been was completed." (Revelation 6:9, 11)

An old Fanny Crosby hymn draws on the wording of our passage in 5:4 to express this.

> When He comes in the clouds descending,
> And they who loved Him here,
> From their graves shall awake and praise Him
> With joy and not with fear;
> **When the body and the soul are united,**
> **And clothed no more to die,**
> What a shouting there will be when each other's face we see,
> Changed in the twinkling of an eye.[32]

What this intermediate state is like – after death but before the resurrection – we aren't told much, but we look forward to resurrection bodies when Christ returns. And we praise God that our fellowship with Jesus will continue uninterrupted!

Q2. (2 Corinthians 5:6-8) How do Paul's words comfort you when you consider your death? What do Christians believe happens when we die? What will happen to us if we die before Christ returns? What will happen to us when Christ returns?
http://www.joyfulheart.com/forums/index.php?showtopic=1092

Walk by Faith, Not by Sight (5:7)

> "We live by faith, not by sight." (NIV)

> "For we walk by faith, not by sight." (NRSV)

Such a short verse, but it sums up the Christian life so powerfully. "Live". (NIV), "walk" (NRSV, KJV) is *peripateō*, "walk," used figuratively, as "to conduct one's life,

---

[32] "In the Twinkling of an Eye," words: Fanny Crosby (1898), music: William J. Kirkpatrick.

comport oneself, behave, live as habit of conduct."[33]

The way we conduct ourselves is by spiritual sight,[34] seeing things through the Spirit with an eternal perspective. A few verses previous, Paul had written something quite similar:

> "So we fix our eyes not on what is seen, but on what is unseen. For what is seen is temporary, but what is unseen is eternal." (4:18)

A faith perspective marks all mature disciples. Consider these statements of faith:

> "Jesus told [Thomas], 'Because you have seen me, you have believed; blessed are those who have not seen and yet have believed.'" (John 20:29)

> "I have been crucified with Christ and I no longer live, but Christ lives in me. The life I live in the body, I live by faith in the Son of God, who loved me and gave himself for me." (Galatians 2:20)

> "But my righteous one will live by faith. And if he shrinks back, I will not be pleased with him." (Hebrews 10:38, quoting Habakkuk 2:4)

> "Now faith is being sure of what we hope for and certain of what we do not see." (Hebrews 11:1)

> "Though you have not seen him, you love him; and even though you do not see him now, you believe in him and are filled with an inexpressible and glorious joy." (1 Peter 1:8)

We live out our lives here on earth tethered to heaven by the umbilical cord of the Holy Spirit, guided by the teachings of Jesus and his apostles, and expectant that God's promises will surely come to pass.

Q3. (2 Corinthians 5:7) What does it mean to walk by faith, not by sight? Why can't nonbelievers understand this kind of living? What aspects of your life are guided by your senses rather than by your faith? How can you bring a faith perspective into these areas?

http://www.joyfulheart.com/forums/index.php?showtopic=1093

Aiming to Please the Lord (5:9)

Since we are confident that our life is "hidden with Christ in God" (Colossians 3:3)... and since our citizenship is securely established in heaven (Philippians 3:20)...

---

[33] *Peripateō*, BDAG 803, 2aδ.
[34] "Sight" is *eidos*, "the act of looking/seeing, seeing, sight" (BDAG 280, 3).

> "So we make it our goal to please[35] him, whether we are at home in the body or away from it." (5:9)

Pleasing God is now our aim, our ambition in life.[36] Just like pleasing your mom or dad brought joy as a child, now we find joy in pleasing the Lord. Paul wrote:

> "Live as children of light ... and find out what pleases the Lord." (Ephesians 5:8b, 10)

For the disciple, life isn't about us anymore, but about him! We don't serve him in order to get to heaven – that's taken care of – we serve him because we love God. We are freed from worrying about saving ourselves so that we can enjoy a life of loving service pleasing God.

The Judgment Seat of Christ (5:10)

Having said that, however, we never lose sight of the fact that we are accountable to God. There will be a judgment.

> "For we must all appear before **the judgment seat of Christ**, that each one may receive what is due him for the things done while in the body, whether good or bad." (5:10)

The term "judgment seat" is *bēma*, "a dais or platform that required steps to ascend, tribunal." A magistrate would address an assembly from a chair placed on the structure. Here, it refers to the "judicial bench."[37] We also see this term in Paul's letter to the Roman church.

> "You, then, why do you judge your brother? Or why do you look down on your brother? For we will all stand before **God's judgment seat**. It is written: 'As surely as I live,' says the Lord, 'every knee will bow before me; every tongue will confess to God.'" (Romans 14:10-11, quoting Isaiah 45:23)

There, each person will "receive what is due" (NIV) or "receive recompense" (NRSV)[38] from the Lord. There is a fearful passage in Revelation about the judgment:

> "Then I saw a great white throne and him who was seated on it.... And I saw the dead, great and small, standing before the throne, and books were opened. Another book was opened, which is the book of life. The dead were judged according to what they had

---

[35] "Please" (NIV, NRSV), "be accepted" (KJV) is *euarestos*, "pleasing, acceptable," in the Greco-Roman world commonly said of things and especially of persons noted for their civic-minded generosity and who endeavor to do things that are pleasing (BDAG 403).

[36] The phrase, "make it our goal/aim" (NIV, NRSV), "labor" (KJV) is *philotimeomai*, "have as one's ambition, consider it an honor, aspire, with focus on the idea of rendering service" (BDAG 1059).

[37] *Bēma*, BDAG 175.

[38] The word is *komizō*, "to come into possession of something or experience something, carry off, get (for oneself), receive," frequently as recompense (BDAG 557, 3). Used in this sense in 1 Peter 5:4; Colossians 3:25; Ephesians 6:8.

done as recorded in the books.... Each person was judged according to what he had done.... If anyone's name was not found written in the book of life, he was thrown into the lake of fire." (Revelation 20:11-15)

Do we Christians have to appear before Christ's judgment? Haven't we already "passed from death to life" (John 5:24; 1 John 3:14). Paul anticipates Christ's judgment – and vindication (1 Corinthians 4:4). According to Romans 14:10, we too will appear before judgment.

But, praise God, our judgment will not be for salvation. That issue was settled when we put our faith in Christ, received the Holy Spirit, and our position became "in Christ." Our judgment there will be for rewards that we will receive for faithful service (1 Corinthians 3:13-15).

Persuading Men (5:11a)

However, while our verdict has already been pronounced as "pardoned," we have enough fear of God that we know what the verdict will be for our neighbors, family, and friends in the world who don't know Christ.

"Since, then, we know what it is to fear[39] the Lord, we try to persuade men." (5:11a)

"Persuade" is *peithō*, "to cause to come to a particular point of view or course of action," here, "persuade, appeal to."[40] If we truly love people, then we will be concerned about their eternal destiny. Thus, several things motivate our evangelism – which we'll fill out further when we study 5:14.

1. A conviction of the reality of final judgment and eternal punishment, that is, "the judgment seat of Christ" (5:10)
2. A recognition of God's love for us (5:14)
3. An understanding that Christ died for sinners (5:14), and
4. A love for sinners ourselves (5:14).

Q4. (2 Corinthians 5:10-11a) How does Paul's mention of the Judgment Seat of Christ fit the context here? How should our belief that we Christians will appear before the Judgment Seat of Christ to be judged for our works affect (1) our desire to please him? (2) Our motivation to persuade people to receive Christ?
http://www.joyfulheart.com/forums/index.php?showtopic=1094

---

[39] "Fear" (NIV, NRSV), "terror" (KJV) is *phobos*, "something terrible/awe-inspiring, a terror," here, "we know what it is that causes fear of the Lord" (i.e., the judgment to come). (BDAG 1062, 1b).
[40] *Peithō*, BDAG 793, 1b.

Open before You and God (5:11b-12)

Now Paul appeals to the Corinthians to understand the simplicity of his motives so they can answer the distortions of his opponents in Corinth.

> [11b] What we are is plain[41] to God, and I hope it is also plain to your conscience. [12] We are not trying to commend ourselves to you again, but are giving you an opportunity to take pride in us, so that you can answer those who take pride in what is seen rather than in what is in the heart." (5:11b-12)

Out of Our Mind? (5:13)

Now Paul says something curious.

> "If we are out of our mind,[42] it is for the sake of God; if we are in our right mind, it is for you." (5:13)

The verb is *existēmi*, with the basic idea "to become separated from something." The noun form is *existasis*, from which we get our words "ecstasy, ecstatic."

The verse can be taken two ways:

1. His opponents are saying that he is mad. They accused Jesus of this, too (Mark 3:21; John 10:20). Festus accused Paul of this, as well (Acts 26:24-25).
2. His opponents are saying that Paul's ministry isn't truly spiritual because he doesn't have ecstatic experiences.[43]

The first makes more sense to me. But either way, he is deflecting criticism by pointing out his commitment to the Corinthians.

Christ's Love Compels Us (5:13-15)

Now we see the reason that some people may call him crazy or obsessed. He says, "Christ's love compels us." The word translated "compels" (NIV), "urges us on" (NRSV), "constraineth" (KJV) is *synechō*, a word with a variety of meanings, here, "to provide impulse for some activity, urge on, impel."[44] Paul's drive to save whoever he can is motivated by love. The Greek construction "love of Christ" (NRSV, KJV) is ambiguous. It can refer to "love for Christ" (objective genitive) or "Christ's love," the

---

[41] "Plain" (NIV), "well-known" (NRSV), "made manifest" (KJV) is *phaneroō*, "to cause to become known, disclose, show, make known" (BDAG 1048, 2bβ).

[42] "Are out of our mind" (NIV), "are beside ourselves" (KJV) is *existēmi*, in the sense, "'to become separated from something or lose something," it means, of inability to reason normally "lose one's mind, be out of one's senses" (BDAG 350, 2a).

[43] Kruse, p. 121.

[44] *Synechō*, BDAG 970, 7.

love he has *for us* (subjective genitive). My guess is that Paul intended to suggest both, though perhaps love for Christ predominates in his motivational system. After all, it is the first commandment.

Paul is convinced[45] of one proposition:

> "[14] For Christ's love compels us, because we are convinced that one died for all, and therefore all died. [15] And he died for all, that those who live should no longer live for themselves but for him who died for them and was raised again." (5:13-15)

This conviction has several pieces:

1. **One died for all.** Jesus died for the sins of all mankind (1 Timothy 2:6; Matthew 20:28; 1 John 2:2).

2. **All died.** This is more difficult for us to grasp. But if you've studied Paul's writings, you see this clearly. Bruce puts it this way: "One has died as representative of all his people, therefore all of them are deemed to have died in the person of their representative."[46] This involves the idea of "federal headship" which Paul develops in Romans 5:12-6:5.[47] We have been buried with him through baptism (Romans 6:3-4).

3. **We shouldn't live for ourselves any more.** Why? Because we died to ourselves.

4. **We should live for Christ.** He is our life now. We have been united with him in baptism and raised with him to newness of life (Romans 6:3-4), "our life is hidden with Christ in God" (Colossians 3:3).

The classic statement of this conviction is found in Galatians:

> "I have been crucified with Christ and I no longer live, but Christ lives in me. The life I live in the body, I live by faith in the Son of God, who loved me and gave himself for me." (Galatians 2:20)

Christ is your life. He is your present. He is your future. He is your hope of glory. He is the only meaning your life will ultimately have. Embrace him fully now!

Prayer

Thank you, Lord, for the confidence that whether we wake or sleep we look forward to uninterrupted fellowship with you. Lessen our attachment to our physical bodies. Lessen our fear of death, so that we might live fully now in you! In Jesus' name, we

---

[45] "Are convinced" (NIV, NRSV), "judge" (KJV) is the common verb *krinō*, "to make a judgment based on taking various factors into account, judge, think, consider, look upon." (BDAG 568, 3).

[46] Bruce, p. 207.

[47] I delve into this in my book, *The Christ-Powered Life (Romans 5-8)* (JesusWalk, 2008), pp. 36-50.

pray. Amen.

Key Verses

"Therefore we are always confident and know that as long as we are at home in the body we are away from the Lord." (2 Corinthians 5:6)

"We live by faith, not by sight." (2 Corinthians 5:7)

"For we must all appear before the judgment seat of Christ, that each one may receive what is due him for the things done while in the body, whether good or bad." (2 Corinthians 5: 10)

"For Christ's love compels us...." (2 Corinthians 5:14)

7. A Ministry of Reconciliation (5:17-6:2)

This lesson is very much a continuation of the themes of the previous lesson. Paul has talked about Christ's love that compels us to persuade men of the truth of the gospel in light of the judgment. Now he turns to what this salvation looks like in an individual and our role in the process of God's program of reconciliation.

A New Creation in Christ (5:16-17)

Because Christ died for all, Paul now sees each person in a different light.

> "16 So from now on we regard no one from a worldly point of view. Though we once regarded Christ in this way, we do so no longer. 17 Therefore, if anyone is in Christ, he is a new creation; the old has gone, the new has come!" (5:16-17)

So often we judge people according to the various categories we have set up – male / female, hetero / homo, black / white /Asian / Hispanic, white collar / working class / unemployed, married / single / living-together, conservative / moderate / liberal, Republican / Democrat / Independent, child / teen / young adult / middle aged / old. We pigeon-hole people into our own categories and then can't see beyond them to what actually defines them as people. This is a worldly point-of-view.[1] Jesus sees them differently. He sees God at work in them.

Bernardo Daddi, "St. Paul" (1333), tempera on panel, 233.7 x 89.2 cm, National Gallery of Art, Washington, DC.

---

[1] "Worldly/human point of view" (NIV/NRSV) is literally "after the flesh" (KJV), the preposition *kata* with the noun *sarx*, "flesh," here used in the sense of "the outward side of life" as determined by normal perspectives or standards. (BDAG 916, 5).

Paul once regarded Christ as a heretical Jewish rabbi, thankfully executed for his sins, and his followers as dangerous subversives who must be stopped at any cost. But outside Damascus everything changed. Paul cried out, "Who are you, Lord?" And the answer he received turned his world upside down: "I am Jesus, whom you are persecuting" (Acts 9:5).

Paul had what is called a "paradigm shift." That is, the working hypothesis by which he evaluated his world was dramatically altered. Now he saw everything in a new light.

In the same way, Paul says,

> "[16] So from now on we regard no one from a worldly point of view..... [17] Therefore, if anyone is in Christ, he is a new creation; the old has gone, the new has come!" (5:16a, 17)

People who find Jesus and are rescued by him don't just "get religion." They are changed in some fundamental way. Paul calls them "a new creation." "Creation/creature" is *ktisis*, "the result of a creative act, that which is created."[2] The New Testament uses several other words to describe this, including:

- Born again/anew/from above (John 3:3, 5; 1 Peter 1:23; 1 John 3:9; 5:18)
- Made alive, quickened (Ephesians 2:5; John 5:24; 1 John 3:14)
- Regenerated, rebirth (Titus 3:5)
- Washed (1 Corinthians 6:11; Ephesians 5:26; Titus 3:5)
- Renewed (Ephesians 3:10)
- Sealed (2 Corinthians 1:22; Ephesians 1:13; 4:30)

We Christians believe that when Jesus saves us and puts his Holy Spirit in our hearts that a life-altering change has taken place. A new life has been formed by the Creator, which is being nurtured by the Holy Spirit.

If you are discouraged at the little fruit in your life or the little change, look to your Creator! He has put his life within you and set you on a new course. You have changed on the inside. Now just cooperate with him so that the inward change begins to affect and alter your outward life as well. It is a process. It takes time. But the beginning creative work of the Holy Spirit has begun.

This verse brings to mind a simple chorus:

> "I'll never be the same again, oh no,
> I'll never be the same again, oh no,
> Since I found the Lord, I am not the same,
> And I'll never be the same again!"[3]

---

[2] *Ktisis*, BDAG 573, 2a).
[3] Author unknown.

Q1. (2 Corinthians 5:16-17) What does verse 17 teach us about the nature of a new believer? What changes in a person when he puts his faith in Christ? Why don't old habits disappear immediately if everything has become new?
http://www.joyfulheart.com/forums/index.php?showtopic=1095

Reconciliation (5:18-19)

We Christians are not members of an exclusive "born again" club. Far from it! We have a message that he can change anyone! Jesus can rescue and renew anyone! There is hope in Jesus! Now Paul points us to our own personal mission.

> "18 All this is from God, who reconciled us to himself through Christ and gave us the ministry of reconciliation: 19 that God was reconciling the world to himself in Christ, not counting men's sins against them. And he has committed to us the message of reconciliation." (5:18-19)

To reconcile means to exchange hostility for a friendly relationship.[4] To restore to friendship or harmony.[5] Families sometimes have a falling out. Sisters no longer speak to one another. Husbands leave, wives and children are abandoned. Adultery and alcoholism and greed alienate people. Reconciliation is needed, to take what was broken and mend it, to heal a relationship. That's what God has done.

The problem is that many times it isn't just an unfortunate misunderstanding. It is caused and exacerbated by grievous sins. Unless the man is willing to forsake his philandering ways, his wife is unwilling to take him back. Unless the woman deals with her drug addiction, her relationship with her children can never be healed.

Now look at what God did about the sin that was at the root of our estrangement from God.

> "God ... reconciled us to himself through Christ.... that God was reconciling the world to himself in Christ, not counting men's sins against them." (5:18b-19a)

The reason that God could justly stop counting our sins against him is because he had laid those sins on Christ, "the Lamb of God, who takes away the sin of the world" (John 1:29). In two other letters, Paul discusses this act of reconciliation that centers on the cross.

> "For if, when we were God's enemies, we were reconciled to him through the death of his Son, how much more, having been reconciled, shall we be saved through his life!"

---

[4] "Reconciled" is *katallassō*, "the exchange of hostility for a friendly relationship, reconcile" (BDAG 523, a).
[5] *Merriam-Webster's 11th Collegiate Dictionary.*

(Romans 5:10)

"But now he has reconciled you by Christ's physical body through death to present you holy in his sight, without blemish and free from accusation." (Colossians 1:22)

Ambassadors of Reconciliation (5:18-20)

God is the chief Reconciler by sending his Son to bear our sins. But now he delegates to us a role in this reconciliation process.

"All this is from God, who ... gave us the **ministry of reconciliation**[6].... And he has committed to us the **message of reconciliation**. We are therefore **Christ's ambassadors**, as though God were making his appeal through us. We implore you on Christ's behalf: Be reconciled to God." (5:18-20)

Paul discusses three roles that we have in his reconciliation program:

1. Ministry of Reconciliation. "Ministry" is *diakonia*, "functioning in the interest of a larger public, service, office."[7] We have an official capacity to fulfill. In America, the government usually has departments or agencies. But in Europe they're often called ministries. Instead of America's Secretary of State, England has a Foreign Minister. In the same way, we are official representatives, ministers of God's Ministry of Reconciliation.

2. Message of Reconciliation. "Message" (NIV, NRSV), "word" (KJV) is *logos*, here, "a communication whereby the mind finds expression, word."[8] This word or message has been "committed" (NIV, KJV) or "entrusted" (NRSV) to us.[9] *The Message* puts it this way: "God has given us the task of telling everyone what he is doing." (5:19).

3. Ambassadors of Christ. "Ambassador" is the verb *presbeuō*, "be an ambassador/envoy, travel or work as an ambassador."[10] (We get our words "presbyter" and "Presbyterian" from this root.) Literally, this phrase would read, "On behalf of (*hyper*) of Christ we serve as ambassadors...." *Hyper* is a preposition indicating that an activity or event is in some entity's interest, "for, in behalf of, for the sake of someone or something."[11]

An ambassador in a country's foreign service lives in a foreign country, but is

---

[6] "Reconciliation" is *katallagē*, "reestablishment of an interrupted or broken relationship, reconciliation" (BDAG 523).

[7] *Diakonia*, BDAG 230, 3.

[8] *Logos*, BDAG 598, 1aβ.

[9] This is the common verb *tithēmi*, "put, place," with meaning, "fix, establish, set," here, "as he established among us the word of reconciliation" = "entrusted to us" (*Tithēmi*, BDAG 1003, 4b).

[10] *Presbeuō*, BDAG 862.

[11] *Hyper*, BDAG 1030, A1aδ.

charged with communicating clearly his president's or prime minister's words and positions. An ambassador cannot operate in silence, but is a constant voice who bears his kingdom's message. See how personal and direct this communication can be:

> "We are therefore Christ's ambassadors, as **though God were making his appeal through us**. We implore you on Christ's behalf: Be reconciled to God." (5:20)

"Appeal" (NIV, NRSV), "beseech" (KJV) is *parakaleō*, which means here, "to urge strongly, appeal to, urge, exhort, encourage,"[12] and is used in this strong sense also in 12:8. The word could be translated, "to beg." It's that strong!

Dear friends, we may not be foreign missionaries like the Apostle Paul, representing Jesus abroad. But we are very clearly Jesus' personal representatives in our neighborhoods, in our workplaces, in our schools, in our families. There is a sense, when we share the good news with people, that we are conveying Jesus' own personal love for that person. We also convey his authority. This delegation of love, authority, and message is indeed awesome!

> "Peace be with you! As the Father has sent me, I am sending you." (John 20:21)

> "He who listens to you listens to me; he who rejects you rejects me; but he who rejects me rejects him who sent me." (Luke 10:16; cf. Matthew 10:40)

> "I tell you the truth, whoever accepts anyone I send accepts me; and whoever accepts me accepts the one who sent me." (John 13:20)

Perhaps we would prefer to be quiet rather than take upon ourselves this kind of responsibility. But if we remain quiet, then the Kingdom of God has a faithless representative in the workplace, in the family, in the community. We cannot bear the name of Christ with authenticity unless we are willing to represent him as his ambassadors, as inadequate as we may feel we are for this task.

Q2. (2 Corinthians 5:18-20) How have we humans been reconciled to God? What did God do so that reconciliation could take place? In what sense are you an Ambassador of the Kingdom of God? In what sense are you a Minister of Reconciliation for Jesus Christ?

http://www.joyfulheart.com/forums/index.php?showtopic=1096

---

[12] *Parakaleō*, BDAG 765, 2.

Substitutionary Atonement (5:21)

Now Paul shares part of the essential message of reconciliation, that our sins no longer need to be a barrier between us and God.

> "God made him who had no sin to be sin for us, so that in him we might become the righteousness of God." (5:21)

This verse is one of the clearest statements in the entire Bible of the Doctrine of the Substitutionary Atonement (also known as penal substitution or vicarious atonement). This refers to the Bible teaching that Jesus bore the penalty for our sins and took our place, so we didn't have to die for our own sins. A "substitute," of course, is "a person or thing that takes the place or function of another."[13] Let's examine this verse carefully.

Jesus had no sin. In a number of places, the Scripture affirms that Jesus did not sin and had no sin in himself to atone for (Hebrews 4:5; 7:26; 1 Peter 2:22; 1 John 3:5; 2:1; John 14:30; 1 Peter 3:18). This alone sets him apart from any other human, from any other founder of a religion. He uniquely is sinless.[14]

"God made him to be sin." God is the subject of this sentence.[15] God "made"[16] Jesus to be sin. That is, Jesus became the bearer of sin, as would a sacrifice under the Mosaic Law.

"For us" (NIV, KJV), "for our sake" (NRSV) represents the preposition *hyper* (that we examined in verse 20), "for, in behalf of, for the sake of someone or something."[17]

"So that is the conjunction *hina,* a very common marker used to denote purpose, aim, or goal, "in order that, that," in the final sense.[18] God's action was for the expressed purpose to free us from sin.

"In him." We are now looked at by God as fused to Jesus Christ. We are united to him.

"We might become the righteousness of God." The verb is *ginomai,* "be, become," here in the sense, "to experience a change in nature and so indicate entry into a new

---

[13] *Merriam-Webster's 11th Collegiate Dictionary.*

[14] The Roman Catholic Doctrine of the Immaculate Conception teaches that the Virgin Mary was conceived without any stain and therefore free of original (hereditary) sin or personal sin. This was declared a dogma by Pope Pius IX in 1854. The doctrine goes back as early as the fifth century in Syria, but was not embraced by the Eastern Church. This doctrine is not based on Scripture, but elevated Mary and was thought to protect Jesus from the transmission of original sin.

[15] The subject of the verb "he made" is clearly God by context. The end of the previous verse is *theos,* "God."

[16] The verb is the very common *poieō,* "do, make," here (with a double accusative), "make someone or something (into) something" (BDAG 840, 2hβ).

[17] *Hyper,* BDAG 1030, A1a.

[18] *Hina,* BDAG 475, 1a.

condition, become something."[19] The verb is in the Aorist tense which suggests a sudden event, not a gradual process. "Righteousness" is *dikaiosynē*, here, the "quality or state of juridical correctness with focus on redemptive action, righteousness."[20] Because Jesus took our sins upon him, we take upon us his righteousness which comes from God. It was this righteousness that Paul sought. Righteousness obtained by obeying the law could do nothing to atone for sins. Paul expressed the desire to:

> "... be found in him, not having a righteousness of my own that comes from the law, but that which is through faith in Christ – the righteousness that comes from God and is by faith." (Philippians 3:9)

Though our passage teaches the Doctrine of the Substitutionary Atonement quite clearly, it is taught throughout the New Testament. Some of these passages include:

> "The next day John saw Jesus coming toward him and said, 'Look, the Lamb of God, who takes away the sin of the world!'" (John 1:29)

> "He himself bore our sins in his body on the tree, so that we might die to sins and live for righteousness; by his wounds you have been healed." (1 Peter 2:24, alluding to Isaiah 53:5)

> "For Christ died for sins once for all, the righteous for the unrighteous, to bring you to God." (1 Peter 3:18a)

> "He is the atoning sacrifice for our sins, and not only for ours but also for the sins of the whole world." (1 John 2:2)

Q3. (2 Corinthians 5:21) In what sense did Jesus "become sin" on our behalf? In what sense do we "become righteousness"?

http://www.joyfulheart.com/forums/index.php?showtopic=1097

Today Is the Day of Salvation (6:1-2)

You can hear Paul the Preacher in this passage. He is appealing to the Corinthian believers directly. Two verses previous he had said:

> "... As though God were making his appeal (*parakaleō*) through us. We implore (*deomai*) you on Christ's behalf: Be reconciled to God." (5:20)

Now he continues this appeal:

> "As God's fellow workers we urge (*parakaleō*) you not to receive God's grace in vain."

[19] *Ginomai*, BDAG 198, 5a.
[20] *Dikaiosynē*, BDAG 248, 2.

(6:1)

To "receive God's grace in vain" would mean that though they had been pardoned and cleansed by God and had been given a responsibility to share the good news of this reconciliation and atonement, but that they did nothing with it. They stayed silent. Paul isn't implying that the Corinthians had received God's grace in vain. He only exhorts them that there should be good fruit through their ministry to others.

What's more, this is an urgent matter.

> "For he says, 'In the time of my favor I heard you, and in the day of salvation I helped you.' I tell you, now is the time of God's favor, now is the day of salvation." (6:2)

We aren't to put off sharing the good news to a more convenient time – or resist God's speaking to us for another time. Paul cites Isaiah 49:8 here to underscore his appeal. "Now" is the time. "Today" is the day. We aren't to put it off, or God's work in us could be in vain.

This has been a rich chapter. Paul has exhorted the Corinthians of the urgency of Christ's love to see people become Christians, and to experience the new creation of the Holy Spirit. This reconciliation was God's purpose in sending Christ and we are ambassadors of this message. It is a strong message, an urgent message, and one that God is still speaking to us today.

Q4. (2 Corinthians 5:18-6:2) If you, then, are called to be an urgent agent of reconciliation, how is this likely to affect your daily life? How will it affect how people perceive you? How will it affect how God perceives you?
http://www.joyfulheart.com/forums/index.php?showtopic=1098

Prayer

Lord, put in our hearts the compelling love for Jesus that will share his message, speak his words, become ambassadors and reconcilers on his behalf. Thank you for the great price you paid through the sacrifice of Jesus Christ. Use us, we pray, in your grand plan of salvation for those around us. In Jesus' name, we pray. Amen.

Key Verses

> "Therefore, if anyone is in Christ, he is a new creation; the old has gone, the new has come!" (2 Corinthians 5:17)

> "God was reconciling the world to himself in Christ, not counting men's sins against

them. And he has committed to us the message of reconciliation." (2 Corinthians 5:19)

"We are therefore Christ's ambassadors, as though God were making his appeal through us. We implore you on Christ's behalf: Be reconciled to God." (2 Corinthians 5:20)

"God made him who had no sin to be sin for us, so that in him we might become the righteousness of God." (2 Corinthians 5:21)

"I tell you, now is the time of God's favor, now is the day of salvation." (2 Corinthians 6:2b)

8. Hardships, Holiness, and Joy (6:3-7:16)

In this lesson we'll cover a lot of ground – two chapters. But you'll find that most of chapter 7 is narrative, rather than teaching, so we'll go over most of that rather quickly. In this lesson I've included three topics:

1. God's help in spite of intense hardships (6:3-13)
2. Personal holiness, separation from sinful practices (6:14-7:1)
3. Paul's joy due to Titus' encouraging report (7:2-16)

We'll begin with Paul's account of his extreme hardships. He's not bragging. Rather he is bringing some reality to his claim to be the founding apostle of the Corinthian church. At present, some "super-apostles" are seeking to discredit him and slander him so people will follow them instead. In his defense, Paul talks about the weakness and suffering he's experienced and how they bolster his claim to authenticity.

James J. Tissot, "St. Paul" (1896), watercolor, Brooklyn Museum, New York.

A No-Stumbling-Blocks Policy (6:3)

"We put no stumbling block in anyone's path, so that our ministry will not be discredited."[1] (6:3)

There are some leaders who have quirks or prejudices that are hard to get used to. I'm sure Paul had his own idiosyncrasies, but he did his level best to remove any obstacle[2] that would keep people from coming to know the Lord. He had a no-stumbling-blocks policy so that his message would have the widest possible appeal. He

---

[1] "Be discredited" (NIV), "find fault" (NRSV), "be blamed" (KJV) is *mōmaomai*, "find fault with, criticize, censure, blame," from *mōmos*, "blame" (BDAG 663).

[2] "Stumbling block" (NIV), "obstacle" (NRSV), "offence" (KJV) is *proskopē*, "an occasion for taking offense or for making a misstep" (BDAG 882). From *proskoptō*, literally "bruise as a result of stumbling."

even refused to let the church support him so that money wouldn't be an obstacle to anyone. If his audience was Jewish, he would speak like a Jew. If his hearers were Gentiles, he would keep his Jewishness in the background. In an earlier letter to the Corinthians he said:

> "I have become all things to all men so that by all possible means I might save some." (1 Corinthians 9:22b)

In the verses that follow, we begin to see what this policy cost him in sheer pain.

Commended by Hardships (6:4-5)

> "4 Rather, as servants of God we commend[3] ourselves in every way: in great endurance; in troubles, hardships and distresses; 5 in beatings, imprisonments and riots; in hard work, sleepless nights and hunger...." (6:3-5)

Let's look at some of these more closely.

"Endurance" (NIV, NRSV), "patience" (KJV) is "the capacity to hold out or bear up in the face of difficulty."[4] It can be translated as "patience, endurance, fortitude, steadfastness, perseverance." Paul didn't quit.

"Troubles" (NIV), **"afflictions"** (NRSV, KJV) comes from the root idea of "pressing, pressure." Here it is used in the metaphorical sense: "trouble that inflicts distress, oppression, affliction, tribulation."[5] Have you ever been under extreme pressure for a long period of time? Then you know what Paul experienced.

"Distresses" (NIV, KJV), **"calamities"** (NRSV) expresses the idea of "narrowness." Here it means, "a set of stressful circumstances, distress, difficulty, anguish, trouble."[6] If you've ever felt boxed in, confined, then you've experienced distress.

"Beatings" (NIV, NRSV), "stripes" (KJV) is "a sudden hard stroke with some instrument, blow, stroke."[7] Perhaps you've experienced beatings as a child or as a spouse. Then you know.

"Imprisonments"[8] – in Paul's case, false imprisonment – is part of the cost of preaching the gospel when it is unpopular. Some of our brothers and sisters in the Muslim countries and China have experienced this.

"Riots" (NIV, NRSV), "tumults" (KJV) refers to an "unsettled state of affairs, distur-

---

[3] "Commended" (NIV, NRSV), "approving" (KJV) is *synistēmi*, "to provide evidence of a personal characteristic or claim through action, demonstrate, show, bring out something" (BDAG 793, 3).

[4] *Hypomonē*, BDAG 1039, 1.

[5] *Thlipsis*, BDAG 457, 1.

[6] *Stenochōria*, BDAG 943.

[7] *Plēgē*, BDAG 825, 1.

[8] "Imprisonments" is *phylakē*, "guarding," then, "the place where guarding is done, prison" (BDAG 1067, 3).

bance, tumult," probably of mob action in Paul's case.[9] Paul didn't hide in a corner; sometimes his opponents started riots to try to get him run out of town.

"Hard work" (NIV), **"labors"** (NRSV, KJV). Paul had to earn his own living by the sweat of his brow making tents out of goatskins. He would work long hours, then preach in the evening until he was dead tired.

"Sleepless nights" (NIV, NRSV), **"watchings"** (KJV).[10] You've experienced sleeplessness because of pressure you were experiencing. Paul was often awake at night.

"Hunger" (NIV, NRSV), **"fastings"** (KJV)[11] was common. When he was travelling, there may have been no place to stop for a meal. He may also have experienced hunger because he didn't have enough money to purchase food and no friends in the city who would invite him in.

Sometimes we put Bible characters on an unreal kind of pedestal, as if they weren't made of flesh and blood. Yes, they had hardships, we think, but angels were always around to ease their discomfort. After all, they were holy men and women. But the truth is that holy men and women, particularly those who will not be deterred from their mission, undergo a great deal of suffering so that they can be faithful to their call. What are you willing to endure to do Christ's will?

Commended by a Godly Character and Spiritual Ministry (6:6-7)

Paul reviewed the sufferings that authenticated his apostleship. Now he talks about character.

> "[6] ... In purity, understanding, patience and kindness; in the Holy Spirit and in sincere love; [7] in truthful speech and in the power of God; with weapons of righteousness in the right hand and in the left...." (6:6-7)

"Purity/pureness" can be seen as "uprightness of life,"[12] moral purity. If we don't live holy lives, people – especially unbelievers that we want to witness to – won't take us seriously. Purity of thought and life is a clear objective for us.

"Understanding" (NIV), **"knowledge"** (NRSV, KJV) is "comprehension or intellec-

---

[9] *Akatastasia*, BDAG 35, 1.

[10] *Agrypnia*, "the state of remaining awake because one is unable to go to sleep, sleeplessness" (BDAG 16, 1), from *a-*, "not" + *hypnos*, "sleep."

[11] *Nēsteia*, "the experience of being without sufficient food, going hungry," generally, of hunger brought about by necessity, though in other contexts it refers to deliberately going without food, fasting (BDAG 673, 1).

[12] *Hagnotēs*, Thayer 54, "purity, sincerity," BDAG 13. The basic idea of the word is "what awakens awe" (F. Hauck, *hagnos, ktl.,* TDNT 1:122-124).

tual grasp of something, knowledge."[13] This knowledge also spills over into knowing God himself, not just facts or wisdom.

"Patience" (NIV, NRSV), "longsuffering" (KJV) refers to the "state of being able to bear up under provocation, forbearance, patience toward others."[14] Does your patience give others confidence in your faith?

"Kindness" is "the quality of being helpful or beneficial, goodness, kindness, generosity," also, "readily generous in disposition."[15]

"Sincere/genuine love" (NIV, NRSV), "love unfeigned" (KJV) is two words, *agapē*, "self-giving love" and *anypokritos*, "pertaining to being without pretense, genuine, sincere," literally, "without play-acting."[16]

"Weapons" (NIV, NRSV), "armour" (KJV) refers to "an instrument designed to make ready for military engagement, weapon." The sword would normally be in the right hand, with the shield in the left, so "weapons of righteousness in the right hand and in the left" refer to "the weapons of righteousness for offense and defense."[17]

How does your character recommend you to the people you're trying to reach for Christ? Is your character strong and pure, or does it need some work?

Commended through Paradoxical Ministry (6:8-10)

Next, Paul introduces a series of word pairs that are paradoxical. As the list continues, he shares what he is accused of vs. the opposite, which is the actual truth.

> "[8] ... Through glory and dishonor, bad report and good report; genuine, yet regarded as impostors; [9] known, yet regarded as unknown; dying, and yet we live on; beaten, and yet not killed; [10] sorrowful, yet always rejoicing; poor, yet making many rich; having nothing, and yet possessing everything." (6:8-10)

Glory and dishonor. Sometimes Paul has been honored, but just as often he has experienced "a state of dishonor or disrespect."[18]

Bad report and good report. "Bad report" (NIV) refers to "the act of detracting from or damaging another's reputation, defamation, slander, calumny."[19] "Good report" (NIV) is the opposite: a "favorable expression about something, good report, good

---

[13] *Gnōsis*, BDAG 203, 1.
[14] *Makrothymia*, BDAG 612, 2a.
[15] *Chrēstotēs*, BDAG 1090, 2.
[16] *Anypokritos*, BDAG 91.
[17] *Hoplon* BDAG 716, 2a.
[18] *Atimia*, BDAG 149.
[19] *Dysphēmia*, BDAG 265. From the root *phēmē*, "report, news."

repute."[20] Paul has been the victim of slander as well as praise. Realize that not everything you hear about a Christian leader is necessarily true – or false. Be careful how you form opinions about others.

As impostors, and yet are true (NRSV).[21] Back in Corinth, his opponents had undermined and trashed his reputation – yet *he* was the genuine apostle and *they* were the impostors.

Known, yet regarded as unknown. Paul continues with the irony. He is known throughout Christendom as an apostle, yet in Corinth, his opponents seek to portray him as a nobody.

Dying, and yet we live on. Paul had been left for dead (Acts 14:19), but he lived.

Beaten, and yet not killed. Paul tells us in 11:23-25 that he was flogged, lashed, and beaten with rods time after time. Yet he lived to tell the story.

Sorrowful, yet always rejoicing.[22] Paul had his ups and downs, his share of sorrows, yet he chose to rejoice in spite of his troubles. He practiced what he preached:

> "Rejoice in the Lord always. I will say it again: Rejoice!" (Philippians 4:4)

> "Be joyful always; pray continually; give thanks in all circumstances, for this is God's will for you in Christ Jesus." (1 Thessalonians 5:16-18)

Poor, yet making many rich. Paul wasn't a rich man or independently wealthy, though a great deal of money passed through his hands through the course of his ministry. But he enriched others spiritually and helped them enjoy the true riches.[23] This reminds me of John Wesley (1703-1791), founder of Methodism, who, though he received a huge income later in life, severely limited his expenditures and gave away nearly everything to the poor, living extremely modestly himself. He had discovered the joy of making others rich. He had nothing to prove to himself or anyone else.

Having nothing, and yet possessing[24] everything. Paul was like Jesus who had "no place to lay his head" (Luke 9:58b). Yet he was heir to his Father's entire estate!

> "We are heirs – heirs of God and co-heirs with Christ." (Romans 8:17)

> "All things are yours." (1 Corinthians 3:21-23)

---

[20] *Euphēmia*, BDAG 414.

[21] "Impostors" (NIV, NRSV), "deceivers" (KJV), is the adjective *planos*, "pertaining to causing someone to be mistaken," here as a substantive, "deceiver, impostor" (BDAG 822, b).

[22] "Sorrowful" is *lypeō*, "be sad, be distressed, grieve" (BDAG 604, 2b). "Rejoicing" is *chairō*, "to be in a state of happiness and well-being, rejoice, be glad" (BDAG 1074, 1).

[23] "Making rich" is *ploutizō*, "to cause to be relatively high on a scale of opulence, make wealthy," here, "to cause to abound in something, make rich," in imagery, of spiritual riches (BDAG 832).

[24] "Possessing" is *katechō*, "to keep in one's possession, possess" (BDAG 533, 3).

Open Wide Your Hearts (6:11-13)

Finally, after sharing this list, Paul appeals to the Corinthians to open their hearts to him once more.

> "11 We have spoken freely[25] to you, Corinthians, and opened wide[26] our hearts[27] to you. 12 We are not withholding our affection from you, but you are withholding[28] yours from us. 13 As a fair exchange – I speak as to my children – open wide your hearts also." (6:11-13).

Q1. (2 Corinthians 6:3-13) Why do you think Paul shares so much about his various struggles with the Corinthians? How does this help them accept his apostleship as authentic? Have you ever complained about what you've had to put up with in your ministry? How does it compare to what Paul faced?
http://www.joyfulheart.com/forums/index.php?showtopic=1099

Don't Yoke Yourselves to Unbelievers (6:14-16)

Paul has just shared insights into his life and character. Now he calls on the Corinthians to guard their own character.

As I've mentioned before, Corinth had an international reputation for sexual immorality. In Corinth's Temple of Aphrodite were 1,000 female prostitutes. The coined Greek word "to Corinthianize" meant to practice immorality; the phrase "Corinthian girl" designated a prostitute. The Corinthian believers, both male and female, faced powerful sexual temptations. Late in this letter Paul expresses grief over

> "... many who have sinned earlier and have not repented of the impurity, sexual sin and debauchery in which they have indulged." (12:21)

So Paul begins this section with a command:

> "Do not be yoked together with unbelievers." (6:14a)

Verse 14a is often quoted as teaching that believers should not marry unbelievers. But is that what it means? Let's look carefully, then come to a conclusion at the end of the passage.

---

[25] *Anoigō*, "open," here in the sense, "to be candid, be open" (BDAG 85, 7).

[26] "Opened wide" is *platynō*, "to cause something to be broad, make broad, enlarge," here, figuratively of warm affection (BDAG 823).

[27] Literally, "our mouth has opened to you."

[28] "Withholding" (NIV), "restricted" (NRSV), "straitened" (KJV) is *stenochōreō*, "to confine or restrict to a narrow space, crowd, cramp, confine, restrict" (BDAG 942).

"Yoked together" (NIV), "mismatched" (NRSV), "unequally yoked" (KJV) is *heterozygeō*, referring to draft animals that need different kinds of yokes, because they are of different species such as an ox and a donkey (Leviticus 19:19). The word means, "be unevenly yoked, be mismated with someone."[29] You believers need to be careful that you're not too closely tied to unbelievers, Paul says.

> "[14b] For what do righteousness and wickedness have in common? Or what fellowship can light have with darkness? [15] What harmony is there between Christ and Belial? What does a believer have in common with an unbeliever? [16] What agreement is there between the temple of God and idols? For we are the temple of the living God." (6:14-16a)

Paul uses five words to describe a close relationship – a closeness that can hurt the believers.

1. **"In common"** (NIV), **"partnership"** (NRSV), "fellowship" (KJV) has the basic idea of "sharing, participation."[30]
2. **"Fellowship"** (NIV, NRSV), "communion" (KJV) is *koinōnia*, "close association involving mutual interests and sharing, association, communion, fellowship, close relationship."[31] This refers to a relationship built upon common interests.
3. **"Harmony"** (NIV), "agreement" (NRSV), "concord" (KJV) is *symphōnēsis* (from which get our word "symphony") "a state of shared interests, agreement."[32]
4. **"In common"** (NIV), **"share"** (NRSV), "part" (KJV) is *meris*, "share, portion."[33]
5. **"Agreement"** is from a word that originally meant "a putting together or joint deposit (of votes)," hence, "approval, assent, agreement."[34]

Paul's argument is that believers and unbelievers really *don't* have so much in common any more. He contrasts word pairs here, too:

1. Righteousness vs. wickedness
2. Light vs. darkness
3. Christ vs. Belial. (Belial is a name of Satan.)[35]
4. Believer vs. unbeliever
5. Temple of God vs. idols.

---

[29] *Heterozygeō*, BDAG 399.
[30] *Metochē*, BDAG 643. From *metechō*, "to be or become partaker; to partake" (Thayer, 407).
[31] *Koinōnia*, BDAG 552, 1.
[32] *Symphōnēsis*, BDAG 963.
[33] *Meris*, BDAG 632, 2.
[34] *Synkatathesis*, Thayer 592. "Agreement, union" (BDAG 953).
[35] *Belial* is a transliteration of a Hebrew word meaning "worthlessness, wickedness" (Thayer 100).

You Are the Temple of God (6:16a)

Now Paul makes an astounding statement: "For we are the temple of the living God" (6:16a). Because of the Corinthians' strong ties with unbelievers, they had been flirting with idol worship and its related sexual temptations – especially prominent in Corinth.

So Paul reminds them that the temple they should be concerned about is not the fancy temples of Corinth, but God himself: "For we are the temple of the living God" (16:16a). This is not a new concept to the Corinthians, for in his first letter Paul compared both individuals and the church itself to a temple:

> "Don't you know that you yourselves are God's temple and that God's Spirit lives in you?" (1 Corinthians 3:16, reference to the church)

> "Do you not know that your body is a temple of the Holy Spirit, who is in you, whom you have received from God?" (1 Corinthians 6:19, a reference to an individual's physical body in relationship to prostitutes)

Old Testament Promises (6:16b-18)

In what sense are believers like temples of God? Paul explains by quoting three Old Testament passages.

1. God walks among believers (16:16b)

> "I will live with them and walk among them,
> and I will be their God,
> and they will be my people."
> (6:16b; adapted from Leviticus 26:12; Jeremiah 32:38; Ezekiel 37:27)

2. Believers are holy themselves (6:17)

> "Therefore come out[36] from them[37] and be separate,[38] says the Lord.
> Touch no unclean thing, and I will receive you." (6:17; quoting Isaiah 52:11)

3. Believers are God's own special children (6:18)

> "I will be a Father to you,
> and you will be my sons and daughters." (6:18, adapted from 1 Samuel 7:14)

If you'll recall, throughout the Old Testament, God's people struggled with the idolatry of the peoples of the lands where they lived. Baal worship enticed many into

---

[36] "Come out" is *exerchomai*, "come out," here in the sense of to discontinue an association, "depart," also at 1 John 2:19 (BDAG 348, 4).

[37] "Among" (KJV) is *mesos*, "midst," here, "pertaining to a position within a group, without focus on mediate position, among"(BDAG 635, 2b).

[38] "Be separate" is *aphorizō*, "to remove one party from other parties so as to discourage or eliminate contact, separate, take away" (BDAG 158, 1).

both idolatry and the sexual immorality that accompanied this false religion. Ashtoreth poles prompted goddess worship. Again and again the prophets called the people from this to a worship of the true God, Yahweh.

The Christians in Corinth had similar temptations – and similar promises from God.

Q2. (2 Corinthians 6:14-18) What are the reasons Paul gives us – both in his letter and by quoting Old Testament scriptures – that we should live holy lives? What kinds of temptations did the Corinthians face in their notorious city.
http://www.joyfulheart.com/forums/index.php?showtopic=1100

Let Us Purify Ourselves (7:1a)

In light of the Old Testament promises that Paul has just quoted, he calls the Corinthians to holiness:

> "Since we have these promises, dear friends, let us purify ourselves from everything that contaminates body and spirit, perfecting holiness out of reverence for God." (7:1)

The phrase translated, "everything that contaminates" (NIV), "defilement" (NRSV), "filthiness" (KJV) is a strong word from a root meaning "to stain, sully, defile, debauch."[39]

Notice that the contamination is to both body[40] and spirit, indicating that both idolatry – and the sexual sins that accompany it – take what is white and pure and clean and defile it. The only remedy is deep cleansing[41] as well as separation from the contaminants.

Perfecting Holiness (7:1b)

The goal of this purification is "perfecting holiness out of reverence for God" (7:1b).

"Perfecting" (NIV, KJV), "making perfect" (NRSV) is *epiteleō*, "to bring about a result according to plan or objective, complete, accomplish, perform, bring about."[42] Paul is seeking a maturing or perfecting of their faith, not wanting to see them continually

---

[39] *Molysmos*, "defilement," figuratively, in sacred and moral context (BDAG 657), from the verb *molunō*, meaning "to stain, sully, defile, debauch" (Liddell-Scott).

[40] "Body" (NIV, NRSV), "flesh" (KJV) is *sarx*, here, "the physical body as a functioning entity, body, physical body" (BDAG 915, 2a).

[41] "Purify" (NIV), "cleanse" (NRSV, KJV) is *katharizō*, here of moral and cultic cleansing, "cleanse, purify" from sin (BDAG 489, 3bα).

[42] *Epiteleō*, BDAG 383, 2.

dragged down into a pit of degradation by their adolescent behavior.

"Holiness" is a state of separation to God, being separated from what is common and unclean. Those who are bought by God and are God's possessions are set apart for his use and pleasure exclusively. The Corinthians have remained entangled in activities and allegiances that are absolutely contrary to God's nature. They are unholy! Paul calls them to perfect holiness.

One of the chief motivators to holiness should be "the fear[43] of God." This involves both a fear of punishment as well as a reverence and respect for God that keeps a person from entanglement with sin. Holiness is one of the major themes in both the Old and New Testaments. Holiness is our purpose and destiny.

> "For he chose us in him before the creation of the world to be **holy** and blameless in his sight." (Ephesians 1:4)
>
> "May he strengthen your hearts so that you will be blameless and **holy** in the presence of our God and Father when our Lord Jesus comes with all his holy ones." (1 Thessalonians 3:13)
>
> "For God did not call us to be impure, but to live a **holy life**." (1 Thessalonians 4:7, in the context of immoral sexual behavior)
>
> "Make every effort to live in peace with all men and to **be holy**; without **holiness** no one will see the Lord." (Hebrews 12:14)
>
> "As obedient children, do not conform to the evil desires you had when you lived in ignorance. [15] But just as he who called you is **holy**, so be **holy** in all you do; for it is written: '**Be holy**, because I am holy.'" (1 Peter 1:14-16)

What Kind of Separation Is Required?

A misunderstanding of this command, "Come out from them and be separate," has spawned (6:17a) a kind of holier-than-thou brand of separatism in certain sectors of the Christian church. Let me clarify what this command *does not* mean and what it *does* mean.

First, our passage isn't talking about separation from believers, but about separation from the idolatry and sexual immorality of the pagans in Corinth. There is a time, of course, to separate from believers. In an earlier letter to the Corinthian church, Paul clarified his teaching:

> "[9] I have written you in my letter not to associate with sexually immoral people – [10] not at all meaning the people of this world who are immoral, or the greedy and swindlers, or

---

[43] "Reverence" (NIV), "fear" (NRSV, KJV) is *phobos*, "fear," here in the sense of "reverence, respect" (BDAG 1062, 2bα).

idolaters. In that case you would have to leave this world.

[11] But now I am writing you that you must not associate with anyone who calls himself a brother but is sexually immoral or greedy, an idolater or a slanderer, a drunkard or a swindler. With such a man do not even eat." (1 Corinthians 5:9-11)

In the 1 Corinthians 5 passage, Paul says clearly that we aren't to associate with believers who continue to practice immorality. Elsewhere, the New Testament teaches to separate ourselves from divisive people (Romans 16:17), idle brothers (2 Thessalonians 3:6, 14), and false teachers (2 John 10).

Some Christians are so separatist that they refuse to associate with Billy Graham because he cooperated with liberal Christian churches. This is known as "second-degree separation" – that is, separation from anyone who will not separate from the things we believe are wrong. Dear friends, this kind of militant separatism breaks the primary law of "love one another." It is judgmental and exactly the kind of separatism practiced by the Pharisees in Jesus' day.

Again, our passage in 2 Corinthians does *not* teach separation from believers (though there's a time for that). Separation from believers is not the point or the purpose of this passage.

Notice in the passage quoted above from 1 Corinthians, Paul does *not* require separation from unbelievers. It isn't practical:

"In that case you would have to leave this world." (1 Corinthians 5:10b)

Indeed, we should retain friendships with unbelievers! Otherwise, we wouldn't be able to influence them for Christ.

Consider Jesus' example. He associated with the sinners of his day: tax collectors, prostitutes, and others. He went to their homes and enjoyed their parties. This passage doesn't teach us to separate from unbelievers per se.

But it does command us to separate ourselves from people and associations that will lead us into sin. Paul's concern was that the Corinthian Christians still participated in the pagan feasts and their attendant sexual immorality.

When we become Christians, we *must* cut ties with things that will lead us back into sin! Recently I observed a Christian outreach aimed at musicians. One of the leaders had been deeply involved in this culture – and the alcoholism and drug use and promiscuity that attended it. I'm afraid that this leader wasn't strong enough to influence his former friends; they influenced him and enticed him back!

If you've been involved in drinking and drug use with non-Christian friends, you can't be with them when they drink and use drugs! Why? Because the old associations are very likely to drag you down again. You can still be their friends – if they'll have you – but you can't be around them when they are sinning. You've got to separate yourself from sin and the people who would tempt you to fall back into sin! That's what Paul is talking about here.

To summarize, does being unequally yoked mean that we shouldn't marry an unbeliever? Paul teaches this elsewhere (1 Corinthians 7:39). But the context here is that we should separate ourselves from those who would lead us back into the sin and degradation of our former lives.

Q3. (2 Corinthians 6:14-7:1) What kind of separation is Paul calling the Corinthians to? How can they strike a balance between separating themselves from sinful practices that mess up their spiritual lives while at the same time maintaining friendships with pagan neighbors and co-workers?
http://www.joyfulheart.com/forums/index.php?showtopic=1101

A Plea for Open Hearts (7:2)

Now Paul returns to his appeal to the Corinthians to reconcile with him and begin again the warm fellowship they had once experienced before his opponents had slandered and undermined his reputation.

> "Make room for us in your hearts. We have wronged no one, we have corrupted no one, we have exploited no one." (7:2)

He lists three ways that his character testifies to his faithfulness. But he's obviously contrasting himself to his opponents who did exploit and take advantage of the Corinthians (12:17-18).

1. **"Wronged"**[44]
2. **"Corrupted"**[45]
3. **"Exploited"** (NIV), **"take advantage of"** (NRSV), "defrauded" (KJV)[46]

---

[44] *Adikeō*, "do wrong to someone, treat someone unjustly" (BDAG 20, 1c).

[45] *Phtheirō*, "to cause harm to in a physical manner or in outward circumstances, destroy, ruin, corrupt, spoil," that is, to "ruin financially someone" or "ruin or corrupt someone," by erroneous teaching or immorality (BDAG 1054, 1a or 2a).

[46] *Pleonekteō*, "to take advantage of, exploit, outwit, defraud, cheat someone."BDAG 824, 1a. This word also occurs in 12:17-18.

Paul Is Encouraged by the Corinthians (7:3-4)

Paul has asked them to open their hearts, but he doesn't want them to take this as a judgment on them, so he explains just how much he loves them.

> "³ I do not say this to condemn you; I have said before that you have such a place in our hearts that we would live or die with you. ⁴ I have great confidence in you; I take great pride in you. ⁴⁷I am greatly encouraged; in all our troubles my joy knows no bounds." (7:3-4)

Fightings Without and Fears Within (7:5)

Now he talks a bit about the struggles he has recently gone through.

> "For when we came into Macedonia, this body of ours had no rest, but we were harassed at every turn – conflicts on the outside, fears within." (7:5)

These were both physical[48] and psychological struggles. He talks about being harassed,[49] as well as various conflicts[50] in Macedonia. This had gone on non-stop, without any rest.[51]

I think that it's interesting that Paul admits to fears[52] during this time. To hear some people teach, you'd think that real Christians don't experience fear, which is the opposite of faith. The reality is that we often experience fear. Fear is a reaction to danger that is hard-wired into our human bodies to pour adrenaline into our bloodstream to prepare us to defend ourselves. But fear can also continue on, eating into our confidence, if we let it. Praise God, through faith we face our fears, take courage, and don't allow our fears to control us. Paul didn't.

Q4. (2 Corinthians 7:5) What are the distinctions between fear, faith, and courage? Why is being honest about our fears better than pretending we don't have any fears? How did Paul deal with his fears?

http://www.joyfulheart.com/forums/index.php?showtopic=1102

---

[47] "Troubles" (NIV), "affliction" (NRSV), "tribulation" (KJV) is *thlipsis*, "trouble that inflicts distress, oppression, affliction, tribulation" (BDAG 457, 1). The word is common elsewhere in 2 Corinthians.

[48] "Body" (NIV, NRSV), "flesh" (KJV) is *sarx*, "the physical body as functioning entity, body, physical body" (BDAG 915, 2a).

[49] "Harassed" (NIV), "afflicted" (NRSV), "troubled" (KJV) is *thlibō*, "to make narrow," here, "to cause to be troubled, oppress, afflict someone" (BDAG 457, 3).

[50] "Conflicts" (NIV), "disputes" (NRSV), "fightings" (KJV) is *machē*, in the New Testament only in the plural and only of battles fought without actual weapons: "fighting, quarrels, strife, disputes" (BDAG 622).

[51] "Rest" (NIV) is *anesis*, "relief from something onerous or troublesome, rest, relaxation, relief" (BDAG 77, 2).

[52] "Fears" is *phobos*, "fear, alarm, fright" (BDAG 1062, 2aα).

The Comfort of Titus' Coming (7:6-7)

You see a little bit of Paul's humanity in the next couple of verses. Paul has been struggling, but the presence of his co-worker, who has just returned from Corinth, brings tremendous encouragement to him.

> "⁶ But God, who **comforts** the downcast,⁵³ **comforted** us by the coming of Titus, ⁷ and not only by his coming but also by the **comfort** you had given him. He told us about your longing⁵⁴ for me, your deep sorrow,⁵⁵ your ardent concern⁵⁶ for me, so that my joy was greater than ever." (7:6-7)

Paul alluded to this comfort he had received at the beginning of the letter:

> "Praise be to ... the God of all comfort, who **comforts** us in all our troubles, so that we can **comfort** those in any trouble with the **comfort** we ourselves have received from God." (1:3-4)

Part of that comfort was learning that the Corinthians still loved and appreciated him (7:7). Paul refers to their positive reaction to his "severe letter" again in verse 11.

Sorrow that Leads to Repentance (7:8-10)

Now he discusses this "severe letter" and its results.

> "⁸ Even if I caused you sorrow⁵⁷ by my letter, I do not regret⁵⁸ it. Though I did regret it – I see that my letter hurt⁵⁹ you, but only for a little while – ⁹ yet now I am happy, not because you were made sorry, but because your sorrow led you to repentance. For you became sorrowful as God intended and so were not harmed⁶⁰ in any way by us. ¹⁰ Godly sorrow brings repentance that leads to salvation and leaves no regret, but worldly

---

[53] "Downcast" (NIV, NRSV), "those that are cast down" is *tapeinos*, with the basic meaning of "low," that is used figuratively here: "pertaining to being of low social status or to relative inability to cope, lowly, undistinguished, of no account" (BDAG 989, 1).

[54] "Longing" (NIV, NRSV), "earnest desire" (KJV) is *epipothēsis*, "yearning desire for, longing," here and at verse 11 (BDAG 372).

[55] "Deep sorrow" (NIV), "mourning" (NRSV, KJV) is *odyrmos*, "lamentation, mourning" (BDAG 692).

[56] "Ardent concern" (NIV), "zeal" (NRSV), "fervent mind" (KJV) is *zēlos*, "intense positive interest in something, zeal, ardor, marked by a sense of dedication," also at 9:2 (BDAG 427, 1).

[57] "Caused sorrow/made sorry" is *lypeō*, "to cause severe mental or emotional distress, vex, irritate, offend, insult someone" (BDAG 604, 1).

[58] "Regret" (NIV, NRSV), "repent" (KJV) is *metamelomai*, "to have regrets about something, in the sense that one wishes it could be undone, be very sorry, regret" (BDAG 639, 1), from *meta-*, "exchange, transfer, transmutation" + *melomai*, "be a cause of concern."

[59] "Hurt" (NIV), "grieved" (NRSV), "made sorry" (KJV) is *lypeō*.

[60] "Harmed" (NIV, NRSV), "receive damage" (KJV) is *zēmioō*, "to experience the loss of something," with implication of undergoing hardship or suffering, "suffer damage/loss, forfeit, sustain injury" (BDAG 428, 1).

sorrow brings death." (7:8-10)

Paul is sorry that he had to be so strong in this letter, but it had the desired fruit: godly repentance,[61] a change of mind and heart in Corinth.

Sometimes parents need to be harsh when their children are rebellious in order to correct them. Love that is gentle is possible when it is reciprocated. But sometimes "tough love" is called for. It's not fun for the parent, pastor, or apostle, but can bring about the desired repentance when administered consistently and with the right motive.

Eagerness to Clear their Name (7:11-13a)

Now Paul describes the reaction to his letter. The Corinthians bent over backwards to clear themselves from any charge.

"[11] See what this godly sorrow[62] has produced in you: what earnestness,[63] what eagerness to clear yourselves,[64] what indignation,[65] what alarm,[66] what longing,[67] what concern,[68] what readiness to see justice done.[69] At every point you have proved yourselves to be innocent[70] in this matter. [12] So even though I wrote to you, it was not on account of the one who did the wrong or of the injured party, but rather that before God you could see for yourselves how devoted to us you are. [13] By all this we are encouraged." (7:11-13a)

Titus' Good Report (7:13b-16)

Paul praises the Lord for the good news that Titus had brought, but also to see how

---

[61] "Repentance" is *metanoia*, basically, "a change of mind," then "repentance, turning about, conversion" (BDAG 643).

[62] "Godly sorrow" is literally "sorrow (*lypeō*) according to God" using *kata*, here, "marker of norm of similarity or homogeneity, according to, in accordance with, in conformity with, according to," to introduce the norm that governs something, in this case, God (BDAG 512, 5aα).

[63] "Earnestness" (NIV, NRSV), "carefulness" (KJV) is *spoudē*, "earnest commitment in discharge of an obligation or experience of a relationship, eagerness, earnestness, diligence, willingness, zeal" (BDAG 939, 2).

[64] "Eagerness to clear yourselves" (NIV, NRSV) is *apologia*, "generally, of eagerness to defend oneself" (BDAG 117, 2b).

[65] *Aganaktēsis*, "indignation" (BDAG 5).

[66] "Alarm" (NIV, NRSV), "fear" (KJV) is *phobos*, "fear, alarm, fright" (BDAG 1062, 2aα).

[67] "Longing" (NIV, NRSV), "vehement desire" (KJV) is *epipothēsis*, "yearning desire for, longing" (BDAG 377).

[68] "Concern" (NIV), "zeal" (NRSV, KJV) is *zēlos*, "intense positive interest in something, zeal, ardor, marked by a sense of dedication" (BDAG 422, 1).

[69] "Readiness to see justice done" (NIV), "punishment" (NRSV), "revenge" (KJV) is *ekdikēsis*, "penalty inflicted on wrongdoers," absolutely, "punishment" (of Paul's opponent) (BDAG 302, 3).

[70] "Innocent" (NIV), "guiltless" (NRSV), "clear" (KJV) is *hagnos*, "pure, holy" (BDAG 13, a).

blessed Titus was by this assignment, because it was quite sensitive and could have gone badly.

> "13b In addition to our own encouragement, we were especially delighted to see how happy Titus was, because his spirit[71] has been refreshed[72] by all of you. 14 I had boasted to him about you, and you have not embarrassed me. But just as everything we said to you was true, so our boasting about you to Titus has proved to be true as well. 15 And his affection for you is all the greater when he remembers that you were all obedient,[73] receiving him with fear and trembling. 16 I am glad I can have complete confidence in you." (7:13b-16)

What does it mean for the church to be "obedient"? It means that they had become responsive once again to Paul's ministry and to his apostolic authority and commands. I've seen churches that are rebellious to pastoral authority and I've seen obedient ones. Only obedient churches can be united and productive in ministry.

In this lesson we've watched what Paul endured in spite of intense hardships. We've heard his plea for personal holiness, and we've seen his encouragement at Titus' report. In all of this he has sought to set before the Corinthians healthy examples of Christian leadership so they can become healthier as a church and in their own personal lives. Twenty centuries later, Paul's life is an example that brings conviction to our own lives as well. Thank you, Paul, for hanging in there – for Christ and for us.

Prayer

Father, I pray that you'd put in my heart the same kind of courage that rose up in the heart of your apostle. Forgive me for complaining. Forgive me for sometimes blurring the lines between your holiness and the world I live in. Forgive me for giving into my fears when all along you were seeking to challenge me to faith. Forgive me and grow me into Christ's image. In His name, I pray. Amen.

Key Verses

> "Do not be yoked together with unbelievers." (2 Corinthians 6:14)

> "For we are the temple of the living God. As God has said: 'I will live with them and walk among them, and I will be their God, and they will be my people.'" (2 Corinthians 6:16)

---

[71] "Spirit" (NIV, KJV), "mind" (NRSV) is *pneuma*.

[72] "Refreshed" (NIV, KJV), "set at rest" (NRSV) is *anapauō*, "to cause someone to gain relief from toil, cause to rest, give (someone) rest, refresh, revive" (BDAG 69, 1).

[73] "Obedient/obedience" is *hypakoē*, "a state of being in compliance, obedience," that is, one listens and follows instructions (BDAG 1028, 1b).

"Therefore come out from them and be separate, says the Lord. Touch no unclean thing, and I will receive you." (2 Corinthians 6:17)

"Since we have these promises, dear friends, let us purify ourselves from everything that contaminates body and spirit, perfecting holiness out of reverence for God." (2 Corinthians 7:1)

9. Generosity Modeled and Encouraged (8:1-9:5)

"St. Paul" statue, bronze, in front of St. Isaac's Cathedral, St. Petersburg, Russia.

In this lesson, Paul is seeking to finalize preparations for the Corinthian church to receive a collection "to make a contribution for the poor among the saints in Jerusalem." (Romans 15:25). For several years, Paul has been working with churches in Macedonia and Achaia to take up an offering to relieve the extreme poverty in Judea.

This project had been on Paul's heart for a long time. After his first missionary journey, when discussing with the apostles in Jerusalem,

"They asked ... that we should continue to remember the poor, the very thing I was eager to do." (Galatians 2:10)

In a previous letter to the Corinthians, Paul had mentioned the offering.

"[1] Now about the collection for God's people: Do what I told the Galatian churches to do. [2] On the first day of every week, each one of you should set aside a sum of money in keeping with his income, saving it up, so that when I come no collections will have to be made. [3] Then, when I arrive, I will give letters of introduction to the men you approve and send them with your gift to Jerusalem. [4] If it seems advisable for me to go also, they will accompany me." (1 Corinthians 16:1-4)

Now the time has come to complete the offering, since representatives of the Macedonian churches would be coming to Corinth shortly and Paul wants to make sure everything is ready. Then Paul will arrive and together they will carry the cash to Jerusalem (Acts 24:17).

It appears in this chapter, however, that Paul is concerned that the Corinthians won't be ready after all. They had started well, but needed additional prompting and encouragement.

The Generosity of the Macedonian Churches (8:1-5)

So Paul begins his encouragement by sharing the example of other churches that are giving generously for this collection. Paul is writing this letter from Macedonia and boasts about the generosity he is seeing there (7:5-7).

> "¹ And now, brothers, we want you to know about the grace that God has given the Macedonian churches. ² Out of the most severe trial, their overflowing joy and their extreme poverty welled up in rich generosity." (8:1-2)

As Paul writes, the churches in Macedonia – probably Thessalonica and Philippi, and perhaps Berea – were undergoing a terrible time of persecution and the poverty that prevails at such a time, probably related to Paul's own difficulties there (7:5).

Paul describes the Macedonian's problem as "the most severe trial" (NIV), a "severe ordeal of affliction" (NRSV), combining two words, one upon another, to indicate the severity of the experience: *dokimē*, "a testing process, test, ordeal,"[1] and *thlipsis*, "pressure, oppression, affliction, tribulation."[2] (We've examined both of these words previously.) Combined with their trials is the word *bathos*, "extreme" (NIV, NRSV) or "deep" (KJV)[3] describing their poverty.[4] This is a level of poverty hard for us to imagine. We might use the expression "dirt poor" to describe it.

But despite the severity of their persecution and the depth of their poverty, the Macedonian Christians are exhibiting unexpected joy and generosity. The phrase "overflowing joy" (NIV), "abundant joy" (NRSV) employs the modifier *perisseia*, "that which is beyond the regular or expected amount, surplus, abundance."[5] Paul uses a related verb to describe the spontaneous overflow[6] of their generosity.

This generosity itself comes with a modifier:[7] "rich generosity" (NIV), "wealth of generosity" (NRSV), "riches of their liberality" (KJV). They aren't just generous, they are amazingly generous! *Haplotēs*, translated "generosity" (NIV, NRSV), "liberality" (KJV), has the root idea of "simplicity, sincerity,"[8] but here probably carries the idea of "open-

---

[1] *Dokimē*, BDAG 256,1. Also at 2:9 and 9:13.

[2] *Thlipsis*, BDAG 457, 1.

[3] *Bathos*, BDAG 162, 2.

[4] "Poverty" is *ptōcheia*, "state of being deficient in means of support, poverty" (BDAG 896), also used in verse 9.

[5] *Perisseia*, BDAG 804.

[6] "Welled up" (NIV), "overflowed" (NRSV), "abounded" (KJV) is *perisseuō*, "to be in abundance, abound," here "to be extremely rich or abundant, overflow" (BDAG 805, 1aγ).

[7] *Ploutos*, "plentiful supply of something, a wealth, abundance" (BDAG 832, 2).

[8] Barrett translates the phrase, "the wealth of their simple-hearted goodness" (p. 219). The same word in Romans 12:8 he translates as "whole-heartedly," that is, "being without *arrière-pensée* [ulterior motive] in one's gifts" (C.K. Barrett, *The Epistle to the Romans* (Harper's New Testament Commentaries; Harper &

heartedness," hence, "generosity, liberality."[9]

Paul continues,

> "[3] For I testify that they gave as much as they were able, and even beyond their ability. Entirely on their own, [4] they urgently pleaded with us for the privilege of sharing in this service to the saints. [5] And they did not do as we expected, but they gave themselves first to the Lord and then to us in keeping with God's will." (8:3-5)

They gave "according to their means" (*kata dynamin*), a phrase very common in papyrus documents from that era, especially in marriage contracts where a husband promises to provide food and clothing for his wife "according to his means."[10] This is what Paul recommended to the Corinthians previously:

> "On the first day of every week, each one of you should set aside a sum of money **in keeping with his income**...." (1 Corinthians 16:2)

"In keeping with his income" (NIV), "as God has prospered him" (KJV) translates the passive verb, *euodoō*, "have things turn out well, prosper, succeed."[11] To the degree that he prospers, he should give.

But here in 2 Corinthians, Paul notes that the Macedonians went beyond giving according to their ability. They gave "even beyond their ability. Entirely on their own[12]...." In other words, they weren't motivated by clever offering appeals, but out of their own volition, they got caught up in the joy of giving to relieve the poverty of others – while the Macedonians themselves were utterly poor. Amazing!

Row, 1957), p. 238-239. Danker contends that "the sense of 'sincere concern, simple goodness' is sufficient for all these passages" (BDAG 104, 2).

[9] Liddell-Scott, *Greek Lexicon*, sees a meaning "open-heartedness," hence, "liberality" (*in loc.*). The sense "generosity" is favored by Bruce and others based on parallels in Josephus, *Antiquities* 7, 13, 4 ("[David] took [Aruna's] generosity (*haplotēs*) and magnanimity (*megalopsuxia*, "greatness of soul, highmindedness, generosity") loudly, and accepted his good-will...."), and *Testament of Issachar*, 3, 8. Also at Romans 12:8, and 2 Corinthians 9:11, 13.

[10] Kruse, p. 151. *Dynamis*, "power," here means "ability to carry out something, capability" (BDAG 263, 2).

[11] *Euodoō*, BDAG 410. Danker translates the phrase, "save as much as he gains." But Fee notes that the Christian community contained a number of slaves who might have no income at all. He sees the verb as "intentionally ambiguous, and does not mean that each should lay aside all his or her 'profits,' which a literal translation of the Greek text would allow, but that in accordance with 'whatever success or prosperity may have come their way that week,' each should set aside something for this collection. There is no hint of a tithe or proportional giving; the gift is simply to be related to their ability from week to week as they have been prospered by God" (Gordon D. Fee, *The First Epistle to the Corinthians* (New International Commentary; Eerdmans, 1987), p. 814). The NRSV's translation "whatever extra you earn," misses the sense of it, I think.

[12] "Entirely on their own" (NIV), "voluntarily" (NRSV), "willing of themselves" (KJV) is *authairetos*, "pertaining to being self-chosen, of one's own accord," also in 8:17 (BDAG 150).

More than that, it sounds like Paul may not have even decided to ask them to give, because it says they "urgently pleaded" (NIV), "begging us earnestly" (NRSV), "praying us with much intreaty" (KJV)[13] "...for the privilege of sharing in this service to the saints." They didn't want to be left out of the blessing of being a blessing!

This reminds me of the poor widow who gave two small coins as her offering in the temple. Her love for God was so great that she gave all she had. Jesus commented to his disciples on her generosity in the face of deep poverty:

> "I tell you the truth, this poor widow has put in more than all the others. All these people gave their gifts out of their wealth; but she out of her poverty put in all she had to live on." (Luke 21:3-4)

Jesus held her up as an example to his disciples.

Q1. (2 Corinthians 8:1-5) Why is it so difficult to give when we are stressed by circumstances and bills and pressures? What can we learn from the example of the Macedonians and the poor widow? How will this lesson affect your own giving?
http://www.joyfulheart.com/forums/index.php?showtopic=1103

The Grace of Giving

It's interesting to observe that in five places in our passage, giving is referred to as "grace":

	NIV	NRSV	KJV
Verse 4	"privilege"	"privilege"	"gift"
Verse 7	"act of grace"	"generous undertaking"	"grace"
Verse 8	"grace of giving"	"generous undertaking"	"grace"
Verse 9	"grace"	"generous act"	"grace"
Verse 19	"offering"	"generous undertaking"	"grace"

The word is *charis*, which has the root idea of "a beneficent disposition toward someone, favor, grace, gracious care or help, goodwill." Here, it has the sense of a "practical

---

[13] This intense phrase is formed from three words used together: *polys*, "much" + *paraklēsis*, "strong request, appeal" (BDAG 766, 2) + *deomai*, "to ask for something pleadingly, request" (BDAG 218, aβ).

application of goodwill, (a sign of) favor, gracious deed or gift, benefaction."[14]

Those who see giving as a chore, a necessary evil, a tax, an exaction, have missed the spirit of giving and of blessing that should be part of a Christian's value system. The Macedonians viewed this offering as a "service" (NIV), a "ministry" (NRSV, cf. KJV) of theirs to those less fortunate.[15] This was their opportunity to show solidarity with their brothers and sisters in the mother church, a "participation, sharing," a sense of fellowship.[16] The Church in Judea had blessed them with the gospel; now they were giving back.

Q2. (2 Corinthians 8:4, 7-9, 19) What does grace have to do with giving? What does giving look like when it isn't accompanied by grace? What does it look like when grace prompts your giving?
http://www.joyfulheart.com/forums/index.php?showtopic=1104

Match the Macedonians' Generosity (8:6-8)

> "[6] So we urged Titus, since he had earlier made a beginning, to bring also to completion this act of grace on your part. [7] But just as you excel in everything – in faith, in speech, in knowledge, in complete earnestness and in your love for us – see that you also excel in this grace of giving." (8:6-7)

The Corinthians had begun to give according to Paul's direction in 1 Corinthians 16:1-4, and through Titus' ministry with them. But now is the time to wrap it up, to bring the offering to a completion so they would be ready to send it off without a big push to give right at the end. Now he complements them about their record of excelling.[17] I don't think Paul is speaking sarcastically here; rather he is encouraging them to extend their example of spiritual excellence to giving as well. The grace of giving can't be commanded, but it can be encouraged and stimulated by the example of others. He says,

---

[14] *Charis*, BDAG 1079, 3a.

[15] *Diakonia*, "service," is defined here as, "service rendered in an intermediary capacity, mediation, assignment," also used with this sense in 9:1 (BDAG 230, 1).

[16] *Koinōnia*, BDAG 553, 4.

[17] "Excel" (NIV, NRSV), "abound" (KJV) is *perisseuō*, here, "be outstanding, be prominent, excel in something" (BDAG 805, 1bβ).

"I am not commanding you, but I want to test the sincerity of your love by comparing[18]
it with the earnestness of others." (8:8)

Paul makes no apology for using the example of the Macedonian's giving to stimulate
the Corinthians' giving. You could look at it cynically as a way to engage their pride –
and you might be a little bit right.

But one thing I have learned in discipling Christians for decades is that believers
normally rise only as high as the level of commitment and devotion they see in other
Christians that they respect. People imitate what they see directly or hear about (1
Corinthians 11:1). If you've visited various churches, you may have seen some pretty
"dead" churches, as well as some churches that have a profoundly "faith-filled"
environment in which Christians grow quickly.

So to stimulate their faith, Paul shares the example of some on-fire saints in Macedonia who are characterized by their zeal. "Earnestness" (NIV), "eagerness" (NRSV),
"diligence" (KJV) in verse 7 and "earnestness" (NIV, NRSV), "forwardness" (KJV) in
verse 8 is *spoudē*, "earnest commitment in discharge of an obligation or experience of a
relationship, eagerness, earnestness, diligence, willingness, zeal."[19]

Your zeal in giving, says Paul, will be a good way to demonstrate or test[20] your love
by contrasting it with the loving zeal of the Macedonians.

Christ's Generosity in Poverty Made Us Rich (8:9)

But Paul doesn't stop with giving the Corinthians the example of the Macedonians.
Rather, he points to the example of Christ himself:

"For you know the grace of our Lord Jesus Christ, that though he was rich, yet for your
sakes he became poor, so that you through his poverty might become rich." (8:9)

Jesus Was Poor Here on Earth

I've heard people who ought to know better, try to support the Prosperity Teaching
using this verse. They somehow "prove" that the historic Jesus was wealthy during this
time on earth. That is false, according to the Gospels.

Jesus' parents were so poor that Jesus was born in a stable. They had to offer the
poor-man's sacrifice of two pigeons when Jesus was dedicated in the Temple at 40 days
of age (Luke 2:22-24; Leviticus 12:8). While the Holy Family received extravagant gifts

[18] "Compare" (NIV) isn't in the text but is implied by the context.
[19] *Spoudē*, BDAG 939, 2.
[20] "Test" (NIV, NRSV), "prove" (KJV) is *dokimazō*, here, "to draw a conclusion about worth on the basis of
testing, prove, approve ... accept as proved, approve" (BDAG 255, 2b).

from the Magi, these were probably used up by their sojourn in Egypt, for Joseph was known in Nazareth as a carpenter (that is, a working craftsman, Matthew 13:55), not as a wealthy man who didn't have to work. As a carpenter himself (Mark 6:3), Jesus probably made a little more income than a subsistence farmer, but he was by no means rich. During his ministry, he was probably supported by a group of wealthy women (Luke 8:1-3) and received the hospitality of people in towns and villages, but of his own wealth, he said, "The Son of Man has no place to lay his head" (Matthew 8:20).

Christ Humbled Himself

So what does Paul mean when he says "though he was rich, yet for your sakes he became poor" (8:9)? Paul is talking about spiritual things, not material things!

This is probably best taught in Paul's majestic hymn about Christ in Philippians 2:

> "6 Who, being in very nature God,
> did not consider equality with God something to be grasped,
> 7 but made himself nothing,
> taking the very nature of a servant,
> being made in human likeness.
> 8 And being found in appearance as a man,
> he humbled himself and became obedient to death–
> even death on a cross!" (Philippians 2:6-8)

Christ, the Creator of the Universe (John 1:3; Colossians 1:16-17), voluntarily laid down his crown and radiant glory shining brighter than the sun, and took on the mortal body and the humble garb of a poor Jewish carpenter. He emptied himself of all his divine prerogatives and humbled himself – and ultimately died for us and for our sins. This is grace, unmerited favor that we neither can earn or deserve!

Paul builds on this truth in our passage:

> "For you know the grace of our Lord Jesus Christ,
> that though he was rich,
> yet for your sakes he became poor,
> so that you through his poverty
> might become rich." (8:9)

The riches we received are the "the riches of his glorious inheritance in the saints" (Ephesians 1:18), where we have all things in Christ and are heirs to everything he possesses. Yet in this life, our material lives may be "for richer, for poorer." We know what the true riches really are and those are what we long for!

Q3. (2 Corinthians 8:9) What riches did Christ have according to this verse? How did he become poor? In what way were we poor? In what way have we become rich?
http://www.joyfulheart.com/forums/index.php?showtopic=1105

Complete the Giving You Began (8:10-11)

Now after pointing to Christ's supreme example of giving, Paul continues:

"10 And here is my advice about what is best for you in this matter: Last year you were the first not only to give but also to have the desire to do so. 11 Now finish the work, so that your eager willingness to do it may be matched by your completion of it, according to your means." (8:10-11)

They should finish the collection so that their initial enthusiasm[21] will be matched by actual execution until completion.[22]

Give According to Your Blessing (8:12-15)

Paul takes pains to explain himself with clarity.

"12 For if the willingness is there, the gift is acceptable[23] according to what one has, not according to what he does not have. 13 Our desire is not that others might be relieved[24] while you are hard pressed,[25] but that there might be equality. 14 At the present time your plenty will supply what they need, so that in turn their plenty will supply what you need. Then there will be equality, 15 as it is written:

'He who gathered much did not have too much,
and he who gathered little did not have too little.'" (8:12-15)

We're only expected to give what we have, he says, not what we don't have. The idea isn't to impoverish the relatively well-off Corinthians so that the Jerusalem saints can

---

[21] "Eager willingness" (NIV), "eagerness" (NRSV), "a readiness to will" (KJV) is two words: *prothymia*, "exceptional interest in being of service, willingness, readiness, goodwill" (BDAG 870), also used in the next verse, and *thelō*, "want," here, "to have something in mind for oneself, of purpose, resolve, will, wish, want, be ready" (BDAG 442, 2).

[22] "Completion" (NIV, NRSV), "performance" (KJV) is *epiteleō*, "to finish something begun, end, bring to an end, finish" (BDAG 383, 1).

[23] "Acceptable/accepted" is *euprosdektos*, "pertaining to being capable of eliciting favorable acceptance, acceptable" (BDAG 410, 1a).

[24] "Relieved/relief" (NIV, NRSV), "eased" (KJV) is *anesis*, "relief from something onerous or troublesome, rest, relaxation, relief" (BDAG 772).

[25] "Hard pressed" (NIV), "pressure" (NRSV), "burdened" (KJV) is *thlipsis*, "trouble that inflicts distress, affliction," here, "difficult circumstances" (BDAG 457, 1).

become rich. The goal is an equitable distribution.

Does the Bible Advocate Socialism or Communism?

What does Paul mean when he seeks a goal of "equality" (NIV, KJV) or "fair balance" (NRSV) in verse 13 and 14? The Greek noun is *isotēs*, "state of matters being held in proper balance, equality."[26] Is he teaching some kind of socialism? No. What he is teaching is sacrificial love in action.

The infant church had seen this kind of love in their earliest days in Jerusalem.

> "All the believers were together and had everything in common. Selling their possessions and goods, they gave to anyone as he had need." (Acts 2:44-45)

"In common" is *koinos*, "pertaining to being of mutual interest or shared collectively, communal, common," that is, they loved each other so much that they voluntarily shared what they had with those in need.

> "All the believers were one in heart and mind. No one claimed that any of his possessions was his own, but they shared everything they had ... and much grace was upon them all. There were no needy persons among them. For from time to time those who owned lands or houses sold them, brought the money from the sales and put it at the apostles' feet, and it was distributed to anyone as he had need." (Acts 4:32-35)

This was not forced; it was love at work in the real world. Barnabas voluntarily sold some extra property to provide money to help those in need (Acts 4:36-37). Notice that Ananias and Sapphira weren't faulted for keeping back some of the proceeds of their sale, which would have been okay, but only for "lying to the Holy Spirit," pretending that they had given *all* of the proceeds for the poor (Acts 5:1-11).

Socialism and communism involve a forced redistribution of wealth. Scriptural giving out of love to relieve the poor is entirely voluntary; it cannot and should not be commanded (8:8). Such giving is a grace, not a law.

Gathering Just the Amount Needed (8:14-15)

"At the present time," Paul writes, "your plenty will supply what they need, so that in turn their plenty will supply what you need." You help them now when you have extra, and when you are hit with disaster, they'll help you. In fact, in his letter to the Romans, Paul observes:

> "For Macedonia and Achaia were pleased to make a contribution for the poor among the saints in Jerusalem. They were pleased to do it, and indeed they **owe** it to them. For if

---

[26] *Isotēs*, BDAG 483, 1.

the Gentiles have shared in the Jews' spiritual blessings, they **owe** it to the Jews to share with them their material blessings." (Romans 15:25-27)

There's a sense in which the Jerusalem church has sacrificed to send out the gospel full of spiritual blessings to the Gentiles; now it is only fair that the Gentiles share material blessings with the mother church in their time of need.

Paul concludes this part of his argument, by referring to the days of the Exodus when manna came down from heaven.

"He who gathered much did not have too much,
and he who gathered little did not have too little." (8:15, quoting Exodus 16:18)

Some people gathered a lot of manna; others gathered only a little, the Bible says. But when it was measured, the amount each had gathered was just what he and his family needed. No one gained by gathering more than they needed; that which was kept over to the next day spoiled anyway. Each family got what they needed, not more or less. It is that kind of equitable distribution that Paul seeks in the family of God, motivated entirely by love.

Representatives Who Will Carry the Offering to Jerusalem (8:16-19)

Paul explains that the offering will be conveyed to Jerusalem by representatives of the various churches, responsible men who are well-known to the Corinthians.

> [16] I thank God, who put into the heart of Titus the same concern I have for you. [17] For Titus not only welcomed our appeal, but he is coming to you with much enthusiasm and on his own initiative. [18] And we are sending along with him the brother who is praised by all the churches for his service to the gospel. [19] What is more, he was chosen by the churches to accompany us as we carry the offering, which we administer in order to honor the Lord himself and to show our eagerness to help." (8:16-19)

We Are Transparent in Financial Matters (8:20-21)

Paul interrupts his introduction of the conveyers of the gift by an explanation of why these precautions are being taken.

> "[20] We want to avoid any criticism of the way we administer this liberal gift. [21] For we are taking pains to do what is right, not only in the eyes of the Lord but also in the eyes of men." (8:20-21)

In Paul's day and in ours, people have seen so much corruption hiding behind the guise of religion that they are skeptical. So, to avoid any criticism,[27] Paul is planning

---

[27] "Criticism" (NIV), "blame" (NRSV, KJV) is *mōmaomai*, "find fault with, criticize, censure, blame someone"

ahead of time[28] for a clear, open, and transparent way of handling this large amount of money.[29]

There is a time to live our lives before Christ, and not to please men (Acts 4:19; 5:29). But how we live reflects on the gospel and on our Lord. So when possible, we need to take whatever precautions are necessary to demonstrate that are we are acting above reproach – especially about such often abused matters as money, sex, and power. Pastors and church leaders who don't take extra precautions to protect themselves in these areas are asking for both temptation and accusations of wrongdoing.

Q4. (2 Corinthians 8:21-22) What is the balance between living our lives wholly before God without being men-pleasers, and doing what is right in the sight of men?
http://www.joyfulheart.com/forums/index.php?showtopic=1106

Show Honor to Representatives from the Churches (8:22-24)

Now Paul continues to lay out the qualifications of those who will be accompanying the offering to its destination.

> "22 In addition, we are sending with them our brother who has often proved to us in many ways that he is zealous, and now even more so because of his great confidence in you. 23 As for Titus, he is my partner[30] and fellow worker[31] among you; as for our brothers, they are representatives of the churches and an honor to Christ." (8:22-23)

These men are called "representatives" (NIV), "messengers" (NRSV, KJV) of the churches. The word is *apostolos*, "sent ones," here referring to "messengers without extraordinary status...." That is, they are not "apostles" used as a technical term, but rather serve in the more general sense of a "delegate, envoy, messenger."[32] They have

---

(BDAG 663).

[28] "Taking pains" (NIV), "intend" (NRSV), "providing for honest things" (KJV) is two words, *pronoeō*, "to think about something beforehand" (BDAG 872) and *kalos*, "good things."

[29] "Liberal/generous gift" (NIV/NRSV), "abundance" (KJV) is *hadrotēs*, "abundance," from *hadros*, "thick, stout, full-grown, strong, rich" (BDAG 21; Thayer, p. 12).

[30] "Partner" is *koinōnos*, "one who takes part in something with someone, companion, partner, sharer" (BDAG 553, 1d).

[31] "Fellow worker" (NIV), "co-worker" (NRSV), "fellow helper" (KJV) is *synergos*, "pertaining to working together with, helping," as substantive, "helper, fellow-worker" (BDAG 969). We get the English word "synergy" from this root.

[32] *Apostolos*, BDAG 122, 1.

been selected by the churches for this particular mission of conveying the money safely and securely to Jerusalem.

Finally, Paul exhorts the Corinthians,

> "Therefore show these men the proof[33] of your love and the reason for our pride in you, so that the churches can see it." (8:24)

In other words, when these men come from Macedonia representing the churches there, don't give them any cause to send back to their churches the report that the Corinthians weren't ready or weren't generous. Respect those whom these men represent.

Boasting to the Macedonians (9:1-4)

> "[1] There is no need for me to write to you about this service to the saints. [2] For I know your eagerness to help, and I have been boasting about it to the Macedonians, telling them that since last year you in Achaia were ready to give;[34] and your enthusiasm has stirred most of them to action.[35] [3] But I am sending the brothers in order that our boasting about you in this matter should not prove hollow,[36] but that you may be ready, as I said you would be. [4] For if any Macedonians come with me and find you unprepared, we – not to say anything about you – would be ashamed of having been so confident." (9:1-4)

Paul begins this section by saying, "There's no need for me to write you about the collection." And, in a sense, this was true. They had shown initial enthusiasm for the project and had started well. But it appears that they had somewhat bogged down, and Paul is concerned that the representatives of the Macedonian churches will appear only to find them unprepared. Since Paul has been bragging to the Macedonian churches about their enthusiasm, if they don't follow through, Paul will be embarrassed and so will the Corinthians.

Time to Complete Your Generous Gift (9:5)

Thus, Paul needs to write to them about this after all – just to make sure things are

[33] "Proof" is *endeixis*, "something that compels acceptance of something mentally or emotionally, demonstration, proof" (BDAG 332, 2).

[34] "Ready to give" (NIV), "ready" (NRSV, KJV) is *paraskeuazō*, "to cause something to be ready, prepare," here in the perfect voice, "be ready." (BDAG 772). The negative of this word is used in verse 4, *aparaskeuastos*, "not ready, unprepared" (a military technical term) (BDAG 97).

[35] "Stirred to action" (NIV), "stirred up" (NRSV), "provoked" (KJV) is *erethizō*, "to cause someone to react in a way that suggests acceptance of a challenge, arouse, provoke," here in a good sense (BDAG 393).

[36] "Hollow" (NIV), "in vain" (NRSV), "empty" (KJV) is *kenoō*, "to empty," here, "to cause to be without result or effect, destroy, render void or of no effect" (BDAG 539, 2).

ready on time.

> "So I thought it necessary to urge the brothers to visit you in advance and finish the arrangements for the generous gift you had promised. Then it will be ready as a generous gift, not as one grudgingly given." (9:5)

The word describing their "generous gift" is a word used for blessing, for praise.[37] Their gift will be a great blessing to the believers in Jerusalem. The gift is an act of blessing.

However, Paul wants it to be given in the right spirit. If they wait until the last minute and then play "hurry-up," everyone will come to resent[38] the gift, since they would have to ask for a lot of money quickly. Planning a capital funds program or a plan to raise weekly giving for the budget is a lot of work. But when people learn to give regularly – each Sunday worked for these people who may have been paid weekly – then the giving is easy, a matter of a good habit, and people enjoy the process of giving. Paul is urging the Corinthians to follow through on the counsel he had given in his earlier letter:

> "On the first day of every week, each one of you should set aside a sum of money in keeping with his income, saving it up, so that when I come no collections will have to be made." (1 Corinthians 16:2)

Prayer

Father, we humans are often so selfish, it's hard for us when we're first learning to give to your work. Teach us what genuine sacrifice really means as we contemplate Jesus emptying of himself to become poor for our sakes. Teach our hearts so that we may become like You. In Jesus' name, we pray. Amen.

Key Verses

> "For you know the grace of our Lord Jesus Christ, that though he was rich, yet for your sakes he became poor, so that you through his poverty might become rich." (2 Corinthians 8:9)

> "For we are taking pains to do what is right, not only in the eyes of the Lord but also in the eyes of men." (2 Corinthians 8:21)

---

[37] "Generous gift" (NIV), "bountiful gift" (NRSV), "a matter of bounty" (KJV) is *eulogia*, usually translated "praise, blessing" in the New Testament. But here, since the concept of blessing connotes the idea of bounty, the word also bears the meaning, "generous gift, bounty" (BDAG 408, 4).

[38] "One grudgingly given" (NIV), "an extortion" (NRSV), "of covetousness" (KJV) is *pleonexia*, "the state of desiring to have more than one's due, greediness, insatiableness, avarice, covetousness." Danker says of this verse, "the context calls for the pregnant meaning, a gift that is grudgingly granted by avarice; extortion" (BDAG 824).

10. Sowing Generously (9:6-15)

Vincent Van Gogh, "The Sower" (after Millet), (1889), oil on canvas, 80 x 64 cm, Niarchos Collection, Zurich.

In the previous lesson, we looked at various motivations to give towards the collection to relieve the poverty of the believers in Jerusalem. In this lesson we examine some of the spiritual principles that underlie giving throughout the Old and New Testaments.

The Law of Sowing and Reaping (9:6)

The Law of Sowing and Reaping, the Law of Spiritual Causality teaches that there is an underlying cause for our relative degree of blessing from God or non-blessing.

"Remember this:
Whoever sows sparingly will also reap sparingly,
and whoever sows generously will also reap generously." (9:6)

"Sparingly" is *pheidomenōs*, "in a scanty or meager manner, sparingly," from *pheidomai*, "to be miserly."[1] "Generously" (NIV), "bountifully" (NRSV, KJV) is *eulogia*, "blessing," which we saw in the previous verse (9:5). Here, the idea is "sowing for blessing." Since the concept of blessing connotes the idea of bounty, *eulogia* also bears the meaning, "generous gift, bounty."[2]

Too many times we give out of a sense of poverty and loss rather than a sense of bounty. My dear friend, are you giving with bounty in mind or with meagerness in

[1] *Pheidomenōs*, BDAG 1051.
[2] *Eulogia*, BDAG 408, 4.

mind? What is your attitude in giving? What is your practice in giving?

Paul seems to be stating a law of nature that has spiritual ramifications as well. When you sow your field trying to put in as little seed as possible, the harvest will be meager. But when you sow your field with the maximum harvest in mind, then you won't scrimp on the seed, knowing that what you give now will come back to you many-fold. It is a matter of having a farmer's common sense about sowing.

A Proverb of Generosity (Proverbs 11:24-25)

We see this principle often in the Old Testament. Here's the principle in a proverb:

"[24] One man gives freely, yet gains even more;
another withholds unduly, but comes to poverty.
[25] A generous man will prosper;
he who refreshes others will himself be refreshed." (Proverbs 11:24-25)

Principles of Blessing and Tithing (Malachi 3:10-12)

Consider the promises in Malachi that result from tithing:

"'[10] Bring the whole tithe into the storehouse,
that there may be food in my house.
Test me in this,' says the LORD Almighty,
'and see if I will not throw open the floodgates of heaven
and pour out so much blessing
that you will not have room enough for it.
[11] I will prevent pests from devouring your crops,
and the vines in your fields will not cast their fruit,'
says the LORD Almighty.
[12] 'Then all the nations will call you blessed,
for yours will be a delightful land,' says the LORD Almighty." (Malachi 3:10-12)

The tithe (that is, 10% of one's income) *belonged* to the Lord according to the Mosaic Law. It was his, not theirs. Thus, when people did not give the tithe to the Lord, they were guilty of robbing God, since they kept back what belonged to him. As a result they experienced a curse.

But look at the promised results of tithing:
- Abundant blessing (10b).
- Protection from pests and crops not maturing[3] (11).

---

[3] *Shākal*, "be bereaved, make childless, miscarry." Here it is used figuratively of unproductive land (Victor P. Hamilton, *shākal*, TWOT #2385).

- A reputation of being blessed (12a).
- A land of delight[4] (12b).

These blessings seem to be *material* blessings promised to the people of God, not just *spiritual*, though having God delight in you is certainly a spiritual blessing. The cause of the blessing is bringing the full tithe, not just a fraction of it.

The Result of Failing to Put God First in Giving (Haggai 1:2-11)

Take a look at Haggai, written during the period right after the nation returned from exile. The people were intent on building their own homes, but neglected repairing the house of God. It's a long passage, but sobering and instructive:

"[2] This is what the LORD Almighty says:
'These people say, "The time has not yet come for the LORD's house to be built."'

[3] Then the word of the LORD came through the prophet Haggai:
[4] 'Is it a time for you yourselves to be living in your paneled houses,
while this house remains a ruin?'
[5] Now this is what the LORD Almighty says:

'Give careful thought to your ways.
[6] **You have planted much, but have harvested little.**
You eat, but never have enough.
You drink, but never have your fill.
You put on clothes, but are not warm.
You earn wages, only to put them in a purse with holes in it.'

[7] This is what the LORD Almighty says:
'Give careful thought to your ways.
[8] Go up into the mountains and bring down timber
and build the house,
so that I may take pleasure in it and be honored,'
says the LORD.

[9] 'You expected much, but see, it turned out to be little.**
What you brought home, I blew away. Why?'
declares the LORD Almighty.
'Because of my house,
which remains a ruin,
while each of you is busy with his own house.
[10] Therefore, **because of you** the heavens have withheld their dew

---

[4] "The basic meaning is "to feel great favor towards something ... take delight in, be pleased with, desire" (Leon J. Wood, *hēpes*, TWOT #712).

and the earth its crops.

¹¹ I called for a drought on the fields and the mountains,
on the grain, the new wine, the oil
and whatever the ground produces,
on men and cattle, and on the labor of your hands.'" (Haggai 1:2-11)

Haggai is talking about a cause and effect with regard to giving.

Jesus' Teaching on Giving and Blessing (Luke 6:37-38)

We see the same kind of teaching from Jesus about cause and effect – including in the area of giving:

"³⁷ Do not judge, and you will not be judged.
Do not condemn, and you will not be condemned.
Forgive, and you will be forgiven.

³⁸ Give, and it will be given to you.
A good measure, pressed down, shaken together and running over,
will be poured into your lap.
For with the measure you use, it will be measured to you." (Luke 6:37-38)

When Jesus talks about the measure you use, he means: If you give with a big scoop or a cup completely full, then you'll receive with the same big scoop and full cup. If you give with a tiny scoop or just a pinch, you'll receive just a tiny blessing. The blessing is related directly to the giving – which is what Paul is teaching us in 2 Corinthians:

"Remember this:
Whoever sows sparingly will also reap sparingly,
and whoever sows generously
will also reap generously." (9:6)

There is a definite law of cause and effect in giving to God!

Q1. (2 Corinthians 9:6) Does the Scripture teach that material blessing results from giving generously to God's work? Why are we so careful to reinterpret this as referring mainly to spiritual blessing? If you compared your own actual giving to God's work to a tithe (10%) of your income, would it look generous?
http://www.joyfulheart.com/forums/index.php?showtopic=1107

Freedom and Joy in Giving (9:7)

As you are preparing the collection to be sent to Jerusalem shortly, Paul says, I don't want you to be under any kind of pressure to give – especially last-minute pressure to give! Why? Because pressure doesn't produce good fruit.

> "Each man should give what he has decided in his heart to give,
>   not reluctantly or under compulsion,
>   for God loves a cheerful giver." (9:7)

"Decided in his heart" (NIV), "made up your mind" (NRSV), "purposeth in his heart" (KJV) is *proaireō*, in the middle voice, "to reach a decision beforehand, choose (for oneself), commit oneself to, prefer."[5] In other words, you should be giving to this collection because you've thought it through and want to be a part of it. Christian giving should be motivated by thoughtful discipleship and love for Jesus, not by guilt or greed – motivations too often promoted by churches, as we'll see below.

Now Paul mentions two wrong motivations for giving:

1. **Reluctance.** "Reluctantly" (NIV, NRSV), "grudgingly" (KJV) is *lypē*, "pain of mind or spirit, grief, sorrow, affliction," here, with the preposition *ek*, "out of," it means "reluctantly."[6] If you're giving, but really don't want to, stop! If it pains you to give, don't! Giving out of inner reluctance isn't real worship anyway; it's conforming outwardly to someone's expectations for us. Rather, worship is an inward response of love for God. Pray that God will increase your love for him so your reluctance to give will evaporate.

2. **Pressure.** "Under compulsion" (NIV, NRSV), "of necessity" (KJV) is *anankē*, "necessity or constraint as inherent in the nature of things, necessity, pressure of any kind," a divine dispensation, some hoped-for advantage, custom, duty, etc. Here, "under pressure."[7] It's amazing to me how pastors will use guilt as a motivator to worship – for worship is what giving is supposed to be. How can you worship out of guilt? Usually, pressure is exerted to get you to do something you really don't want to do because of your reluctance.

I've witnessed offerings preceded by a 20-minute harangue. I've also been in churches where at offering time people line up, walk to the front, and make their offering under the watchful eye of the pastor. I can see offering being a time of joyful celebration that might be characterized by a parade, but I'm afraid that it is sometimes just a way to pressure people into giving something for the sake of appearances. Passing the offering plate can provide pressure to give, too. Some churches place an offering box in the back of the church so that people can give when they leave, greatly reducing the

[5] *Proaireō*, BDAG 865.
[6] *Lypē*, BDAG 605.
[7] *Anankē*, BDAG 61, 1.

pressure. The offering might be a little less, but not much. (I've heard that it doesn't affect how much is given!) People who give reluctantly or under pressure never give much anyway!

What God is looking for is a heart that is happy because it is able to give to God and to his work – a "cheerful giver." "Cheerful" is *hilaros*, "pertaining to being full of cheer, cheerful, glad, happy," here, "one who gives cheerfully, gladly (= without reluctance)."[8] As we are teaching people to give, we need to focus on positive motivations, such as love and joy, rather than fear and guilt.

Q2. (2 Corinthians 9:7) Why do you think pastors or other church leaders use guilt to try to compel people to give more? Can greed be behind their pressure? Why is pressure incompatible with worship? What does cheerfulness while giving say about the condition of a person's heart?
http://www.joyfulheart.com/forums/index.php?showtopic=1108

God Can Cause You to Abound (9:8)

One of the greatest obstacles to giving is fear – fear that if we give to God, we won't have enough for ourselves. This isn't greed, which is a different motivation, but garden-variety fear. Fear is the opposite of faith. When we have faith that God will supply our needs, then we give without fear. Look at this promise:

"And God is able to make all grace **abound** to you, so that in all things at all times,
having all that you need, you will **abound** in every good work." (9:8)

"Grace" (*charis*), you recall, is the word Paul has uses in 2 Corinthians 8 and 9 to describe the offering being collected (a "work of grace"). He is saying that God can bless you financially in an abundant way. The word "abound" (KJV, NIV) and the phrases, "in abundance, share abundantly" (NRSV) is *perisseuō*, "abound," which occurs twice in verse 8. Here it means, "have an abundance, abound, be rich," "have ample means for every enterprise."[9]

The phrase "all that you need" (NIV), "enough of everything" (NRSV), "all sufficiency" (KJV) is the adjective *pas*, "all" and the noun *autarkeia*. The basic idea of the word is

[8] *Hilaros*, BDAG 473. Though our English word "hilarious" comes from this word, it means "extremely funny" in English. English "hilarity" is "boisterous and high-spirited merriment or laughter," which goes well beyond the Greek meaning of "cheerful" (*Merriam-Webster's 11th Collegiate Dictionary*).
[9] *Perisseuō*, BDAG 805, 1bα.

"self-sufficiency" in the sense of "independence." Here, it means, a "state of having what is adequate, sufficiency, a competence."[10]

Notice these two words: "abound, have an abundance" and "sufficiency, having enough." Greed wants to have plenty – more than what is needed, so that you'll have enough if you get in a hard place again. But faith that overcomes the fear of want only needs "enough," because it trusts God to supply what is needed in the future. In the Sermon on the Mount,

- Jesus teaches us to pray, "Give us this day our daily bread" (Matthew 6:11)
- Jesus teaches us, "Do not store up treasures for yourselves on earth" (Matthew 6:19)
- Jesus teaches us, "Do not worry about your life.... but seek first his kingdom and his righteousness, and all these things will be given to you as well." (Matthew 6:33)
- Jesus teaches us, "Do not worry about tomorrow, for tomorrow will worry about itself. Each day has enough trouble of its own." (Matthew 6:34)

When becoming rich is our goal, we get off the path that Jesus leads us on. Now God may, in his wisdom, make you rich. But when becoming rich or hoarding wealth becomes your goal, you've missed out on God's will for you.

So what is the promise in verse 8? That if you give, God will give you more than enough for your own needs and sufficient for you to do other good works as well. He will give you enough for yourself *plus* enough to help others in some kind of good work.

The Righteous Man

To drive home his point, Paul quotes from Psalm 112:9.

"As it is written:
  'He has scattered abroad his gifts to the poor;
  his righteousness endures forever.'" (9:9)

Paul's point is clear when you read the context of this Psalm about the faith of a righteous man:

"[6] Surely he will never be shaken;
a righteous man will be remembered forever.
[7] He will have no fear of bad news;
his heart is steadfast, trusting in the LORD.
[8] His heart is secure, he will have no fear;

---

[10] *Autarkeia,* BDAG 152.

> in the end he will look in triumph on his foes.
> [9] He has scattered abroad his gifts to the poor,
> his righteousness endures forever;
> his horn will be lifted high in honor." (Psalm 112:6-9)

The righteous man in the psalm is full of faith and unafraid. Therefore, through his faith and confidence in the Lord "he has scattered abroad his gifts to the poor," since he knows that the Lord will supply his needs.

Another promise comes to mind that Paul shared with the Philippian church that had helped to support him on his missionary trips:

> "And my God will meet[11] all your needs[12] according to his glorious riches in Christ Jesus." (Philippians 4:19)

If all this sounds similar to the Prosperity Teaching common in our time, it is because the Prosperity Teaching isn't wholly false. It has helped many people understand God's desire to prosper his people financially – and that's a good thing. However, Prosperity Teaching includes distortions that tend to get people out of balance in their faith. For more on this, see Appendix 2. A Brief Critique of the Prosperity Message.

God's Supply, Increase, and Enlargement (9:10-11)

Paul continues:

> "[10] Now he who supplies seed to the sower and bread for food will also supply and increase your store of seed and will enlarge the harvest of your righteousness. [11] You will be made rich in every way so that you can be generous on every occasion, and through us your generosity will result in thanksgiving to God." (9:10-11)

How does God supply[13] seed to the sower? By giving a harvest large enough so that there is not only enough "bread for food," but also enough seed to plant next year's crop. The farmer sows the seed; God gives the increase.

Now look at the promise:

> "He ... will also supply[14] and increase[15] your store of seed and will enlarge[16] the harvest

---

[11] *Plēroō*, "to make full, fill (full)" (BDAG 827, 1a).

[12] *Chreia*, "that which is lacking and needed, need, lack, want, difficulty" (BDAG 1088, 2a).

[13] "Supplies" (NIV, NRSV), "ministereth" (KJV) is *epichorēgeō*, "to convey as a gift, give, grant" (BDAG 387, 1).

[14] "Will supply" (NIV, NRSV), "minister" (KJV) is *chorēgeō*, originally "lead a chorus" or "pay the expenses for training a chorus," then generally "defray the expenses of something, provide, supply (in abundance)" (BDAG 1087).

[15] "Increase" (NIV), "multiply" (NRSV, KJV), is *plēthynō*, "to cause to become greater in number, increase, multiply" (BDAG 826, 1a).

of your righteousness." (9:10b)

God will not only supply you seed, but increase or multiply your store of seed. What is seed for? To plant, not to eat. So God is not increasing your general wealth so that you have more than you need. Rather, he is increasing your "seed" so you have more to give for his Kingdom purposes. This way you can see a greater "harvest of your righteousness," that is, you can do more and greater good works that result from you being a righteous person.

It is in the context of having more to give, that Paul says the same thing another way:

> "You will be made rich in every way so that you can be generous on every occasion, and through us your generosity will result in thanksgiving to God." (9:11)

"Made rich" (NIV), "enriched" (NRSV, KJV) is *ploutizō*, "to cause to be relatively high on a scale of opulence, make wealthy," then figuratively, "to cause to abound in something, make rich."[17]   The question is: What kind of riches is Paul talking about? Spiritual riches? Yes. Financial riches? Yes, since he says, "you will be made rich *in every way*." Does this mean that you will become financially wealthy if you give to God? Perhaps, but it *does* mean that he will give you more finances than you require for your own family's needs, "so that you can be generous[18] on every occasion." The whole point here is not accumulating personal financial wealth. It is God blessing you so you'll have more than enough yourself, so that you can continue to give generously. Your faith begins a cycle of giving that you should not interrupt by your greed. If it flows in, it must also continue to flow out for this promise to be continually renewed and reactivated.

Q3. (2 Corinthians 9:10-11) According to these verses, what is the purpose of God increasing your "store of seed"? How do greed and generosity differ from each other? What is God's promise here to generous givers?

http://www.joyfulheart.com/forums/index.php?showtopic=1109

Your Giving Will Prompt Praise (9:12-15)

Paul's final encouragement to giving is that the Corinthians' gift will prompt great

---

[16] "Enlarge" (NIV), "increase" (NRSV, KJV) is *auxanō*, "to cause to become greater in extent, size, state, or quality, grow something, cause to grow, increase" (BDAG 153, 1).

[17] *Ploutizō*, BDAG 833, 2.

[18] "So that you can be generous" (NIV), "for your generosity" (NRSV), "bountifulness" (KJV) is *haplotēs*, which we discussed in the previous lesson, "generosity, liberality" (BDAG 104).

praise towards God to rise up from the recipients.

> "[12] This service that you perform[19] is not only supplying[20] the needs[21] of God's people but is also overflowing in many expressions of thanks to God. [13] Because of the service by which you have proved[22] yourselves, men will praise God for the obedience[23] that accompanies your confession[24] of the gospel of Christ, and for your generosity in sharing with them and with everyone else. [14] And in their prayers for you their hearts will go out to you,[25] because of the surpassing grace God has given you. [15] Thanks be to God for his indescribable gift!" (9:12-15)

Notice how at the end of this section, Paul turns the focus back to God:

1. **God's surpassing grace**, grace that goes beyond, exceeds, outdoes anything imaginable.[26]
2. **God's indescribable[27] gift**, indescribable because of the incredible love that prompted it and the majesty and station of the sacrifice for our sin, the very and only Son of God himself!

The words "grace" (*charis*) and "gift" (*dōrea*), nearly synonymous here, remind us that

---

[19] Verse 12 uses two nouns to describe service, which NRSV translates "the rendering of this ministry." The first noun is *diakonia*, "ministry, service." The second is *leitourgia*, "service of a personal nature, help, assistance, service," with some sort of religious connotation (BDAG 592, 2). We get our word "liturgy" from this word. The two words together might be literally translated, "the ministry of this religious service."

[20] "Supplies" is *prosanaplēroō*, "to fill up or replenish besides, supply something," also used in 11:9 (BDAG 876).

[21] "Needs" (NIV, NRSV), "want" (KJV) is *hysterēma*, "the lack of what is needed or desirable," frequently in contrast to abundance, "need, want, deficiency" (BDAG 1044, 1).

[22] The KJV's curious phrase, "... whiles by the experiment of this ministration," is better explained by the NIV: "... because of the service by which you have proved yourselves." In other words, the believers in Jerusalem will then realize what giving this offering has accomplished in your own Christian character and maturity. The offering is proof of God's work in you. The noun is *dokimē*, "the experience of going through a test with special reference to the result, standing a test, character" (BDAG 256, 2). Also at 2:9 and 8:2.

[23] "Obedience" (NIV, NRSV), "professed subjection" (KJV) is *hypotagē*, "the state of submissiveness, subjection, subordination." (BDAG 1041).

[24] "Confession" (NIV, NRSV), "professed" (KJV), *homologia*, "expression of allegiance as an action, professing, confessing," here, with the idea, "the subjection of your professing of the gospel" = "your professing of the gospel finds expression in obedient subjection to its requirements" (BDAG 709, 1).

[25] "Their hearts will go out to you" (NIV), "long for you" (NRSV), "long after you" (KJV) is *epipotheō*, "to have a strong desire for something, with implication of need, long for, desire something" from *epi-*, "accumulation, increase, addition" + *potheō*, "long for" (BDAG 377).

[26] *Hyperballō*, "to attain a degree that extraordinarily exceeds a point on a scale of extent, go beyond, surpass, outdo" (BDAG 1032).

[27] "Indescribable" (NIV, NRSV), "unspeakable" (KJV) is *anekdiēgētos*, from *a-*, "not" + *ekdiēgeomai*, "to narrate in full or wholly," then, "to relate, tell, declare" (Thayer, 193).

our salvation isn't because we have been deserving, but that it flows wholly from his amazing love for us, and the generous gift that *He* has given. Our own gifts, no matter how generous, pale in comparison!

> "But God demonstrates his own love for us in this: While we were still sinners, Christ died for us." (Romans 5:8)

Praise the Lord!

Q4. (2 Corinthians 9:12-15) Why should our giving prompt thanksgiving? How is our giving a demonstration of God's grace? Why is God's gift of Jesus termed "surpassing"? Why is God's gift of Jesus termed "indescribable"?
http://www.joyfulheart.com/forums/index.php?showtopic=1110

Prayer

Lord, thank you for teaching us the principles of giving to your Kingdom work. Since giving is a quality that describes your character throughout the Scriptures, we want to learn to be giving people so that we can be your disciples. In Jesus' name, we pray. Amen.

Key Verses

> "Remember this: Whoever sows sparingly will also reap sparingly, and whoever sows generously will also reap generously." (2 Corinthians 9:6)

> "Each man should give what he has decided in his heart to give, not reluctantly or under compulsion, for God loves a cheerful giver." (2 Corinthians 9:7)

> "Thanks be to God for his indescribable gift!" (2 Corinthians 9:15)

11. Paul's Defense of His Ministry (10-11)

Imagine how frustrating it would be if you had founded a congregation and then had to watch from afar as imposters and charlatans destroyed what you had spent years building. What would you feel like?

A Change in Tone

Up through 2 Corinthians 9, Paul has kept a fairly upbeat attitude, especially in 7:11-16 where he described the Corinthians' positive reaction to his "severe letter" and to Titus' visit. But in chapters 10-13, he seems to take the gloves off and lambasts his opponents who are ruining the church.

This is certainly a change in tone! As we discussed in the Introduction, some feel that this change indicates the inclusion of another letter at this point. But I think it is more likely that Paul has just received additional communication concerning the Corinthians and feels he needs to change his tone.

Albrecht Dürer, detail of St. Paul from "The Four Holy Men (Mark and Paul)" (1526), oil on panel, 215 x 76 cm, Alte Pinakothek, Munich.

I've chosen to tackle two chapters in this one lesson, since much of the material is polemic, rather than teaching. We'll go through much of it rapidly, but slow down when we come to some of Paul's spiritual insights.

Paul's Boldness (10:1-2)

Does it require arrogance to correct someone? Of course not! Parents have to correct children all the time and do so without the ugliness of pride. But Paul wants to make sure that his readers don't mistake sternness for pride, so he begins with humility.

"[1] By the meekness[1] and gentleness[2] of Christ, I appeal to you – I, Paul, who am 'timid'[3]

---

[1] "Meekness" is *prautēs*, "the quality of not being overly impressed by a sense of one's self-importance, gentleness, humility, courtesy, considerateness, meekness," in the older favorable sense (BDAG 862).

[2] "Gentleness" is *epieikeia*, "the quality of making allowances despite facts that might suggest reason for a different reaction, clemency, gentleness, graciousness, courtesy, indulgence, tolerance" (BDAG 372).

[3] "Timid" (NIV), "humble" (NRSV), "base" (KJV) is *tapeinos*, "low," here, "pertaining to being servile in

when face to face with you, but 'bold' when away! [2] I beg you that when I come I may not have to be as bold as I expect to be toward some people who think that we live by the standards of this world." (10:1-2)

If you catch a hint of irony here, you're right. The NIV version includes the words "timid" and "bold" in quotes, since they represent a misunderstanding by the Corinthians of Paul's true character. Paul warns them that they will see this boldness face-to-face unless there is repentance and change. He uses three words, one after another, to underscore his determination:

1. **"Bold"** (NIV), is *tharreō*, "to have certainty in a matter, be confident, be courageous."[4]

2. **"Confidence"** (KJV) is *pepoithēsis*, "a state of certainty about something to the extent of placing reliance on, trust, confidence."[5]

3. **"Daring"** (KJV) is *tolmaō*, "to show boldness or resolution in the face of danger, opposition, or a problem, dare, bring oneself to do something," here "bring oneself to, presume."[6]

At this point in the letter, Paul begins to establish that he is coming to Corinth and that they need to prepare for his coming. This warning is repeated several more times as well (10:6; 12:14, 20, 21; 13:1, 2, 10).

Watch Paul's power-in-weakness approach. Though they imagine that he is soft-spoken and not trained in rhetoric, Paul warns that when he comes he will do whatever it takes and use all his apostolic authority to set things in order and protect the church.

Spiritual Warfare (10:3-6)

Now we come to a passage that discusses warfare, both spiritual and verbal:

"[3] For though we live in the world, we do not wage war as the world does. [4] The weapons we fight with are not the weapons of the world. On the contrary, they have divine power to demolish strongholds. [5] We demolish arguments and every pretension that sets itself up against the knowledge of God, and we take captive every thought to make it obedient to Christ. [6] And we will be ready to punish every act of disobedience, once your obedience is complete." (10:3-6)

---

manner, pliant, subservient, abject," a negative quality in a judgment pronounced by Paul's opponents upon him (BDAG 989, 2).

[4] *Tharreō*, BDAG 444.

[5] *Pepoithēsis*, BDAG 796, 1b. The word doesn't appear separately in the NIV and NRSV translations, but underlies them.

[6] *Tolmaō*, BDAG 1010, 1aβ.

Paul uses the vocabulary of armed conflict. The words "wage war" (NIV, NRSV), "war" (KJV) is *strateuō*, which has the basic meaning of "serve in the army, undertake a campaign." Here it carries the figurative meaning, "to engage in a conflict, wage battle, fight."[7] The related noun *strateia*, "military engagement," is used in verse 4.[8] Paul's opponents may have expected him to be powerless to stop them, but Paul is declaring all-out war with victory for the truth as the only possible outcome.

The weapons he will use are not human[9] weapons,[10] says Paul, but spiritual weapons endued with divine power.[11]

Now he uses the language of siege-warfare, coming against a fortress, destroying its defenses, breaching its walls, and taking its citizens captive.

- **"Strongholds"** is *ochyrōma*, "a strong military installation, fortress,"[12] a high, walled city that is prepared to outlast and defend itself from any attacker.
- **"Pulling down"** (KJV) "demolish" (NIV), "destroy" (NRSV), is *kathairesis*, "causing destruction by tearing down."[13] It refers to how fortress walls are literally pulled down with ropes and cables so that conquering troops can enter the city and then prevent that city from defending itself in the future.

The strongholds that will fall here, however, are not physical, but logical and spiritual.

- **"Arguments"** (NIV, NRSV), "imaginations" (KJV) is *logismos*, "the product of a cognitive process, calculation, reasoning, reflection, thought," here perhaps, "sophistries."[14] Paul's opponents have their plausible reasons why they are right and Paul should be discredited, but these arguments will not stand the light of day when he arrives.
- **"Pretension"** (NIV), "proud obstacle" (NRSV), "high thing" (KJV)[15] describes the proud arrogance of Paul's opponents. These pretenders have exalted[16]

---

[7] *Strateuō*, BDAG 947, 2.

[8] "Warfare" (NRSV, KJV) is *strateia*, "military engagement, expedition, campaign" (BDAG 947).

[9] "Human" (NIV, NRSV), "carnal" (KJV) is *sarx* in the sense of "earthly, mediocre, merely human, worldly" (BDAG 914, 2).

[10] "Weapons" is *hoplon*, which we saw in 6:7. Originally, "tool," then, "an instrument designed to make ready for military engagement, weapon." (BDAG 716, 2b). Also at Romans 13:12; 2 Corinthians 6:7.

[11] "Divine power" (NIV, NRSV) is literally, "mighty through God" (KJV), using the adjective *dynatos*, "able, capable, powerful," of beings and their attributes" (BDAG 264, 1bβ).

[12] *Ochyrōma*, BDAG 746. The word derives from *ochuroō*, "to fortify."

[13] *Kathairesis*, BDAG 487, 1. "Demolish" (NIV), "destroy" (NRSV), "casting down" (KJV) is *kathaireō*, "to destroy by tearing down, tear down, destroy, overpower" (BDAG 488, 2).

[14] *Logismos*, BDAG 598, 1.

[15] *Hypsōma*, "height," here figuratively, "that which postures arrogantly, arrogance" (BDAG 1046, 2).

[16] "Sets itself up" (NIV), "raised up" (NRSV), "exalteth itself" (KJV) is *epairō*, "lift up, hold up," then by extension, "to offer resistance to, be in opposition, rise up" (BDAG 357, 2).

themselves and their teachings, but they will not last long.

The siege will end with the rebellion being destroyed.

- **"Take captive"** (NIV, NRSV), "bringing into captivity" (KJV) is *aichmalōtizō*, "to cause someone to become a prisoner of war, take captive," here used figuratively.[17]

- **"Obedience/obedient"** (KJV, NIV), "to obey" (NRSV) is *hypakoē*, "a state of being in compliance, obedience" (one listens and follows instructions).[18] Rather than being rebellious, the offenders will submit again to God's Word.

- **"Punish"** (NIV, NRSV), "revenge" (KJV) is *ekdikeō*, "grant justice," here in the negative sense, "to inflict appropriate penalty for wrong done, punish, take vengeance for."[19] Sometimes we shy away from punishment out of fear that we will be vindictive. But where clear rebellion isn't followed by true justice, it sends a message that you can get away with trashing apostolic authority and setting up your own authority in its place. That God will bring final justice is the message of the Bible, especially Revelation. Earlier, the Corinthian church had punished offenders (1 Corinthians 5:1-5; 2 Corinthians 2:5-11). This will be no different.

Paul has set his opponents – and the church – on notice that he will return and deal swiftly and decisively with any disorder.

Is this passage about the force of Paul's mind and logic to cut his opponents' position to pieces? I don't think so. I think he is talking about a spiritual stronghold that stands behind his opponents' pretensions. He is relying on "divine power" to do the job, not his own sharp mind. He is seeking spiritual victory that will set the church free and make it healthy. Any discerning pastor knows that this happens through much prayer, not through human brilliance and a forceful personality.

Q1. (2 Corinthians 10:3-6) Why does Paul liken his dealing with his opponents in Corinth with reducing a city wall by siege and then taking its citizens captive? Is Paul talking about a victory by the use of incisive logic or is there a spiritual stronghold here, one that derives its power from Satan's kingdom?

http://www.joyfulheart.com/forums/index.php?showtopic=1111

---

[17] *Aichmalōtizō*, BDAG 31, 1b.

[18] *Hypakoē*, BDAG 1028, 1b.

[19] *Ekdikeō*, BDAG 300, 2.

Paul's Apostolic Authority (10:7-8)

Paul is talking about his apostolic authority, a spiritual gift and ministry, as he makes clear in the next verses.

> "[7] You are looking only on the surface of things. If anyone is confident that he belongs to Christ, he should consider again that we belong to Christ just as much as he. [8] For even if I boast somewhat freely about the authority the Lord gave us for building you up[20] rather than pulling you down,[21] I will not be ashamed of it." (10:7-8)

In the American church we have passed through an era where spiritual leaders down-played their authority. Pastors were taught to be facilitators, not leaders. But we must not be ashamed of spiritual authority. It is God's authority channeled through human vessels to guide and protect his church.

Forceful by Letter and in Person (10:9-12)

Paul states again that what he expresses in his letters he will execute when he is present.

> "[9] I do not want to seem to be trying to frighten you with my letters. [10] For some say, 'His letters are weighty and forceful, but in person he is unimpressive and his speaking amounts to nothing.' [11] Such people should realize that what we are in our letters when we are absent, we will be in our actions when we are present." (10:9-11)

Now he warns against his opponents who are trying to put themselves on the same level of authority as the founding apostle of the church. Such comparisons are false and foolish!

> "We do not dare to classify or compare[22] ourselves with some who commend themselves. When they measure themselves by themselves and compare themselves with themselves, they are not wise." (10:12)

Paul's Field of Ministry (10:13-15a)

Paul's opponents had boasted of their great authority, but they were out of line. They were boasting about the field of labor that God has assigned Paul.

> "[13] We, however, will not boast beyond proper limits,[23] but will confine our boasting to

---

[20] "Building up" (NIV, NRSV), "edification" (KJV) is *oikodomē*, "the process of building, building, construction," here figurative of spiritual strengthening, "edifying, edification, building up" (BDAG 696, 1bα).

[21] "Pulling down" (NIV), "destruction" (KJV) is *kathairesis*, which we saw in verse 4.

[22] "Compare" is *synkrinō*, "to draw a conclusion by comparing, compare" (BDAG 953, 2a).

[23] "Beyond limits" (NIV) in verses 13 and 15 is *ametros*, "immeasurable," here, "boast beyond limits, illimitably" (BDAG 53).

the field[24] God has assigned to us, a field that reaches even to you. [14] We are not going too far in our boasting, as would be the case if we had not come to you, for we did get as far as you with the gospel of Christ. [15] Neither do we go beyond our limits by boasting of work done by others." (10:13-15a)

His opponents' boasts are petty. What's more, Paul's field of ministry extended far beyond Corinth.

"[15b] Our hope is that, as your faith continues to grow, our area of activity among you will greatly expand, [16] so that we can preach the gospel in the regions[25] beyond you. For we do not want to boast about work already done in another man's territory. [17] But, 'Let him who boasts boast in the Lord.' [18] For it is not the one who commends himself who is approved, but the one whom the Lord commends." (10:15b-18)

Led Astray from Pure Devotion to Christ (11:1-3)

Now, Paul turns to another subject, one that must pain him greatly. His opponents have hurt this precious congregation and diverted their love for Christ.

"[1] I hope you will put up with a little of my foolishness; but you are already doing that. [2] I am jealous for you with a godly jealousy. I promised you to one husband, to Christ, so that I might present you as a pure virgin to him. [3] But I am afraid that just as Eve was deceived by the serpent's cunning, your minds may somehow be led astray from your sincere and pure devotion to Christ." (11:1-3)

The word "jealous" here isn't like that of a jilted lover. Rather, the Greek word *zēloō* means, "be positively and intensely interested in something, strive, desire, exert oneself earnestly, be dedicated," here, "be deeply interested in someone, court someone's favor, make much of," with implication of desiring the other to be on one's own side.[26]

Paul is deeply committed to the Corinthians. He has to stand by and watch from afar as his opponents ruin the strong foundation he has laid in Corinth for Christ (1 Corinthians 3:10-16).

Paul illustrates his concern with two contrasting images:

1. **A pure virgin** being presented to a husband.
2. **Eve being seduced** by the serpent in the Garden of Eden.

Two words describe the actions of his opponents:

1. **"Cunning"** (NIV, NRSV), "beguiled" (KJV) is *exapataō*, "to cause someone to

---

[24] "Field" (NIV, NRSV), "measure" (KJV) is *metron*, "measure," here figuratively, "according to the measure of the limit (= within the limits) which God has apportioned us (as a measure)" (BDAG 644, 2b).

[25] "Regions" (NIV, KJV), "lands" (NRSV) in verse 16 is not in the text, but implied by the context.

[26] *Zēloō*, BDAG 427, 1b. *Zelos*, "intense positive interest in something, zeal, ardor," marked by a sense of dedication (BDAG 427, 1).

accept false ideas about something, deceive, cheat, someone."[27]

2. **"Led astray"** (NIV, NRSV), "corrupted" (KJV) is *phtheirō*, literally, "destroy, ruin, corrupt, spoil," such as, to seduce a virgin. Figuratively, this word means, "to cause deterioration of the inner life, ruin, corrupt."[28]

Then he uses two words to describe the desired state of the church, the Bride of Christ:

1. **"Sincere"** (NIV, NRSV) is *haplotēs*, "simplicity, sincerity, uprightness, frankness."[29]

2. **"Pure devotion"** (NIV, NRSV), *hagnotēs*, "purity, sincerity."[30]

Do these words represent your relationship to Christ and that of your congregation?

Gullible and Easily Deceived (11:4-5)

Paul is grieved that the congregation is so easily duped by pretenders. His words are heavy with irony.

> "[4] For if someone comes to you and preaches **a Jesus other** than the Jesus we preached, or if you receive a **different spirit** from the one you received, or a different gospel from the one you accepted, you put up with[31] it easily enough. [5] But I do not think I am in the least inferior[32] to those 'super-apostles. [33]'" (11:4-5)

Paul had written similarly to the Galatian church:

> "I am astonished that you are so quickly deserting the one who called you by the grace of Christ and are turning to **a different gospel** – [7] which is really no gospel at all. Evidently some people are throwing you into confusion and are trying to pervert the gospel of Christ." (Galatians 1:6-7)

These so-called "super-apostles" in Corinth were distorting the gospel and deceiving the people. Though they claimed to be as good or better than Paul, they were in fact false prophets and pompous charlatans!

---

[27] *Exapataō*, BDAG 345.

[28] *Phtheirō*, BDAG 1054, 2b.

[29] *Haplotēs*, BDAG 104, 1. We've seen this word previously in 1:12; 8:2; 9:11, 13.

[30] *Hagnotēs*, BDAG 13, also found in 6:6. This word is not contained in some ancient Greek manuscripts. The longer reading used in the NIV and RSV translations has strong manuscript support (p⁴⁶ Aleph* B G 33 syr cop etc.), but the shorter reading (KJV) is also strong, so the United Bible Societies Committee enclosed the longer reading in brackets with a {C} rating – "considerable degree of doubt" (Metzger, p. 583-584).

[31] "Put up with" (NIV), "submit to" (NRSV), "bear with" (KJV) is *anechō*, "to regard with tolerance, endure, bear with, put up with" (BDAG 78, 1).

[32] "Be inferior" (NIV, NRSV), "be behind" (KJV) is *hystereō*, "to be behind," here, "to be lower in status, be less than, inferior to" (BDAG 1043, 4).

[33] "Super-" (NIV, NRSV), "very chiefest" (KJV) is *hyperlian*, "exceedingly, beyond measure" (BDAG 1033).

Q2. (2 Corinthians 11:1-5) What does it feel like when a congregation loses its pure devotion to Jesus Christ, and instead takes on other motivations for its religious observance? In what ways is this like the church at Ephesus losing its "first love" (Revelation 2:4)? How can this purity of devotion be restored?
http://www.joyfulheart.com/forums/index.php?showtopic=1112

Was Paul an Untrained Speaker? (11:6)

> "I may not be a trained speaker, but I do have knowledge. We have made this perfectly clear to you in every way." (11:6)

Several times Paul has acknowledged what his opponents accuse him of, of not being a trained speaker (1 Corinthians 1:21; 2:1-4; 2 Corinthians 10:1, 10). Was he boring? We do know that a young man fell asleep during one of his messages and fell out of a third-story window (Acts 20:7-12). But let's give Paul the benefit of the doubt! This was during a late-night service, far past the young man's bedtime.

Paul certainly is able to put words together in a clear, convincing manner. However, by Greek standards, he is "untrained" (NRSV), "rude" (KJV). The word is *idiōtēs* (from which we get our word "idiot"), "a person who is relatively unskilled or inexperienced in some activity or field of knowledge, layperson, amateur" in contrast to an expert or specialist of any kind.[34]

In ancient Greece, rhetoric was a high art form, the art and study of the use of language with persuasive effect. Aristotle (384-322 BC) systematized what was known about rhetoric in his time. The three persuasive audience appeals were *logos* (appeal to reason), *pathos* (appeal to emotions), and *ethos* (appeal to character). There were five canons of rhetoric: invention or discovery, arrangement, style, memory, and delivery.

Paul was a highly trained rabbi, schooled in Jerusalem under the great Rabbi Gamaliel (Acts 22:3). He knew the Scriptures backward and forward. He had a sharp and creative mind. He was a skilled communicator so far as Jewish hearers were concerned. But he was not trained in Greek rhetoric, and so his sermons sounded rude and unskilled to his hearers in Corinth. Once he had told them:

> "My message and my preaching were not with wise and persuasive words, but with a demonstration of the Spirit's power, so that your faith might not rest on men's wisdom, but on God's power." (1 Corinthians 2:4-5)

---

[34] *Idiōtēs*, BDAG 468, 1.

However, while Paul didn't possess rhetorical skills, he possessed something far more important – he knew what he was talking about and he knew the One he proclaimed.

"I may not be a trained speaker, but **I do have knowledge**." (11:6)

Paul's Refusal to Ask for Support (11:7-9)

Now Paul turns to another topic raised by the presence of these pseudo-apostles who dominated the Corinthian church. They apparently demanded money from the people and exploited them, in contrast to Paul and his associates (11:19; 12:17-18). Since Paul had never been paid by the church for his ministry in Corinth, they may have felt that, if he were a *real* teacher, he wouldn't have lowered himself to do manual labor to support himself. Perhaps they resented his careful financial independence of them. Perhaps Paul is trying to contrast his own scrupulousness concerning being a financial burden with the exploitation practiced by the false apostles. In any case, he explains himself.

"[7] Was it a sin for me to lower[35] myself in order to elevate you by preaching the gospel of God to you free of charge? [8] I robbed other churches by receiving support from them so as to serve you. [9] And when I was with you and needed something, I was not a burden to anyone, for the brothers who came from Macedonia supplied what I needed. I have kept myself from being a burden to you in any way, and will continue to do so." (11:7-9)

Paul obviously felt that to expect payment might "hinder" (1 Corinthians 9:12b) the furtherance of the gospel in Corinth.[36] He was concerned that he would be a "burden" on them (2 Corinthians 11:9). This word, *katanarkaō*, meant, properly, "to cause to grow numb or torpid, inactive," to the detriment of one. Here it means, "to weigh heavily upon, be burdensome to."[37] Paul was willing to do anything to further the gospel – in this case, not require the Corinthians to support him.

He was able to do this for two reasons: First, because the Macedonian churches – in particular, Philippi – provided him support[38] and supplied[39] his needs.

"Moreover, as you Philippians know, in the early days of your acquaintance with the gospel, when I set out from Macedonia, not one church **shared with me in the matter of giving and receiving**, except you only; for even when I was in Thessalonica, you sent me aid again and again when I was in need." (Philippians 4:15-16)

---

[35] "Lower" (NIV), "humbling" (NRSV), "abasing" (KJV) is *tapeinoō*, "to cause someone to lose prestige or status, humble, humiliate, abase" (BDAG 990, 2a).

[36] "Hinder" (NIV, KJV), "put an obstacle" (NRSV) is *enkopē*, "that which holds back the progress of something, hindrance" (BDAG 274).

[37] *Katanarkaō*, Thayer, 334; BDAG 522.

[38] "Support" (NIV, NRSV), "wages" (KJV) is *opsōnion*, "pay, wages" (BDAG 747, 1b).

[39] "Supplied" is *prosanaplēroō*, "to fill up or replenish besides, supply" (BDAG 876), also at 9:12.

Second, Paul worked as a tentmaker in Corinth, where he met Priscilla and Aquilla (Acts 18:2-3). Furthermore, he worked not only in Corinth, but in Ephesus (Acts 20:34), Thessalonica (1 Thessalonians 2:9; 2 Thessalonians 3:8), and perhaps elsewhere, too.

Paul took a particular pride in being able to preach the gospel "free of charge" (NIV, NRSV), "freely" (KJV), without any payment.[40] In 1 Corinthians he had explained to them his motivations – perhaps it had been a sore spot[41] then, too.

> "... We put up with anything rather than hinder the gospel of Christ.... I would rather die than have anyone deprive me of this boast.... If I preach voluntarily, I have a reward; if not voluntarily, I am simply discharging the trust committed to me. [18] What then is my reward? Just this: that in preaching the gospel I may **offer it free of charge**, and so not make use of my rights in preaching it." (1 Corinthians 9:12b, 15b, 17-18)

Full-time Christian Ministry vs. Bi-Vocational Ministry

In our day, the "best" calling according to many seems to be to what is termed "full-time Christian ministry," that is, doing Christian work full-time, rather than part-time. But Paul, though he vigorously argued for the right to receive compensation for ministry (1 Corinthians 9:3-14), chose not to take advantage of this right. He did "secular" work deliberately, rather than spend full-time in ministry. Was he somehow a lesser Christian worker because of it? No!

I really believe that some of the great heroes of the Christian faith in our time are bi-vocational pastors, who work full-time and then take on the labors of pastoral ministry or missionary service, not because they are paid for it, but because they are called to it. It is not a way of making a living for them; it is a way of life.

Certainly, getting a regular paycheck from a church or parachurch organization enables a person to devote more time and focus to ministry. And in many situations, that full-time commitment is needed to help the church or mission.

But paid ministry comes with a cost. In the case of parish ministry, it makes the pastor dependent upon keeping the congregation happy so he can continue to receive a check and support his family. Sometimes, the only right thing to do is to stand your ground for what God has shown you and resist the pressure from wealthy members who insist on their way because they are paying the bills.

One modern response to these pressures is for a pastor or missionary to go out and obtain pledges for support from friends and other churches. But this comes with the high cost of spending time in the home country raising funds when the most pressing

---

[40] *Dōrean*, "pertaining to being freely given, as a gift, without payment, gratis" (BDAG 266, 1).
[41] 1 Corinthians 9:3.

need is for a genuine vacation or to be on the field ministering.

"Tent-making" (so-called from Paul's example) is a viable alternative strategy to receiving a salary from the church or raising one's own support. The downside is that a tentmaker-pastor can work literally "night and day" (1 Thessalonians 2:9), taking away valuable time required to care for the needs of a family, so that the family suffers the loss of time with a parent or spouse. No wonder Paul was single during his missionary journeys!

Dear friends, we're in no position to judge a person's dedication to or effectiveness in ministry by whether they're full-time or bi-vocational or not paid at all. God is the One who sends workers into his harvest field. The final reward for these faithful workers at the end of the harvest, however – including *your* work for him – will be unimaginably great!

Q3. (2 Corinthians 11:7-9) Why do you think Paul refused to require the Corinthians to support him? How did this help his ministry? How did it contribute to them taking him for granted? How can we honor Christian workers, clergy and lay, who give of their time sacrificially to minister for Christ? How will Christ honor them?
http://www.joyfulheart.com/forums/index.php?showtopic=1113

Undermining the Claims of False Apostles (11:10-14)

By defending his lack of exploitation of the Corinthians, Paul sought to expose his opponents' motivations for what they were.

> "¹⁰ As surely as the truth of Christ is in me, nobody in the regions of Achaia will stop this boasting of mine. ¹¹ Why? Because I do not love you? God knows I do! ¹² And I will keep on doing what I am doing in order to cut the ground from under those who want an opportunity to be considered equal with us in the things they boast about." (11:10-11)

Now Paul makes his strongest charges against his opponents.

> "¹³ For such men are false apostles, deceitful workmen, masquerading as apostles of Christ. ¹⁴ And no wonder, for Satan himself masquerades as an angel of light. ¹⁵ It is not surprising, then, if his servants masquerade as servants of righteousness. Their end will be what their actions deserve." (11:13-14)

He charges them with:

1. Being false,[42] that is, bogus,

---

[42] "False apostles" is *pseudapostolos*, "one who claims to be an apostle without the divine commission

2.   Being deceitful,[43] that is, violating trust in an effort to deceive,
3.   Putting on a disguise[44] in order to pretend, and
4.   Being Satan's servants.

Finally, he declares that they will be judged for this self-serving deception. Strong language indeed!

Foolish Boasting (11:16-21)

Paul is about to share more of what he has given to serve Christ as an apostle, and so demonstrate the difference between a true apostle and a charlatan. So he spends a few sentences explaining the situation – with great irony:

"[16] I repeat: Let no one take me for a fool. But if you do, then receive me just as you would a fool, so that I may do a little boasting. [17] In this self-confident boasting I am not talking as the Lord would, but as a fool. [18] Since many are boasting in the way the world does, I too will boast. [19] You gladly put up with fools since you are so wise! [20] In fact, you even put up with anyone who enslaves you or exploits you or takes advantage of you or pushes himself forward or slaps you in the face. [21] To my shame I admit that we were too weak for that! What anyone else dares to boast about – I am speaking as a fool – I also dare to boast about." (11:16-21)

Now we get to see the character of Paul's opponents who:

1.   Enslave,[45]

2.   Exploit,[46]

3.   Take advantage of,[47]

4.   Push themselves forward,[48] and

5.   Insult the Corinthians, that is, slap them in the face.

---

necessary for the work, false / spurious / bogus apostle" (BDAG 1096).

[43] "Deceitful" is *dolios*, "pertaining to violation of trust in effort to deceive, deceitful, treacherous" (BDAG 256).

[44] "Masquerading" (NIV), "disguising" (NRSV), "transforming" (KJV) is *metaschēmatizō*, "to feign to be what one is not, change / disguise oneself" (BDAG 643, 2), verses 13, 14, and 15.

[45] "Enslaves" (NIV), "makes slaves of" (NRSV), "bring into bondage" (KJV) is *katadouloō*, "enslave, reduce to slavery" (BDAG 516).

[46] "Exploits" (NIV), "preys upon" (NRSV), "devour" (KJV) is *katesthiō*, literally, "to eat up ravenously, eat up, consume, devour, swallow," figuratively here, "to exploit, rob" (BDAG 532, 2e).

[47] "Takes advantage of" (NIV, NRSV), "take of" (KJV) is *lambanō*, "take," here "if someone puts something over on you, takes advantage of you" (BDAG 583, 3).

[48] "Pushes himself forward" (NIV), "puts on airs" (NRSV), "exalt himself" (KJV) is *epairō*, "lift up," here, "to suggest that one is better than one really is, be presumptuous, put on airs," (BDAG 357, 3).

Paul's Jewish Heritage (11:22)

> "[22] Are they Hebrews? So am I. Are they Israelites? So am I. Are they Abraham's descendants? So am I." (11:22)

From Paul's comments here we deduce that Paul's opponents are Jewish, perhaps come from Jerusalem with purported authority from the church there. We're not sure. Paul had defended himself from Jewish false teachers before in Philippi, a leading church in Macedonia, where he described himself as:

> "... Circumcised on the eighth day, of the people of Israel, of the tribe of Benjamin, a Hebrew of Hebrews; in regard to the law, a Pharisee; as for zeal, persecuting the church; as for legalistic righteousness, faultless." (Philippians 3:5-6)

The Jewish heritage of these "super-apostles" might have impressed the Gentile Corinthians who revered the Old Testament Scriptures, but Paul reminds the church that his pedigree is just as strong.

Paul's Sufferings (11:23-25)

Now Paul continues:

> "[23] Are they servants of Christ? (I am out of my mind to talk like this.) I am more. I have worked much harder, been in prison more frequently, been flogged more severely, and been exposed to death again and again.
>
> [24] Five times I received from the Jews the forty lashes minus one. [25] Three times I was beaten with rods, once I was stoned, three times I was shipwrecked, I spent a night and a day in the open sea." (11:23-25)

Most of what we know about Paul's trials we learn from the Book of Acts. But that record only touches the highlights, not every time Paul had been arrested and punished.

I wonder what kind of shape his body was in after all this? He was:

- **"Flogged"** (NIV, cf. NRSV) in verse 23 is literally "stripes" (KJV), the noun *plēgē*, "a sudden hard stroke with some instrument, blow, stroke," including the blow of a whip.[49]
- **"Beaten with rods"** is *rhabdizō*, of the punishment known formally in Latin legal terminology as *admonitio* as distinct from *catigatio* (a lashing) and *verberatio* (flogging with chains).[50] We know Paul was beaten with rods in Philippi (Acts 16:22).
- **Stoned**. We know that Paul was stoned and left for dead in Lystra on his first

---

[49] *Plēgē*, BDAG 825, 1.
[50] *Rhabdizō*, BDAG 902.

missionary journey (Acts 14:19).

- **Shipwrecked**. Acts only informs us of one shipwreck near Malta when Paul was being transported in chains to Rome (Acts 27), but that took place after 2 Corinthians was written. Paul was no stranger to the hazards of traveling by ship.

Dangers from Travel (11:26)

Travel in Paul's day was risky at best, but Paul was an inveterate traveler.

"I have been constantly on the move. I have been in danger[51] from rivers, in danger from bandits,[52] in danger from my own countrymen, in danger from Gentiles; in danger in the city, in danger in the country, in danger at sea; and in danger from false brothers." (11:26)

If you've ever travelled in your own country, you know to be on the lookout for pickpockets, thieves, and kidnappers. It was far more dangerous to be in a foreign city or out on the roads far from civilization, where bandits or highwaymen made a living swooping down on lonely travelers, beating them up, and taking all they had – like the man the Good Samaritan aided.

Beyond the dangers from a hostile environment, Paul faced danger as a foreigner, but also danger from people who he should have been able to trust. Why did he put up with all this, and then continue to travel from one city to another?

Depravation and Stress (11:27-28)

Then Paul recounts the typical stresses of his life.

"I have labored[53] and toiled[54] and have often gone without sleep;[55] I have known hunger and thirst and have often gone without food; I have been cold and naked. Besides everything else, I face daily the pressure[56] of my concern[57] for all the churches." (11:27-28)

---

[51] "Danger" (NIV), "perils" (KJV) is *kindynos*, "danger, risk" (BDAG 544).

[52] "Bandits" (NIV, NRSV), "robbers" (KJV) is *lēstēs*, "robber, highwayman, bandit" (BDAG 594, 1).

[53] "Labored" (NIV), "toil" (NRSV), "weariness" (KJV) is *kopos*, which can have two meanings determined by context: (1) "a state of discomfort or distress, trouble, difficulty," a transferred sense of *kopos* = "beating" and (2) "activity that is burdensome, work, labor, toil" (BDAG 559).

[54] "Toiled" (NIV), "hardship" (NRSV), "painfulness" (KJV) is *mochthos*, "labor, exertion, hardship" (BDAG 660).

[55] "Gone without sleep" (NIV), "sleepless nights" (NRSV), "watchings" (KJV) is *agrypnia*, "the state of remaining awake because one is unable to go to sleep, sleeplessness" (BDAG 16, 1).

[56] "Pressure" (NIV, NRSV) is *epistasis*, "responsibility for a matter, pressure, care" (BDAG 380, 1). From *epistatēs*, "overseer, master."

[57] "Concern" (NIV), "anxiety" (NRSV), "care" (KJV) is *merimna*, "anxiety, worry, care" (BDAG 632).

This last year has been hard for me – perhaps the hardest year of my ministry in some ways. God brought me through partly because in reading this passage I could see the example of a man so dedicated to his mission that he refused to quit. Nothing, absolutely nothing could deter him from fulfilling his mission. He was willing to face any challenge, any hardship for the sake of the gospel.

When I look at my own struggles, they pale in comparison to what Paul was willing to go through. It has hardened my resolve, it has toughened me for the mission, it has helped me grow up. Christ taught Paul and is teaching me and you about enduring through suffering. When Ananias argued with the Lord about going to Saul's quarters after Saul's encounter with the risen Christ on the road to Damascus, God told Ananias:

> "Go, for he is an instrument whom I have chosen to bring my name before Gentiles and kings and before the people of Israel; I myself will show him **how much he must suffer** for the sake of my name." (Acts 9:15-16)

Dear friend, has suffering caused you to quit what you were doing for the Lord? Have you been hurt by church people and now you don't even go to church? Are you gun-shy, unable to be a part of Christ's church because what you've experienced to the degree that the Lord can't use you? God is speaking to you to learn that He works through your weakness if you don't quit. Friend, it may be time to get back on the horse that threw you – bruises and all. Let Christ heal you, but don't quit on him.

Q4. (2 Corinthians 11:23-28) How do Paul's sufferings help authenticate his claim to be an apostle? What do these sufferings tell us about Paul's commitment? How does this account inspire you – or convict you? How will you be different from having pondered it?

http://www.joyfulheart.com/forums/index.php?showtopic=1114

Boasting in Weakness (11:29-30)

Paul says to the Corinthians: I've been faithful, even though it has been difficult. These are some of the marks of a true apostle!

> "²⁹ Who is weak, and I do not feel weak? Who is led into sin, and I do not inwardly burn? ³⁰ If I must boast, I will boast of the things that show my weakness." (11:29-30)

I share your weakness, my Corinthian brothers and sisters, says Paul. When someone is led by false teachers into sin, it pains me – I've given so much to see them come to Christ and be set free from their bondages. We'll hear more of Paul's boasting in his weaknesses when we come to 2 Corinthians 12 in the next lesson.

Paul's Escape from Damascus (11:31-33)

This section concludes with Paul's account of a harrowing escape that took place right at the beginning of his ministry. It is also told in Acts 9:22-25.

> "[31] The God and Father of the Lord Jesus, who is to be praised forever, knows that I am not lying. [32] In Damascus the governor under King Aretas had the city of the Damascenes guarded in order to arrest me. [33] But I was lowered in a basket from a window in the wall and slipped through his hands." (11:31-33)

By telling this story, Paul is saying that God is faithful. Even in the most difficult situations, God is able to help us go on. Sometimes it is terribly difficult to go on. Sometimes we feel like Paul felt in Asia:

> "We were so utterly, unbearably crushed that we despaired of life itself. Indeed, we felt that we had received the sentence of death so that we would rely not on ourselves but on God who raises the dead. He who rescued us from so deadly a peril will continue to rescue us; on him we have set our hope that he will rescue us again." (1:8-10)

Look up, dear friend. He will rescue you again, set you on your feet, and make you ready to serve him once more.

Prayer

Father, sometimes ministry – and life itself – seems so hard. Sometimes we don't know if we can bear any more. Thank you for your faithfulness, O Rescuer and Savior and Healer! Dear Lord, some of my brothers and sisters have suffered wounds in your service. Some of them are entrapped in bitterness, wrapped in self-pity, and blame you. Lord, reconcile them again to yourself and heal them, for Jesus' sake. Show them your love once again. Renew their calling in their ears once again, as you did for Peter so long ago when you called him back to feed your sheep.[58] In Jesus' name, I pray. Amen.

Key Verses

> "For the weapons of our warfare are not merely human, but they have divine power to destroy strongholds. We destroy arguments [5] and every proud obstacle raised up against the knowledge of God, and we take every thought captive to obey Christ." (2 Corinthians 10:4-5)

> "Even Satan disguises himself as an angel of light. So it is not strange if his ministers also disguise themselves as ministers of righteousness." (2 Corinthians 10:14b-15a)

---

[58] John 21:15-19.

12. Paul's Vision, Thorn, and Final Words (12-13)

Paul is obviously embarrassed to continue to boast – though he realizes that in order to reestablish his apostolic authority with the Corinthians, he must lay out all of his credentials.

> "I must go on boasting. Although there is nothing to be gained...." (12:1a)

In the previous lesson, we studied Paul's boasting about his sufferings as an apostle (11:21-33). These were designed to prove that the so-called "super apostles" hadn't sacrificed for the gospel's sake. Paul thought it important to link suffering with apostleship, since his opponents spoke eloquently and espoused a "success" image that had completely overtaken the Corinthians.

In this passage, Paul shares an amazing personal revelation and links it with weakness. Paul's authenticity as an apostle is in no way compromised by his own weaknesses and afflictions!

"St. Paul" (c. 799), mosaic fragment, 59.7 x 39.7 x 9 cm, Vatican Museum. Originally decorated the state banquet hall of the papal Lateran Palace. Restored by Giovanni Battista Calandra in 1625.

We're covering two chapters in this final lesson, but most of chapter 13 is concluding remarks that we will cover rather quickly.

Visions and Revelations in the New Testament (12:1)

> "I must go on boasting. Although there is nothing to be gained, I will go on to visions and revelations from the Lord." (12:1)

"Visions" in verse 1 is *optasia*, "an event of a transcendent character that impresses itself vividly on the mind, a vision, celestial sight."[1] "Revelations" is *apokalypsis*, literally,

---

[1] *Optasia*, BDAG 712. A vision is where a deity permits a human being to see, either of the deity personally or of something else usually hidden from mortals.

"uncovering," here, "making fully known, revelation, disclosure."[2]

While visions and revelations may not be as prominent today – at least in American congregations – they were common in the New Testament era. Paul himself had a vision of Christ at his conversion (Acts 22:6-11; 26:12-20; Galatians 1:15-16), had a vision that constituted his "Macedonian call" (Acts 16:9-10), and was encouraged by a vision while in Corinth some years previously (Acts 18:9-10). He contended that his gospel, as well, had been given by revelation (Galatians 1:12).

Boasting of Visions and Revelations (12:2-4)

"[2] I know a man in Christ who fourteen years ago was caught up to the third heaven. Whether it was in the body or out of the body I do not know – God knows. [3] And I know that this man – whether in the body or apart from the body I do not know, but God knows – [4] was caught up to paradise. He heard inexpressible things, things that man is not permitted to tell." (12:2-4)

It's interesting that Paul begins as if the person he is talking about were someone else, though by verses 5-7 it becomes clear that he is talking about himself.

This was a vision of "the third heaven" (12:2), that is, "paradise." In his prayer at the dedication of the temple, Solomon differentiates between heaven and highest heaven (1 Kings 8:27). Some of Paul's first century Jewish contemporaries saw heaven with three, five, or seven levels. But rather than become dogmatic about the structure of heaven, it's probably more helpful to see Paul's third heaven as "an ordinary Hebrew superlative."[3] The term "Paradise" is *paradeisos*, from an Old Persian word, then Hebrew, then transliterated into Greek. It means, "enclosure, garden," and pictures the restoration of the Garden of Eden in the end times. Here it refers to "a transcendent place of blessedness,"[4] essentially a synonym for heaven (Luke 23:43; Revelation 2:7).

Paul isn't sure whether this was an out-of-body experience or not. But he did hear secrets there that he could not repeat.[5] Kruse observes:

"Paul's account of his rapture differs markedly from other such accounts from the

---

[2] *Apokalypsis*, BDAG 112, 1b.

[3] Kruse, p. 201.

[4] *Paradeisos*, BDAG 762, 2.

[5] "Inexpressible" (NIV), "things that are not to be told" (NRSV), "unspeakable" (KJV) is the adjective *arrētos*. The basic meaning is "of something that cannot be expressed, since it is beyond human powers, inexpressible." It is common in ancient inscriptions related to mystery religions describing things too sacred to be divulged (Kruse, p. 203). Here it means, "something that must not be expressed, since it is holy, not to be spoken" (BDAG 134, 2). "Permitted" (NIV, NRSV), "lawful" (KJV) is the impersonal verb *exesti*, "to be authorized for the doing of something, it is right, is authorized, is permitted, is proper" (BDAG 348, 1d).

ancient world, both in its brevity and the absence of any descriptions of what he saw. Paul refers only to what he heard."[6]

Boasting of the Truth (12:5-6)

"[5] I will boast about a man like that, but I will not boast about myself, except about my weaknesses. [6] Even if I should choose to boast, I would not be a fool, because I would be speaking the truth. But I refrain, so no one will think more of me than is warranted by what I do or say." (12:5-6)

Paul seems to separate the man who had seen the vision 14 years previously from the person he is today – one who boasts about his weaknesses. He certainly is not using the vision itself for ammunition against his opponents: I saw a vision, so I am superior. Rather he is telling the story in order to explain what God has shown him about power in weakness.

Paul's Thorn in the Flesh (12:7)

These amazing visions that Paul had seen required him to be humble.

"To keep me from becoming conceited because of these surpassingly great revelations, there was given me a thorn in my flesh, a messenger of Satan, to torment me." (12:7)

Paul was in danger of pride from these astounding[7] revelations. "Conceited" (NIV), "too elated" (NRSV), "exalted above measure" (KJV) is *hyperairō*, "to have an undue sense of one's self-importance, rise up, exalt oneself, be elated."[8] To prevent pride, Paul "was given" a "thorn in the flesh." But what that thorn was and why it was given has caused a great deal of theological controversy.

Part of the controversy centers around the ministry of healing by prayer. To oversimplify the issues a bit, some who teach healing are unwilling to acknowledge that St. Paul could have been sick. Some who don't believe in healing by prayer look to this verse to prove that God can use their sickness for some positive purpose – while the healing faction sees sickness as an evil from Satan. Those are the landmines in the road. Now let's try to work carefully through an interpretation that is true to this text and to the larger teaching of scripture.

---

[6] Kruse, p. 204.

[7] "Surpassingly great" (NIV), "exceptional character" (NRSV), "abundance" (KJV) is the adjective *hyperbolē* (from which we get our word "hyperbole"), "state of exceeding to an extraordinary degree a point on a scale of extent, excess, extraordinary quality / character" (BDAG 1032).

[8] *Hyperairō*, BDAG 1031.

Was the Thorn a Sickness?

A definition of "thorn" doesn't help us. It's just an annoying pointed object[9] – a symbol of something else that is painful and annoying. But what can we learn from this verse?

1. **"Was given"** is the aorist passive of *didōmi*, an extremely common verb meaning, "to give." It can indicate anything from warm generosity to "cause to happen," and all in between. Often when we see this use of the passive voice, it is implied that God is the force behind the event. Certainly, God *allowed* this thorn in the flesh, just as he *allows* sin and sickness to exist in our fallen world. But did he actively send it in order to keep Paul humble? That's the question. This may be just splitting hairs, trying to absolve God from agency for what we deem to be evil.[10] See Romans 8:28 and Genesis 50:20.

2. The thorn is called **"a messenger"** of Satan. "Messenger" is *angelos*, "spirit-being, angel." Often this word refers to one of God's angels, but here the word refers to an "evil spirit."[11]

3. **Satan** is closely identified with this messenger. This isn't just any messenger, but Satan's messenger or agent.[12]

4. The purpose of the thorn was to **"torment"** (NIV, NRSV) or "buffet" (KJV). The verb is *kolaphizō*, literally, "to strike sharply, especially with the hand, strike with the fist, beat, cuff," here figuratively, "to cause physical impairment, torment."[13]

5. **"Weakness"** in verse 9 is *astheneia*, "sickness, disease," then more generally, "incapacity for something or experience of limitation, weakness."[14] The word could mean "sickness, disease," or the more general "weakness," depending upon the context. When Paul was in Galatia, he had some kind of physical weakness – perhaps an eye ailment, though we can't be sure.

   "You know that it was because of a physical (*sarx*) infirmity (*astheneia*) that I first announced the gospel to you; though my condition put you to the test, you did not scorn or despise me, but welcomed me as an angel of God, as Christ Jesus. What has

---

[9] "Thorn" is *skolops*, "originally, "anything pointed," such as a "(pointed) stake," then "something that causes serious annoyance, thorn, splinter, etc.," specifically of an injurious foreign body (BDAG 930).

[10] Imagine the controversy over God sending a lying spirit to Saul (1 Kings 22:23-23; 2 Chronicles 18:21-22). It disturbs our theology.

[11] *Angelos*, BDAG 9, 2c.

[12] Probably the genitive of possession. H.E. Dana and Julius R. Mantey, *A Manual Grammar of the Greek New Testament* (Macmillan, 1927, 1955), §85-86, §90(2).

[13] *Kolaphizō*, BDAG 555, 2.

[14] *Astheneia*, BDAG 142, 2a.

become of the goodwill you felt? For I testify that, had it been possible, you would have torn out your eyes and given them to me." (Galatians 4:13-15, NRSV)

6. **Paul's body** is affected by this thorn or weakness, since both here and in Galatians the weakness is closely related to *sarx*, which refers here to "the material that covers the bones of a human or animal body, flesh."[15]

From this analysis, I can't escape the conclusion personally that Paul's "thorn in the flesh" was some kind of physical ailment or disease that afflicted his body.

Is Sickness from Satan?

This isn't the place to argue for or against the proposition that Satan brings sickness, not God. That would require a detailed argument that ultimately depends upon the underlying assumptions that the interpreter makes. However, let me make a few observations:

1. **Jesus' healing miracles were signs of the Kingdom** (Luke 10:9), that healing is part of the salvation he brought. It is not necessary to contend that there is "healing in the atonement" to see that the word "saved" (*sōzō*) is used in the gospels for physical healing sometimes (Matthew 9:21-22; Mark 5:23, 28, 34; 6:56; 10:52; Luke 8:36, 48, 50; 17:19; 18:42; Acts 4:9; 14:9).

2. **Jesus rebuked Satan and evil spirits** in order to bring about healing in many cases, which would be consistent with them being the immediate cause of the illness (Luke 4:35, 39, 41; 9:42).

3. **Jesus taught his disciples to pray for the sick and to cast out demons**, and expected this kind of healing and deliverance activity to continue (Mark 16:17-18, longer ending; Luke 9:1; 10:9, 17).

4. **Healing and works of miracles are gifts of the Spirit** (1 Corinthians 12:9-10, 28), and we have no indication that they are to pass away until Jesus comes and brings perfection into our fallen world (1 Corinthians 13:10). Indeed, a fair-minded view of history indicates that these gifts continued in the early church, as well as throughout church history. Some people in our own day exercise the gift of healing, sometimes with great power and effect.

5. **God didn't heal all sicknesses** – even in the apostolic circle (Romans 8:18, 23; 2 Corinthians 4:16; Philippians 2:27; 1 Timothy 5:23; 2 Timothy 4:20).

6. **A healer's own sickness is not incompatible with a powerful healing ministry**. For example, those familiar with the life of British Pentecostal healer

---

[15] *Sarx*, BDAG 914, 1.

Smith Wigglesworth (1859-1947) know that through Christ's power he performed mighty healings while he himself was in intense pain from kidney stones.

I don't know all the answers to the paradoxes raised and obvious inconsistencies of these observations. But I know when Christ comes he will replace our imperfect ministry of healing with the resounding wholeness of resurrection bodies. Resurrection is the ultimate physical healing.

Based on my exegesis of 12:7-10, I conclude that by the "thorn in the flesh," Paul was referring to some kind of physical ailment. And, instead of healing it, God used it to work in Paul's character. Can God heal? Yes, absolutely and often! Does he always heal? No. Can God use physical ailments to form Christ's character in us. Yes, I think that's the meaning of this passage.

Q1. (2 Corinthians 12:7) _Why_ was this "thorn in the flesh" given to Paul? What purpose did God want to achieve through this in Paul's character? How can something be both used by God _and_ be caused by Satan's destructive work? How does this verse relate to Romans 8:28 and Genesis 50:20?
http://www.joyfulheart.com/forums/index.php?showtopic=1115

My Power Is Made Perfect in Weakness (12:8-9a)

No matter what kind of sickness Paul had, he certainly didn't want it. Moreover, he came to God again and again in earnest prayer for healing.

> "Three times I pleaded with the Lord to take it away from me." (12:8)

"Pleaded" (NIV), "appealed to" (NRSV), "besought" (KJV) is _parakaleō_, here, "to make a strong request for something, request, implore, entreat."[16] This was earnest, believing prayer. For two of these prayer sessions, God gave him no answer. But on the third, God answered.

> "But he said to me, 'My grace is sufficient for you, for my power is made perfect in weakness.'" (12:9a)

"Grace," of course, is _charis_, which has the basic idea of "a beneficent disposition toward someone, favor." But in some passages, the connotation seems to be "exceptional effect produced by generosity, favor." In some places, Danker notes, "_charis_ is evidently

---

[16] _Parakaleō_, BDAG 765, 3.

to be understood in a very concrete sense. It is hardly to be differentiated from *dynamis* ('power') or from *gnōsis* ('knowledge'] or *doxa* ['glory']."[17]

"Sufficient" is *arkeō*, It is an old Greek word, rich in meaning, says Robertson.[18] The basic idea is "to be possessed of unfailing strength." Then "to be strong, to suffice, to be enough" (as against any danger, hence, "to defend, ward off," used in Homer).[19]

"For" (*gar*) introduces the cause or reason for this statement.[20]

"My Power," literally, "the power" is the noun *dynamis* (from which we get our words "dynamo" and "dynamic"), which means, "potential for functioning in some way, power, might, strength, force, capability."[21] With God, power can be a synonym for any of his deeds of power and his unlimited resources, such as the signs of an apostle – signs, wonders and miracles (12:12).

"In weakness," *astheneia*, the word we discussed above, which could refer to sickness or any other kind of weakness – physical, psychological, financial, you name it.

"Is made perfect," is the passive of the verb *teleō*, which has the basic meaning of "bring to an end, finish, complete." Here it carries the connotation, "find consummation, reach perfection."[22] When you're playing tennis there is a sweet spot on the racket that will send back the perfect shot. When playing sports you can get in "the zone" or "a groove" where you play at your best or beyond. Our weakness and dependence on God creates God's "sweet spot" in which he

> "is able to do exceeding abundantly above all that we ask or think, according to **the power that worketh in us**." (Ephesians 3:20, KJV)

God's Power in Us

Let's pause for a moment and consider some of the scriptures that speak of God's mighty power in us.

> "He **gives strength to the weary**
> and **increases the power of the weak**.
> Even youths grow tired and weary,
> and young men stumble and fall;
> but those who hope in the LORD will renew their strength.

---

[17] *Charis*, BDAG 1079, 4.
[18] Robertson, *Word Pictures, in loc.*
[19] *Arkeō*, Thayer 73. "Be enough, sufficient, adequate" (BDAG 133). "To be strong enough, suffice" (Liddell-Scott).
[20] *Gar*, BDAG 189, 1a.
[21] *Dynamis*, BDAG 262, 1a.
[22] *Teleō*, BDAG 997, 1.

> They will soar on wings like eagles;
> they will run and not grow weary,
> they will walk and not be faint." (Isaiah 40:29-31)

> "I have learned to be content whatever the circumstances.... I have learned the secret of being content in any and every situation, whether well fed or hungry, whether living in plenty or in want. **I can do everything through him who gives me strength**." (Philippians 4:11b-13)

> "I pray also that the eyes of your heart may be enlightened in order that you may know ... his incomparably **great power for**[23] **us who believe**. That power is like the working of his mighty strength, which he exerted in Christ when he raised him from the dead...." (Ephesians 1:18-20)

> "I pray that out of his glorious riches he may **strengthen you with power** through his Spirit in your inner being." (Ephesians 3:16)

> "Finally, **be strong in the Lord and in his mighty power**." (Ephesians 6:10)

> "... **Being strengthened with all power according to his glorious might** so that you may have great endurance and patience...." (Colossians 1:11)

> "So that we may present everyone perfect in Christ ... I labor, **struggling with all his energy** (*energeia*), which so powerfully works in me." (Colossians 1:28-29)

When I Weak, then I Am Strong (12:9b-10)

The answer God gave was "No" – not the answer Paul was seeking. But when God's answer came, it seems that Paul cherished it the rest of his life. For he says,

> "9b Therefore I will boast all the more gladly about my weaknesses, so that Christ's power may rest on me. 10 That is why, for Christ's sake, I delight in weaknesses, in insults,[24] in hardships,[25] in persecutions,[26] in difficulties.[27] For when I am weak, then I am strong." (12:9-10)

Have you ever had a revelation from God that seemed to open your eyes all at once

---

[23] *Eis*, "extension involving a goal or place, into, in, toward, to" (BDAG 288, 1). KJV translates it here as "to us-ward," clumsy but evocative. "In us" (RSV), "toward us" (NASB), "for us" (NIV, NRSV).

[24] "Insults" (NIV, NRSV), "reproaches" (KJV) is *hybris* (from which we get our word "hubris," exaggerated pride or self-confidence), "insolence, arrogance," then "the experience of insolence, shame, insult, mistreatment" (BDAG 1022, 2).

[25] "Hardships" (NIV, NRSV), "necessities" (KJV) is *ananke*, "a state of distress or trouble, distress, calamity, pressure," or even, "compulsion by forcible means, torture" (BDAG 61, 2 and 3).

[26] "Persecutions" is *diogmos*, "a program or process designed to harass and oppress someone, persecution" (BDAG 253).

[27] "Difficulties" (NIV), "calamities" (NRSV), "distresses" (KJV) is *stenochoria*, literally, "narrowness," but here figuratively, "a set of stressful circumstances, distress, difficulty, anguish, trouble" (BDAG 943).

so you suddenly had understanding where before it didn't make any sense? For Paul, this was one of those times.

Instead of resenting God's answer, he exulted in it. "I will boast all the more gladly[28] about my weaknesses," he says. In the next verse he "delights" in all the things we would normally complain about. *Eudokeō* means, "to take pleasure or find satisfaction in something, be well pleased, take delight, like, approve."[29]

Now, when he encounters weaknesses, insults, hardships, persecutions, and difficulties, he gets excited because he knows that, "when I am weak, then I am strong" (12:10b). These are no longer problems to Paul, but opportunities in which to see God's power in action.

In the last century, Watchman Nee (1903-1972) wrote a book entitled, *The Normal Christian Life* (1938-1939), in which he contended that what was "normal" in the early church that we should expect as the norm today. O Lord, bring such a profound revelation to our hearts that your power in our weakness might be our norm, not something out-of-the-ordinary!

If Paul's word sounds a bit strange to us, it is! We don't see many people who have such a faith and enthusiasm for God that Paul had. Perhaps God will transform you into this kind of person who delights in weakness (and its attendant power) so you can be an encouragement and inspiration to your church.

Q2. (2 Corinthians 12:10) What was the life-changing lesson that Paul learned from God when God denied his prayer? How does our self-sufficiency limit God's power through our lives? Can we become dependent upon God without having to experience some "thorn in the flesh" ourselves?
http://www.joyfulheart.com/forums/index.php?showtopic=1116

The Signs of an Apostle (12:11-12)

Now Paul resumes talking about his boastings that began with 11:16. He feels a little embarrassed that he had to recount all his sufferings and weaknesses, but it was necessary.

"I have made a fool of myself, but you drove me to it. I ought to have been commended

---

[28] "Most gladly" (KJV) is *hēdeōs*, "pertaining to being pleased in connection with something, gladly" (BDAG 434).

[29] *Eudokeō*, BDAG 404, 2b.

by you, for I am not in the least inferior to the 'super-apostles,' even though I am nothing." (12:11)

Paul has been seeking to demonstrate that he is a true apostle, in spite of the accusations
and slander of the "super-apostles" that had gained sway in Corinth. Now he mentions
the miraculous power that God has used through him.

> "The things that mark an apostle – signs, wonders and miracles – were done[30] among
> you with great perseverance." (12:12)

- **"Signs"** is the plural of *sēmeion*, "an event that is an indication or confirmation
  of intervention by transcendent powers, miracle, portent."[31]
- **"Wonders"** is *teras*, "something that astounds because of transcendent association, prodigy, portent, omen, wonder."[32]
- **"Miracles"** (NIV), **"mighty works/deeds"** (NRSV, KJV) is *dynamis*, "a deed
  that exhibits ability to function powerfully, deed of power, miracle, wonder."[33]

These power gifts were performed not just once in a while, but "with great perseverance." "Perseverance" (NIV), "patience" (NRSV, KJV) is *hypomonē*, "the capacity to hold
out or bear up in the face of difficulty, patience, endurance, fortitude, steadfastness,
perseverance."[34]

Paul says that signs, wonders, and miracles "mark" an apostle. They are "signs" or
indications that a person is an apostle.[35] Does this mean that a person who ministers
with frequent signs, wonders, and miracles is an apostle? Not necessarily, but it could
be. We know that, "Stephen, a man full of God's grace and power, did great wonders
and miraculous signs among the people" (Acts 6:8), and he seemed to be a servant of the
church or deacon, rather than an apostle. Philip the Evangelist did "miraculous signs" at
Samaria (Acts 8:6-7), but he wasn't recognized as an apostle.

Does this mean that all apostles will operate in signs, wonders, and miracles? Not
necessarily, but it's likely. Paul's point is, however, that God *hadn't* performed these
signs through the so-called "super-apostles," but he *had* through Paul. This was another
proof that he was indeed a genuine apostle.

---

[30] "Done" (NIV), "performed" (NRSV), "worked" (KJV) is *katergazomai*, "to bring about a result by doing
something, achieve, accomplish, do something" (BDAG 533, 2).

[31] *Sēmeion*, BDAG 920, 2aα.

[32] *Teras*, BDAG 999.

[33] *Dynamis*, BDAG 263, 3.

[34] *Hypomonē*, BDAG 1039, 1.

[35] *Sēmeion* is used here in a different sense than it is used later in the verse. Here it means, "a sign or
distinguishing mark whereby something. is known, sign, token, indication" (BDAG 920, 1).

Expending His Resources for the Corinthians (12:13-15)

One of the issues that the Corinthians apparently found difficult to understand was why Paul didn't ask support from them during his ministry there, but rather worked with his hands or received support from other churches. He had explained himself in 1 Corinthians 9:3-18, as well as previously in this letter. But he feels he needs to mention it again – with a bit of irony.

> "13 How were you inferior to the other churches, except that I was never a burden to you? Forgive me this wrong! 14 Now I am ready to visit you for the third time, and I will not be a burden[36] to you, because what I want is not your possessions but you. After all, children should not have to save up for their parents, but parents for their children. 15 So I will very gladly spend for you everything I have and expend myself as well. If I love you more, will you love me less? (12:13-15)

The "super-apostles," however, *were* after the Corinthians' money. Paul needed to differentiate himself from them once again. The irony is on the surface.

> "16 Be that as it may, I have not been a burden[37] to you. Yet, crafty fellow that I am, I caught you by trickery! 17 Did I exploit you through any of the men I sent you? 18 I urged Titus to go to you and I sent our brother with him. Titus did not exploit you, did he? Did we not act in the same spirit and follow the same course?" (12:16-18)

"Exploit" (NIV), "take advantage of" (NRSV), "make a gain" (KJV) is *pleonekteō*, "to take advantage of, exploit, outwit, defraud, cheat someone.[38]

> 19 Have you been thinking all along that we have been defending[39] ourselves to you? We have been speaking in the sight of God as those in Christ; and everything we do, dear friends, is for your strengthening."[40] (12:16-19)

This is not just a defense, says Paul – as if he needed to defend himself to them! He has gone into detail to help bring them understanding and clarity and therefore strengthen them. Sometimes maturity comes through hard lessons.

Concern for the Corinthians' Sin and Disorder (12:20-21)

Paul shifts gears again. He has established afresh his apostolic credentials. Now he warns them that he will fully exercise his apostolic authority to set things in order when

---

[36] "Be a burden" (NIV, NRSV), "be burdensome" (KJV) is *katanarkaō*, "burden, be a burden to" (BDAG 522).

[37] *Katabareō*, "burden, be a burden to" (BDAG 514).

[38] *Pleonekteō*, BDAG 824, 1a.

[39] "Defending" (NIV, NRSV), "excuse" (KJV) is *apologeomai*, "to speak in one's own defense against charges presumed to be false, defend oneself" (BDAG 117).

[40] "Strengthening" (NIV), "building you up" (NRSV), "edifying" (KJV) is *oikodomē*, "edifying, edification, building up" (BDAG 696, 1bα).

he comes again.

> "For I am afraid that when I come I may not find you as I want you to be, and you may not find me as you want me to be." (12:20)

When I return, he is saying, I won't be that "meek" Paul that you might me to be.

The Corinthians' arrogance towards Paul has been based on the premise that somehow they (and their "super-apostles") are superior to Paul. Not so, says Paul. You have serious sin in your midst that you haven't dealt with.

> "I fear that there may be quarreling, jealousy, outbursts of anger, factions, slander, gossip, arrogance and disorder." (12:20)

These are the sins Paul initially singles out:

- **"Quarreling"** (NIV, NRSV), **"debates"** (KJV) is *eris*, "engagement in rivalry, especially with reference to positions taken in a matter, strife, discord, contention."[41]
- **"Jealousy"** (NIV, NRSV), **"envyings"** (KJV) is *zēlos*, here, "intense negative feelings over another's achievements or success, jealousy, envy."[42]
- **"Outbursts of anger"** (NIV), **"anger"** (NRSV), **"wraths"** (KJV) is *thymos*, "a state of intense displeasure, anger, wrath, rage, indignation," in the plural, "outbursts of anger."[43]
- **"Factions"** (NIV), **"selfishness"** (NRSV), **"strifes"** (KJV).[44] In 1 Corinthians 1:11-12; 3:1-9; and 11:18 Paul had rebuked them for their various factions – Paul, Apollos, Christ, rich, poor, etc.
- **"Slander"** (NIV, NRSV), **"backbitings"** (KJV) is *katalalia*, "the act of speaking ill of another, evil speech, slander, defamation, detraction."[45]
- **"Gossip"** (NIV, NRSV), **"whisperings"** (KJV) is *psithyrismos*, "derogatory information about someone that is offered in a tone of confidentiality, (secret) gossip, tale-bearing," from *psithyrizō*, "to whisper."[46]
- **"Arrogance"** (NIV), **"conceit"** (NRSV), **"swellings"** (KJV) is *physiōsis*, elsewhere a medical technical term, literally, "inflated or bloated condition," here,

---

[41] *Eris*, BDAG 392.

[42] *Zēlos*, BDAG 427, 2.

[43] *Thymos*, BDAG 462, 2.

[44] Prior to the New Testament, the word *eritheia* was found only in Aristotle where it denotes a self-seeking pursuit of political office by unfair means. Two possible translations are: (1) strife, contentiousness or (2) selfishness, selfish ambition. So in our passage, where it occurs in the plural, it is either "disputes" or "outbreaks of selfishness" (BDAG 392).

[45] *Katalalia*, BDAG 519.

[46] *Psithyrismos*, BDAG 1098.

"swelled-headedness, pride, conceit."[47]

- **"Disorder"** (NIV, NRSV), "tumults" (KJV) is *akatastasia*. In 6:5 regarding Paul's troubles it was translated, "unsettled state of affairs, disturbance, tumult," perhaps of a riot. But here it is probably, "opposition to established authority, disorder, unruliness."[48]

If you were to be honest, how many of these would you find prevalent in your congregation – not just in one or two people? Their presence indicates a dysfunctional congregation, a kind of organizational sickness.

Q3. (2 Corinthians 12:20) How do you "cure" a church of these kinds of behaviors and sins? How can a "love offensive" begin to change the spirit of a dysfunctional congregation? What is the role of church discipline in a dysfunctional congregation?
http://www.joyfulheart.com/forums/index.php?showtopic=1117

Paul isn't finished. Now he talks about sexual sins:

"... Many who have sinned earlier and have not repented of the impurity, sexual sin and debauchery in which they have indulged."[49] (12:21b)

- **"Impurity"** (NIV, NRSV), "uncleanness" (KJV) is *akatharsia*, "a state of moral corruption, immorality, vileness," used especially of sexual sins.[50] Addiction to pornography, for example, would fit in this category.
- **"Sexual sin"** (NIV), **"sexual immorality"** (NRSV), "fornication" (KJV) is *porneia*, a generic term referring to "unlawful sexual intercourse, prostitution, unchastity, fornication."[51] This word would also encompass homosexual acts.
- **"Debauchery"** (NIV), **"licentiousness"** (NRSV), "lasciviousness" (KJV) is *aselgeia*, "lack of self-constraint which involves one in conduct that violates all bounds of what is socially acceptable, self-abandonment," especially used of sexual excesses.[52]

Sometimes I've heard people minimize sexual sins as no worse than any other sin –

---

[47] *Physiōsis*, BDAG 1070.

[48] *Akatastasia*, BDAG 35.

[49] "Indulged" (NIV), "practiced" (NRSV), "committed" (KJV) is *prassō*, "to bring about or accomplish something through activity, do, accomplish," here, "do, commit something" (BDAG 860, 1a).

[50] *Akatharsia*, BDAG 34, 2. From *a-*, "not" + *kathairō*, "to cleanse."

[51] *Porneia*, BDAG 854, 1.

[52] *Aselgeia*, BDAG 142.

probably to justify their own practices. Friends, we have to take seriously God's word. In a previous letter, Paul taught this church:

> "9 Do you not know that the wicked will not inherit the kingdom of God? Do not be deceived: Neither the sexually immoral nor idolaters nor adulterers nor male prostitutes nor homosexual offenders 10 nor thieves nor the greedy nor drunkards nor slanderers nor swindlers will inherit the kingdom of God. 11 And that is what some of you were. But you were washed, you were sanctified, you were justified in the name of the Lord Jesus Christ and by the Spirit of our God." (1 Corinthians 6:9-11)

God will forgive the repentant, but not those who continue in these known sins without any real struggle to leave them.

The Pain of Correction (12:21a)

Now we come to a curious sentence:

> "I am afraid that when I come again my God will humble me before you, and I will be grieved over many who have sinned earlier[53] and have not repented...." (12:21a)

What does he mean that God will "humble" him? The verb *tapeinoō* in this context means, "to cause someone to lose prestige or status, humble, humiliate, abase."[54] I think he is referring to the public grief that he will be expressing during this apostolic correction process. "Be grieved" (NIV), "have to mourn" (NRSV), "bewail" (KJV) is *pentheō*, "to engage in mourning for one who is dead, ordinarily with traditional rites, mourn over."[55] To be acutely grieved in public is humiliating, something you try to avoid. But Paul is incapable of correcting without feeling and expressing the pain in his heart that his children in the Lord have been recaptured by previous sins and haven't repented.

You never believe your parents when they say, when preparing to spank you, "This is going to hurt me more than it hurts you." But when you're a parent, you understand. That's what's going on here.

Paul's Promise to Set Things in Order (13:1-3a)

Paul has shared his heart. Now he prepares them for an official hearing before the whole church and the judgment of those who persist in sin.

> "This will be my third visit to you. 'Every matter must be established by the testimony

---

[53] "Sinned earlier" (NIV) is *proamartanō*, "sin beforehand" from *pro-*, "before" + *harmatanō*, "to sin" (BDAG 865).

[54] *Tapeinoō*, BDAG 990, 2b.

[55] *Pentheō*, BDAG 795, 2.

of two or three witnesses.'" (13:1)

He is quoting from the Mosaic Law that established procedures in Israelite criminal hearings:

> "One witness is not enough to convict a man accused of any crime or offense he may have committed. A matter must be established by the testimony of two or three witnesses." (Deuteronomy 19:15)

It's kind of like a police officer reading a person being arrested his "Miranda rights." Perhaps the Corinthians are getting the idea that Paul is serious. Now he continues his warning with a verb used to refer to the warnings uttered by the Old Testament prophets[56] – warnings that were fulfilled in terrible finality upon God's sinning people:

> "[2] I already gave you a warning when I was with you the second time. I now repeat it[57] while absent: On my return[58] I will not spare those who sinned earlier or any of the others, [3] since you are demanding[59] proof[60] that Christ is speaking through me." (13:2-3a)

Paul says he won't be lenient at the trial.[61] "Spare" (NIV, KJV), "be lenient" (NRSV) is *pheidomai*, "to save from loss or discomfort, spare someone or something."[62] They are demanding proof that he is an apostle? Well, this will be that proof!

Weakness and Strength (13:3b-14)

Earlier in the letter it seemed like Paul was on the defensive, taking pains to explain himself. But clearly he is on the offensive now. Make no mistake: Christ will act with power through me when I come, says Paul.

> "[3b] He is not weak in dealing with you, but is powerful among you. [4] For to be sure, he was crucified in weakness, yet he lives by God's power. Likewise, we are weak in him, yet by God's power we will live with him to serve you." (13:13b-14)

Paul is alluding here to the Corinthians' perception that Paul is weak when he is with

---

[56] "Warning" (NIV, NRSV), "told" (KJV) is *proeipon*, "to tell beforehand, foretell, tell or proclaim beforehand, warn, of prophetic utterances concerning future events and circumstances" (BDAG 867, 1).

[57] "Repeat" (NIV), "warn" (NRSV), "foretell" (KJV) is *prolegō*, "to say something in advance of an event, tell beforehand or in advance" (BDAG 872, 1).

[58] "On my return" (NIV), "if I come again" (NRSV, KJV) is known in Greek as a Third Class Condition, sometimes known as a "More Probable Future Condition."

[59] "Demanding" (NIV), "desire" (NRSV), "seek" (KJV) is *zēteō*, "search for," here in the sense of, "ask for, request, demand something" (BDAG 428, 4).

[60] "Proof" is *dokimē*, "the experience of going through a test with special reference to the result, standing a test, character," here "desire proof or evidence" (BDAG 256, 2).

[61] Jesus refers to this sort of trial in Matthew 18:17.

[62] *Pheidomai*, BDAG 1051, 1. The verb is also used similarly in 1:23 and in 12:6 in the sense of "refrain."

them, but only powerful in his letters (10:10).

See If You Will Stand the Test (13:5-8)

Up to this point it seems clear that the Corinthians had been examining Paul – and perhaps the "super-apostles" – with regard to their credentials as true apostles. Now Paul turns the tables on them. You should be examining yourselves, he says, not me.

> "5 Examine[63] yourselves to see whether you are in the faith; test[64] yourselves. Do you not realize that Christ Jesus is in you – unless, of course, you fail the test[65]? 6 And I trust that you will discover that we have not failed the test." (13:5-6)

Notice that being "in the faith" and "Christ Jesus is in you" are two sides of the same coin, both ways of saying that a person is an authentic Christian. Paul expects that when they see their own faith, they'll realize that they are in Christ precisely because of Paul, their Apostle, and that for this reason he doesn't "fail the test."

> "7 Now we pray to God that you will not do anything wrong. Not that people will see that we have stood the test but that you will do what is right even though we may seem to have failed. 8 For we cannot do anything against the truth, but only for the truth." (13:7-8)

Whether or not I am proved genuine, says Paul in verse 7b, I want you to do what is right. Barrett says, "Paul is not out to get a verdict in his favor at any cost, but wishes the truth, whether it is favorable to him or not, to prevail."[66]

Authority for Building You Up (13:9-10)

Paul's heart is for his converts, the Corinthians.

> "For we rejoice when we are weak and you are strong. This is what we pray for, that you may become perfect." (13:9, NRSV)

His goal is not for himself, but for their perfection or maturity[67] in Christ. It's for this

---

[63] "Examine" is *peirazō*, "to endeavor to discover the nature or character of something by testing, try, make trial of, put to the test" (BDAG 702, 2a).

[64] "Test" (NIV), "prove" (KJV) is *dokimazō*, "to make a critical examination of something to determine genuineness, put to the test, examine." (BDAG 255, 1). "Examine yourself" is also found in 1 Corinthians 11:28. "Each one should test his own actions. Then he can take pride in himself, without comparing himself to somebody else" (Galatians 6:4).

[65] "Fail (to meet) the test" (NIV, NRSV), "be reprobate" (KJV) is *adokimos*, "not standing the test," then "unqualified, worthless, base" (BDAG 21). Also 1 Corinthians 9:27.

[66] Barrett, p. 339.

[67] "Perfection" (NIV, KJV), "become perfect" (NRSV) is *katartisis*, literally, "a training, discipling, instructing," from *kartizō*, "to fit, equip." Here it refers to "the process of perfecting, maturation" (BDAG 526; Thayer 336; Robertson, *Word Pictures, in loc.*).

very reason – that he seeks their best interest – that he writes this sometimes forceful letter, so that they can get back on course without his having to intervene severely in person.

> "¹⁰ This is why I write these things when I am absent, that when I come I may not have to be harsh⁶⁸ in my use⁶⁹ of authority – the authority the Lord gave me for building you up, not for tearing you down." (13:9-10)

Paul's purpose is to build them up, not condemn them, but they need to understand that he bears apostolic authority from God.⁷⁰

Concluding Words (13:11-13)

> Having delivered his message from God, Paul now offers some closing thoughts.

> "Finally, brothers, good-by. Aim for perfection, listen to my appeal, be of one mind, live in peace. And the God of love and peace will be with you." (13:11)

He delivers four brief commands.

1.   Put things in order (NRSV), "mend your ways" (RSV).⁷¹
2.   Heed my appeal.⁷²
3.   Be of one mind.⁷³
4.   Live in peace.⁷⁴

The Corinthian church has been in some chaos and disagreement, with some siding with the "super-apostles" and others siding with Paul. He calls them to unity and peace.

> "¹² Greet⁷⁵ one another with a holy kiss. ¹³ All the saints send their greetings." (13:12-13)

---

⁶⁸ "Harsh" (NIV), "severe" (NRSV), "sharpness" (KJV) is the adverb *apotomōs*, "severely, rigorously" (BDAG 124). See Titus 1:13.

⁶⁹ "Be" or "use" is *chraomai*, can carry three meanings which might be appropriate here: (1) "make use of, employ," (2) "act proceed," or (3) "treat a person in a certain way" (BDAG 1087, 2 or 3). NIV, NRSV, and KJV translations all seem to adopt definition 1.

⁷⁰ "Authority" (NIV, NRSV), "power" (KJV) is exousia, "authority, capability," here, "the right to control or command, authority, absolute power, warrant" (BDAG 353, 3). Also used in this sense in 10:8.

⁷¹ "Aim for perfection" (NIV), "put things in order" (NRSV), "mend your ways" (RSV), "be perfect" (KJV) is *katartizō*, the root of *katartisis* in 13:9 – "to cause to be in a condition to function well, put in order, restore," here probably, "mend your ways" (BDAG 526, 1a).

⁷² "Listen to my appeal" (NIV, NRSV margin, "encourage one another"), "be of good comfort" (KJV) is *parakaleō*, probably with the passive sense, "be comforted, receive comfort" through words, or a favorable change in the situation (BDAG 764, 4).

⁷³ "Be of one mind" (NIV, KJV), "agree with one another" (NRSV) uses the verb *phroneō*, "to have an opinion with regard to something, think, form or hold an opinion, judge" (BDAG 1065, 1).

⁷⁴ "Live in peace" is *eirēneuō*, "to be at peace," generally of ending a state of enmity or hostilities, here probably, "keep the peace" (BDAG 287, 2b).

In America, men don't usually show affection to other men with a kiss, though the expression exists in parts of Europe, the Middle East, and elsewhere. However, we see kissing several times as an expression of affectionate greeting and respect in Luke's gospel:

- A guest upon entering a home (Luke 7:45).
- The woman thankful for forgiveness (Luke 7:38, 45).
- The father of a son returning home (Luke 15:20).
- The greeting of a friend (Luke 22:47-48).

Paul wants his greeting to them to be conveyed with the affection of a kiss at the conclusion of several of his letters,[76] but with the qualification of a "holy kiss," that is, a kiss without any erotic implications.

Q4. (2 Corinthians 13:12) What is the equivalent of a "holy kiss" in *your* congregation and culture? Why is a warm familial greeting so important in a healthy congregation? Why do people sometimes resist being greeted warmly?
http://www.joyfulheart.com/forums/index.php?showtopic=1118

Trinitarian Benediction (13:14)

Paul concludes with a unique Trinitarian blessing, often used in formal benedictions in our day.

> "May the grace of the Lord Jesus Christ, and the love of God, and the fellowship of the Holy Spirit be with you all." (13:14)

It isn't often in the New Testament that you see all three members of the Godhead spoken of in this co-equal way all together. The other main references are:

> "Therefore go and make disciples of all nations, baptizing them in the name of the Father and of the Son and of the Holy Spirit...." (Matthew 28:19)

> "... Chosen according to the foreknowledge of God the Father, through the sanctifying work of the Spirit, for obedience to Jesus Christ and sprinkling by his blood...." (1 Peter 1:2)

Jehovah's Witnesses and Oneness Pentecostals claim that since the word "Trinity" isn't used in the Bible, the concept can't be real. I disagree. As I have written elsewhere, the

---

[75] "Greet" is *aspazomai*, "to engage in hospitable recognition of another (with varying degrees of intimacy), greet, welcome someone," here, "wish to be remembered, greet, send greetings" (BDAG 144, 1a).
[76] Romans 16:16, 1 Corinthians 16:20, and 1 Thessalonians 5:26. Also 1 Peter 5:14.

New Testament can't be understood properly without some understanding of the relationship between the three members of the Godhead: Father, Son, and Holy Spirit.[77] When you try to cram them all into one Person, you end up distorting the Scriptures by forcing them to say things they don't say. While we're foolish to pretend that we really understand God in Three Persons, yet this is the best explanation we have that is based on the evidence of the New Testament.

Paul's blessing is threefold – one for each Person of the Godhead:

> "May the grace of the Lord Jesus Christ, and the love of God, and the fellowship of the Holy Spirit be with you all." (13:14)

1. **Grace** (*charis*), that is, unmerited favor from Jesus Christ, who gave up his own life to redeem us and make us heirs of God and co-heirs with him for eternity. He did what he didn't have to do for our sakes. That, dear friends, is grace writ large!

2. **Love**, flowing unselfish from the throne of the Father. Most love has some elements of altruism, but is essentially selfish. But not *agapē* love. Our salvation is the result of God loving the world so much that he sent Jesus to save us (John 3:16).

3. **Fellowship** that comes from the Holy Spirit is *koinōnia*, that is sharing, partnership, a relationship that we have in common. The Holy Spirit connects us to God, reveals Christ to us, and is to us a Counselor and Comforter. The fellowship we have with one another results from the Holy Spirit whom we have in common.

At times, 2 Corinthians has been a turbulent letter because of the rocky relationship caused by false apostles between the apostle and his converts. But it has been rich. Because of Paul's ministry to the deficiencies of the Corinthians, you and I are richer. We have understood some of God's abundant gifts: the sealing of the Spirit, living letters written on our hearts, unveiled faces beholding God's glory, the treasure we have in clay jars, the new creation, the ministry of reconciliation, the generous reaping of the giver, and the ability to rejoice – yes, even exult – in our weaknesses. Thank you, Paul. Thank you, Lord. Amen!

Prayer

Father, thank you for this wonderful letter that has blessed me so much over these

---

[77] Ralph F. Wilson, "Four Reasons Why I Believe in the Trinity" (www.joyfulheart.com/scholar/trinity.htm).

last months. Thank you for maturing me as I've studied and meditated and prayed and pondered. Thank you for all the glorious riches you have bestowed on us in Christ Jesus. Thank you for your patience with us, who are at once new creations and yet still growing creatures that seek your perfection. Thank you. In Jesus' name, we thank you. Amen.

Key Verses

"He said to me, 'My grace is sufficient for you, for my power is made perfect in weakness.'" (2 Corinthians 12:9a)

May the grace of the Lord Jesus Christ, and the love of God, and the fellowship of the Holy Spirit be with you all." (2 Corinthians 13:14)

Appendix 1: Handouts for Group Participants

If you're working with a class or small group, feel free to duplicate the following handouts in this appendix at no additional charge. If you'd like to print 8-1/2" x 11" sheets, you can download the free Participant Guide handout sheets at:

www.jesuswalk.com/2corinthians/2corinthians-lesson-handouts.pdf

Discussion Questions

You'll find 3 to 5 questions for each lesson. Each question may include several sub-questions. These are designed to get group members engaged in discussion of the key points of the passage. If you're running short of time, feel free to skip questions or portions of questions.

Introduction to 2 Corinthians

1. The God of All Comfort (1:1-11)
2. Tension with the Corinthians (1:12-2:11)
3. The Fragrance of Christ's Ministering People (2:12-3:6)
4. Being Changed by God's Glory (3:7-18)
5. Treasures in Clay Pots (4:1-18)
6. Walking by Faith, Not by Sight (5:1-16)
7. The Ministry of Reconciliation (5:17-6:2)
8. Hardships, Holiness, and Joy (6:3-7:16)
9. Generosity Modeled and Encouraged (8:1-9:5)
10. Sowing Generously (9:6-15)
11. Paul's Defense of His Ministry (10-11)
12. Paul's Vision, Thorn, and Final Words (12-13)

Introduction to 2 Corinthians

The City of Corinth

Corinth became prosperous from trade – both the trade moving by sea from east and west, but also north and south between Greece and the Peloponnesus. The port of Cenchreae connected the city to the Aegean Sea to the east, while the port of Lechaeum was on the Ionian Sea.

Ruins of the Temple of Apollo, dating to the sixth century BC, can still be seen. Shops and monuments lining the Agora, larger than the Forum in Rome, also persist. At the peak of the Acro-Corinthian mountain stood the Temple of Aphrodite, goddess of love and beauty, where 1,000 female prostitutes served, contributing to the city's reputation for immorality. In fact, the coined Greek word "to Corinthianize" meant to practice immorality and the phrase "Corinthian girl" designated a prostitute.

Temple of Apollo and ruins in Corinth.
Source: BiblePlaces.com

Tentative Chronology of Paul and the Corinthians (50-56 AD)

Below, I've tried to outline in order what we can piece together of Paul's contacts with the Corinthian church.

1. **First Visit** (50-52 AD). Paul first visited Corinth about 50 AD, during the last phase of his second missionary journey, after starting churches in Macedonia – Philippi, Thessalonica, and Berea (Acts 16-17). After leaving Corinth in 52 AD, Paul stops at Ephesus and then returns to Antioch, and from there he goes to Jerusalem (Acts 20:18-22).

2. **"Previous Letter" from Paul**, no longer extant, is written from Ephesus (52 to 55 AD), writes to Corinth rebuking vice and fornication by church members (mentioned in 1 Corinthians 5:9-11).

3. **Report to Paul:** Chloe's people report to Paul about the party spirit and quarrels

at Corinth.

4. **Letter to Paul:** Stephanas, Fortunatas, and Achaicus carry a letter that reports on problems at Corinth with marriage, divorce, food sacrificed to idols, spiritual gifts, and the collection he was organizing for the Jerusalem believers (1 Corinthians 16:17).

5. **Timothy is dispatched** to Corinth to deal with some of the problems (1 Corinthians 4:17; 16:10-11).

6. **1 Corinthians Letter** is written in Spring 55 AD, Paul from Ephesus. At this point Paul is planning a soon visit to Macedonia with a stop in Corinth. (1 Corinthians 4:18-21).

7. **Second visit, the "painful visit,"** is a quick trip to deal with troubles in Corinth that were serious enough to require direct personal confrontation (2:1; 13:2). During this visit Paul was personally attacked by one of the members (2:5; 7:12).

8. **The "severe letter"** from Paul (2:3-4), no longer extant, is written from Ephesus, in which Paul professes his love for them and requires them to discipline the man who had led in defying his apostolic authority. Effective in producing repentance (7:8-12).

9. **Proposed visits** don't come to pass (1 Corinthians 16:1-8).

10. **Paul travels to Troas and Macedonia** amidst various afflictions, but meets Titus there and is encouraged by his good report about the Corinthian church (7:5-7).

11. **"Super-Apostles" challenge Paul's authority**.

12. **2 Corinthians Letter:** Paul sends our 2 Corinthians letter from Macedonia about 56 AD.

13. **Third Visit to Corinth** occurs about 57 AD, with the gift collected to relieve the Jerusalem saints (Acts 19:21-22; Romans 15:26). He stays in Corinth three months, escapes to Macedonia to avoid a Jewish plot, meets companions in Troas (Acts 20:1-5), and leaves for Jerusalem where he is arrested.

Paul's Opponents in Corinth

Who are the visitors to Corinth who try to undermine Paul's authority there? Some have supposed them to be "Gnostics of ecstatic temperament and libertine ethics." Others see them as Judaizers. But most likely they are Palestinian Jews, not Judaizers in the Galatian sense, but perhaps men who tried to impose the authority of the mother church over the Christian world.

Situation

To summarize the situation, Paul is writing to a six-year-old church that he founded in 50-51 AD. Since he moved on, the church has encountered problems, particularly some Jewish Christian leaders who have worked to undermine Paul's influence so they could substitute their own. So in 2 Corinthians, Paul writes about 56 AD to restore his relationship with the church and regain his influence, so he can help them with the problems they are having with holiness and hardship, generosity and church order, and their testimony to the non-Christians around them.

1. The God of All Comfort (1:1-11)

Q1. (2 Corinthians 1:3-7) What kind of comfort do you receive from your faith in God? From your personal daily relationship with God? How might you share the blessing of this kind of comfort with a friend or relative who is currently suffering? What words of comfort can you bring to others?

Q2. (2 Corinthians 1:9-10) How does facing a harrowing crisis help us grow in the Lord? How has a crisis helped your spiritual life? What is the value of learning not to rely on ourselves? What does this do to our pride? How does this improve our effectiveness as God's servants?

Q3. (2 Corinthians 1:10-11) Why does Paul ask people to pray for him? How do the prayers of others have an effect? What happened in your life that has helped you enter into a ministry of intercessory prayer?

Key Verses

"Praise be to the God and Father of our Lord Jesus Christ, the Father of compassion and the God of all comfort, who comforts us in all our troubles, so that we can comfort those in any trouble with the comfort we ourselves have received from God." (2 Corinthians 1:3-4, NIV)

"We were under great pressure, far beyond our ability to endure, so that we despaired even of life. Indeed, in our hearts we felt the sentence of death. But this happened that we might not rely on ourselves but on God, who raises the dead." (2 Corinthians 1:8b-9, NIV)

2. Tension with the Corinthians (1:12-2:11)

Map of Achaia, Macedonia, and Asia in Paul's day

Blessings to us from the Holy Spirit:

1. Established
2. Anointed
3. Marked as God's property
4. Guaranteed eternal life

Q1. (2 Corinthians 1:21b-22) According to this verse, what does the presence of the Holy Spirit in our lives signify? How does the Spirit unite us with God? What is the promise of future blessing inherent in the Spirit's presence?

Q2. (2 Corinthians 1:24) What does it mean to "lord it over" someone? What is the balance between (1) good, strong leadership, (2) micromanaging, and (3) a complete *laissez-faire* approach to leadership? What are the dangers of an authoritative leadership style? What are the dangers of a weak leadership style?

Q3. (2 Corinthians 2:9) How does obedience to servant leaders help the church of Jesus Christ? How does obedience to self-serving leaders hurt the church? Are you obedient to those whom God has placed over you in the Lord? Why or why not? What is the relationship between obedience and church unity?

Q4. (2 Corinthians 2:10-11) How does Satan take advantage of our unforgiveness? What are the symptoms in our own heart of unforgiveness? According to Matthew 6:14-15, how does holding unforgiveness hurt our spiritual lives? What would you have to do to really let go of your resentment and give it to God?

Key Verses

"Now it is God who makes both us and you stand firm in Christ. He anointed us, set his seal of ownership on us, and put his Spirit in our hearts as a deposit, guaranteeing what is to come." (2 Corinthians 1:21-22, NIV)

"I have forgiven in the sight of Christ for your sake, in order that Satan might not outwit us. For we are not unaware of his schemes." (2 Corinthians 2:10b-11, NIV)

3. The Fragrance of Christ's Ministering People (2:12-3:6)

Q1. (2 Corinthians 2:14-16a) In what sense is knowing God fragrant to people who are open to God? In what way is this fragrance repugnant to people who are closed to God? Have you suppressed your "fragrance" because some people are allergic to Christian perfume? If so, how can you regain the fragrance of Christ's gospel?

Q2. (2 Corinthians 3:2-3) In what sense are we "living letters"? In what way can people "read us"? Why is it so important to be authentic, not phony, in our lives? What happens when people "read" something in you that they admire and mention it to you? How might you respond appropriately?

Those in ministry leadership roles should:

1. Know the Scriptures and can interpret them soundly and wisely,
2. Have spiritual gifts for ministry and exercise them with care and wisdom,
3. Are of tested moral character and live a holy life,
4. Have a healthy and growing devotional life,
5. Act properly in terms of money, sex, and power, and
6. Continue in accountability to their elders and peers in the larger Church, so that they don't get off track doctrinally, morally, or spiritually.

Q3. (2 Corinthians 3:4-6) What is the balance between the need for training in ministry (either in the local church or in schools) and personal submission to the Spirit of God? Are you able to "listen to the Spirit's voice" in your own life? Why would this ability be so important in being a competent minister?

Q4. (2 Corinthians 3:6a) Why is a Christian's spiritual health so closely related to his or her involvement in ministry? What are the consequences of dropping out of church – for the believer? For Christ's Kingdom?

Key Verses

"But thanks be to God, who always leads us in triumphal procession in Christ and through us spreads everywhere the fragrance of the knowledge of him. [15] For we are to God the aroma of Christ among those who are being saved and those who are perishing." (2 Corinthians 2:14-15, NIV)

"You yourselves are our letter, written on our hearts, known and read by everybody. You show that you are a letter from Christ, the result of our ministry, written not with ink but with the

Spirit of the living God, not on tablets of stone but on tablets of human hearts." (2 Corinthians 3:2-3, NIV)

"He has made us competent as ministers of a new covenant – not of the letter but of the Spirit; for the letter kills, but the Spirit gives life." (2 Corinthians 3:6, NIV)

4. Being Changed by God's Glory (3:7-18)

Q1. (2 Corinthians 3:7-11) Why did Moses' face glow? Why did he cover it when he was out with the people? Why didn't more people's face glow in Moses' time? What's the difference between the spread of God's glory in Moses' time when compared to our own time?

Q2. (2 Corinthians 3:16-17) Why is the Holy Spirit essential to help people see truth clearly and be able to grasp it? What enables people to come to Christ at all? What kind of freedom does the Spirit give us when we become Christians?

Q3. (2 Corinthians 3:18) Moses glowed by spending time with God on Mt. Sinai, in his tent of meeting, and in the Tabernacle. How can we get a similar glow of the Spirit in our lives? In what way is meditating on Scripture beholding God? Is the low plane of Christianity in our day related to the time we spend in communion with the Lord? What is God leading you to do to increase your glow?

Q4. (2 Corinthians 3:18) Why is character change directly related to time deliberately spent in God's presence? What is the theological word for the process of maturing in Christ? Have you noticed a change in the "degree of glory" you're experiencing now compared to a few years ago? Why or why not?

Key Verses

"Now the Lord is the Spirit, and where the Spirit of the Lord is, there is freedom." (2 Corinthians 3:17, NIV)

"And all of us, with unveiled faces, seeing the glory of the Lord as though reflected in a mirror, are being transformed into the same image from one degree of glory to another; for this comes from the Lord, the Spirit." (2 Corinthians 3:18, NRSV)

5. Treasures in Clay Pots (4:1-18)

Q1. (2 Corinthians 4:1-2) How do questionable ethics and ministry practices hurt the work of Christ? What is Paul's alternative in verse 2b?

Blinded unbelievers

1. The subject is lost people, "unbelievers" (verse 4), "those who are perishing" (verse 3).

2. The culprit is "the god of this age" (John 14:30; 16:11; Ephesians 2:2; 1 John 5:19; Revelation 12:12-13; John 8:44; Ephesians 2:2)

3. Satan's strategy is deception, blinding man's mind.

Fighting blindness

1. We fight with prayer and spiritual weapons (Ephesians 6:10-20) We are open and honest in our own communication (4:2).

2. We declare the good news of Jesus Christ with clarity.

3. We love our unsaved friends intensely.

Q2. (2 Corinthians 4:3-4) Since Satan has blinded people's eyes to the truth, is there any hope for them? What strategies must we use to overcome spiritual blindness? How many people are likely to find Christ without intercessory prayer?

Q3. (2 Corinthians 4:7) What truth is Paul seeking to communicate by this analogy of a treasure in a pottery jar? What does the clay jar represent? What does the treasure represent? What's the paradox here?

Q4. (2 Corinthians 4:8-12) How does it encourage you to know that Paul went through tremendous stress and pressure? What effect did these sufferings have on the way people could see Christ in Paul? Why is pain necessary to spiritual growth? How does our pain allow others to assess our authenticity as Christians?

Q5. (2 Corinthians 4:15-18) In what way do problems and physical deterioration help us toward "an eternal weight of glory"? Why is it so easy to focus on temporal matters to the exclusion of eternal things? Why is a focus on eternal things so important to our spiritual growth? What can we do to help shift our focus?

Key Verses

"The god of this age has blinded the minds of unbelievers, so that they cannot see the light of the gospel of the glory of Christ, who is the image of God." (2 Corinthians 4:18, NIV)

"But we have this treasure in jars of clay to show that this all-surpassing power is from God and not from us." (2 Corinthians 4:7, NIV)

"We are hard pressed on every side, but not crushed; perplexed, but not in despair; persecuted, but not abandoned; struck down, but not destroyed." (2 Corinthians 4:8-9, NIV)

"We always carry around in our body the death of Jesus, so that the life of Jesus may also be revealed in our body." (2 Corinthians 4:10, NIV)

"Therefore we do not lose heart. Though outwardly we are wasting away, yet inwardly we are being renewed day by day." (2 Corinthians 4:16, NIV)

"For our light and momentary troubles are achieving for us an eternal glory that far outweighs them all." (2 Corinthians 4:17, NIV)

"So we fix our eyes not on what is seen, but on what is unseen. For what is seen is temporary, but what is unseen is eternal." (2 Corinthians 4:18, NIV)

6. Walking by Faith, Not by Sight (5:1-16)

Q1. (2 Corinthians 5:1-5) In what sense are our bodies like tents? If we were to truly look forward to our "house not made with hands," how would it affect our daily lives here?

Q2. (2 Corinthians 5:6-8) How do Paul's words comfort you when you consider your death? What do Christians believe happens when we die? What will happen to us if we die before Christ returns? What will happen to us when Christ returns?

Q3. (2 Corinthians 5:7) What does it mean to walk by faith, not by sight? Why can't nonbelievers understand this kind of living? What aspects of your life are guided by your senses rather than by your faith? How can you bring a faith perspective into these areas?

Q4. (2 Corinthians 5:10-11a) How does Paul's mention of the Judgment Seat of Christ fit the context here? How should our belief that we Christians will appear before the Judgment Seat of Christ to be judged for our works affect (1) our desire to please him? (2) Our motivation to persuade people to receive Christ?

Key Verses

"Therefore we are always confident and know that as long as we are at home in the body we are away from the Lord." (2 Corinthians 5:6, NIV)

"We live by faith, not by sight." (2 Corinthians 5:7, NIV)

"For we must all appear before the judgment seat of Christ, that each one may receive what is due him for the things done while in the body, whether good or bad." (2 Corinthians 5: 10, NIV)

"For Christ's love compels us...." (2 Corinthians 5:14, NIV)

7. A Ministry of Reconciliation (5:17-6:2)

"Creation/creature" is *ktisis*, "the result of a creative act, that which is created." The New Testament uses several other words to describe this, including:

- Born again/anew/from above (John 3:3, 5; 1 Peter 1:23; 1 John 3:9; 5:18)
- Made alive, quickened (Ephesians 2:5; John 5:24; 1 John 3:14)
- Regenerated, rebirth (Titus 3:5)
- Washed (1 Corinthians 6:11; Ephesians 5:26; Titus 3:5)
- Renewed (Ephesians 3:10)
- Sealed (2 Corinthians 1:22; Ephesians 1:13; 4:30)

Q1. (2 Corinthians 5:16-17) What does verse 17 teach us about the nature of a new believer? What changes in a person when he puts his faith in Christ? Why don't old habits disappear immediately if everything has become new?

Q2. (2 Corinthians 5:18-20) How have we humans been reconciled to God? What did God do so that reconciliation could take place? In what sense are you an Ambassador of the Kingdom of God? In what sense are you a Minister of Reconciliation for Jesus Christ?

2 Corinthians 5:21 is one of the clearest statements in the entire Bible of the Doctrine of the Substitutionary Atonement (also known as penal substitution or vicarious atonement). This refers to the Bible teaching that Jesus bore the penalty for our sins and took our place, so we didn't have to die for our own sins. A "substitute," of course, is "a person or thing that takes the place or function of another."

Q3. (2 Corinthians 5:21) In what sense did Jesus "become sin" on our behalf? In what sense do we "become righteousness"?

Q4. (2 Corinthians 5:18-6:2) If you, then, are called to be an urgent agent of reconciliation, how is this likely to affect your daily life? How will it affect how people perceive you? How will it affect how God perceives you?

Key Verses

"Therefore, if anyone is in Christ, he is a new creation; the old has gone, the new has come!" (2 Corinthians 5:17, NIV)

"God was reconciling the world to himself in Christ, not counting men's sins against them. And he has committed to us the message of reconciliation." (2 Corinthians 5:19, NIV)

"We are therefore Christ's ambassadors, as though God were making his appeal through us. We implore you on Christ's behalf: Be reconciled to God." (2 Corinthians 5:20, NIV)

"God made him who had no sin to be sin for us, so that in him we might become the righteousness of God." (2 Corinthians 5:21, NIV)

"I tell you, now is the time of God's favor, now is the day of salvation." (2 Corinthians 6:2b, NIV)

8. Hardships, Holiness, and Joy (6:3-7:16)

1. God's help in spite of intense hardships (6:3-13)
2. Personal holiness, separation from sinful practices (6:14-7:1)
3. Paul's joy due to Titus' encouraging report (7:2-16)

Q1. (2 Corinthians 6:3-13) Why do you think Paul shares so much about his various struggles with the Corinthians? How does this help them accept his apostleship as authentic? Have you ever complained about what you've had to put up with in your ministry? How does it compare to what Paul faced?

Paul uses five words to describe a close relationship – a closeness that can hurt the believers.

1. "In common" (NIV), "partnership" (NRSV), "fellowship" (KJV) has the basic idea of "sharing, participation."

2. "Fellowship" (NIV, NRSV), "communion" (KJV) is *koinōnia*, "close association involving mutual interests and sharing, association, communion, fellowship, close relationship." This refers to a relationship built upon common interests.

3. "Harmony" (NIV), "agreement" (NRSV), "concord" (KJV) is *symphōnēsis* (from which get our word "symphony") "a state of shared interests, agreement."

4. "In common" (NIV), "share" (NRSV), "part" (KJV) is *meris*, "share, portion."

5. "Agreement" is from a word that originally meant "a putting together or joint deposit (of votes)," hence, "approval, assent, agreement."

4. God walks among believers (16:16b)
5. Believers are holy themselves (6:17)
6. Believers are God's own special children (6:18)

Q2. (2 Corinthians 6:14-18) What are the reasons Paul gives us – both in his letter and by quoting Old Testament scriptures – that we should live holy lives? What kinds of temptations did the Corinthians face in their notorious city.

Holiness (Ephesians 1:4; 1 Thessalonians 3:13; 4:7; Hebrews 12:14; 1 Peter 1:14-16)

Q3. (2 Corinthians 6:14-7:1) What kind of separation is Paul calling the Corinthians to? How can they strike a balance between separating themselves from sinful practices that mess up their spiritual lives while at the same time maintaining friendships with pagan neighbors and co-workers?

Q4. (2 Corinthians 7:5) What are the distinctions between fear, faith, and courage? Why is being honest about our fears better than pretending we don't have any fears? How did Paul deal with his fears?

Key Verses

"Do not be yoked together with unbelievers." (2 Corinthians 6:14, NIV)

"For we are the temple of the living God. As God has said: 'I will live with them and walk among them, and I will be their God, and they will be my people.'" (2 Corinthians 6:16, NIV)

"Therefore come out from them and be separate, says the Lord. Touch no unclean thing, and I will receive you." (2 Corinthians 6:17, NIV)

"Since we have these promises, dear friends, let us purify ourselves from everything that contaminates body and spirit, perfecting holiness out of reverence for God." (2 Corinthians 7:1, NIV)

9. Generosity Modeled and Encouraged (8:1-9:5)

Q1. (2 Corinthians 8:1-5) Why is it so difficult to give when we are stressed by circumstances and bills and pressures? What can we learn from the example of the Macedonians and the poor widow? How will this lesson affect your own giving?

Giving is referred to as "grace" five places in our text:

	NIV	NRSV	KJV
Verse 4	"privilege"	"privilege"	"gift"
Verse 7	"act of grace"	"generous undertaking"	"grace"
Verse 8	"grace of giving"	"generous undertaking"	"grace"
Verse 9	"grace"	"generous act"	"grace"
Verse 19	"offering"	"generous undertaking"	"grace"

Q2. (2 Corinthians 8:4, 7-9, 19) What does grace have to do with giving? What does giving look like when it isn't accompanied by grace? What does it look like when grace prompts your giving?

Q3. (2 Corinthians 8:9) What riches did Christ have according to this verse? How did he become poor? In what way were we poor? In what way have we become rich?

Q4. (2 Corinthians 8:21-22) What is the balance between living our lives wholly before God without being men-pleasers, and doing what is right in the sight of men?

Key Verses

"For you know the grace of our Lord Jesus Christ, that though he was rich, yet for your sakes he became poor, so that you through his poverty might become rich." (2 Corinthians 8:9, NIV)

"For we are taking pains to do what is right, not only in the eyes of the Lord but also in the eyes of men." (2 Corinthians 8:21, NIV)

10. Sowing Generously (9:6-15)

"Sparingly" is *pheidomenōs*, "in a scanty or meager manner, sparingly," from *pheido-mai*, "to be miserly." "Generously" (NIV), "bountifully" (NRSV, KJV) is *eulogia*, "blessing," which we saw in the previous verse (9:5). Here, the idea is "sowing for blessing." Since the concept of blessing connotes the idea of bounty, *eulogia* also bears the meaning, "generous gift, bounty."

1. Principles of Blessing and Tithing (Malachi 3:10-12)
2. The Result of Failing to Put God First in Giving (Haggai 1:2-11)
3. Jesus' Teaching on Giving and Blessing (Luke 6:37-38)

Q1. (2 Corinthians 9:6) Does the Scripture teach that material blessing results from giving generously to God's work? Why are we so careful to reinterpret this as referring mainly to spiritual blessing? If you compared your own actual giving to God's work to a tithe (10%) of your income, would it look generous?

Correctives for the prosperity message (Appendix 2)

1. The assertion that poverty is the curse Christ frees us from (Malachi 3:9; Deuteronomy 27:26; 28:15-68; Galatians 3:13-14; Genesis 3:17b-19a). Jesus wasn't wealthy (Luke 8:1-3; John 12:6; 13:29).
2. The danger of greed being a primary motivation for giving.
    Do not store up for yourselves treasures on earth (Matthew 6:19-21, 24)
    Desire to become wealthy (1 Timothy 6:6-10)
    Do not love the world (1 John 2:15-16)
3. The related danger of pride when one flaunts one's wealth.

Two wrong motivations for giving:

1. Reluctance. "Reluctantly" (NIV, NRSV), "grudgingly" (KJV) is *lypē*, "pain of mind or spirit, grief, sorrow, affliction," here, with the preposition *ek*, "out of," it means "reluctantly."
2. Pressure. "Under compulsion" (NIV, NRSV), "of necessity" (KJV) is *anankē*, "necessity or constraint as inherent in the nature of things, necessity, pressure of any kind," a divine dispensation, some hoped-for advantage, custom, duty, etc. Here, "under pressure."

"Cheerful" is *hilaros*, "pertaining to being full of cheer, cheerful, glad, happy," here, "one who gives cheerfully, gladly (= without reluctance)."

Q2. (2 Corinthians 9:7) Why do you think pastors or other church leaders use guilt to try to compel people to give more? Can greed be behind their pressure? Why is pressure incompatible with worship? What does cheerfulness while giving say about the condition of a person's heart?

Q3. (2 Corinthians 9:10-11) According to these verses, what is the purpose of God increasing your "store of seed"? How do greed and generosity differ from each other? What is God's promise here to generous givers?

Q4. (2 Corinthians 9:12-15) Why should our giving prompt thanksgiving? How is our giving a demonstration of God's grace? Why is God's gift of Jesus termed "surpassing"? Why is God's gift of Jesus termed "indescribable"?

Key Verses

"Remember this: Whoever sows sparingly will also reap sparingly, and whoever sows generously will also reap generously." (2 Corinthians 9:6, NIV)

"Each man should give what he has decided in his heart to give, not reluctantly or under compulsion, for God loves a cheerful giver." (2 Corinthians 9:7, NIV)

"Thanks be to God for his indescribable gift!" (2 Corinthians 9:15, NIV)

11. Paul's Defense of His Ministry (10-11)

Q1. (2 Corinthians 10:3-6) Why does Paul liken his dealing with his opponents in Corinth with reducing a city wall by siege and then taking its citizens captive? Is Paul talking about a victory by the use of incisive logic or is there a spiritual stronghold here, one that derives its power from Satan's kingdom?

Q2. (2 Corinthians 11:1-5) What does it feel like when a congregation loses its pure devotion to Jesus Christ, and instead takes on other motivations for its religious observance? In what ways is this like the church at Ephesus losing its "first love" (Revelation 2:4)? How can this purity of devotion be restored?

Paul was able to refuse financial compensation from the Corinthians (1 Corinthians 9:12b, 15b, 17-18) because:

1. The Macedonian churches – in particular, Philippi – provided him support and supplied his needs (Philippians 4:15-16)
2. He worked as a tentmaker in Corinth, where he met Priscilla and Aquilla (Acts 18:2-3). Furthermore, he worked not only in Corinth, but in Ephesus (Acts 20:34), Thessalonica (1 Thessalonians 2:9; 2 Thessalonians 3:8), and perhaps elsewhere, too.

Q3. (2 Corinthians 11:7-9) Why do you think Paul refused to require the Corinthians to support him? How did this help his ministry? How did it contribute to them taking him for granted? How can we honor Christian workers, clergy and lay, who give of their time sacrificially to minister for Christ? How will Christ honor them?

Q4. (2 Corinthians 11:23-28) How do Paul's sufferings help authenticate his claim to be an apostle? What do these sufferings tell us about Paul's commitment? How does this account inspire you – or convict you? How will you be different from having pondered it?

Key Verses

"For the weapons of our warfare are not merely human, but they have divine power to destroy strongholds. We destroy arguments [5] and every proud obstacle raised up against the knowledge of God, and we take every thought captive to obey Christ." (2 Corinthians 10:4-5, NIV)

"Even Satan disguises himself as an angel of light. So it is not strange if his ministers also disguise themselves as ministers of righteousness." (2 Corinthians 10:14b-15a, NIV)

12. Paul's Vision, Thorn, and Final Words (12-13)

Is Sickness from Satan?

1. Jesus' healing miracles were signs of the Kingdom (Luke 10:9). "Saved" (*sōzō*) is used in the gospels for physical healing sometimes (Matthew 9:21-22; Mark 5:23, 28, 34; 6:56; 10:52; Luke 8:36, 48, 50; 17:19; 18:42; Acts 4:9; 14:9).

2. Jesus rebuked Satan and evil spirits in order to bring about healing (Luke 4:35, 39, 41; 9:42).

3. Jesus taught his disciples to pray for the sick and to cast out demons (Mark 16:17-18, longer ending; Luke 9:1; 10:9, 17).

4. Healing and works of miracles are gifts of the Spirit (1 Corinthians 12:9-10, 28; 13:10).

5. God didn't heal all sicknesses – even in the apostolic circle (Romans 8:18, 23; 2 Corinthians 4:16; Philippians 2:27; 1 Timothy 5:23; 2 Timothy 4:20).

6. A healer's own sickness is not incompatible with a powerful healing ministry.

Q1. (2 Corinthians 12:7) *Why* was this "thorn in the flesh" given to Paul? What purpose did God want to achieve through this in Paul's character? How can something be both used by God *and* be caused by Satan's destructive work? How does this verse relate to Romans 8:28 and Genesis 50:20?

Q2. (2 Corinthians 12:10) What was the life-changing lesson that Paul learned from God when God denied his prayer? How does our self-sufficiency limit God's power through our lives? Can we become dependent upon God without having to experience some "thorn in the flesh" ourselves?

Q3. (2 Corinthians 12:20) How do you "cure" a church of these kinds of behaviors and sins? How can a "love offensive" begin to change the spirit of a dysfunctional congregation? What is the role of church discipline in a dysfunctional congregation?

Sexual sins (12:21)

1. "Impurity" (NIV, NRSV), "uncleanness" (KJV) is *akatharsia*, "a state of moral corruption, immorality, vileness," used especially of sexual sins. Addiction to pornography, for example, would fit in this category.

2. "Sexual sin" (NIV), "sexual immorality" (NRSV), "fornication" (KJV) is *porneia*, a

generic term referring to "unlawful sexual intercourse, prostitution, unchastity, fornication." This word would also encompass homosexual acts.

3. "Debauchery" (NIV), "licentiousness" (NRSV), "lasciviousness" (KJV) is *aselgeia*, "lack of self-constraint which involves one in conduct that violates all bounds of what is socially acceptable, self-abandonment," especially used of sexual excesses.

Q4. (2 Corinthians 13:12) What is the equivalent of a "holy kiss" in *your* congregation and culture? Why is a warm familial greeting so important in a healthy congregation? Why do people sometimes resist being greeted warmly?

Key Verses

"He said to me, 'My grace is sufficient for you, for my power is made perfect in weakness.'" (2 Corinthians 12:9a, NIV)

May the grace of the Lord Jesus Christ, and the love of God, and the fellowship of the Holy Spirit be with you all." (2 Corinthians 13:14, NIV)

Appendix 2. A Brief Critique of the Prosperity Message

If my interpretation of the promises to givers in 2 Corinthians 9:6-11 sounds something like the prosperity message common in our time, it is because prosperity teaching isn't wholly false. It has helped many people understand God's desire to bless his people and to prosper his people financially – and that's a good thing.

Evelyn Pickering de Morgan (1855-1919), "The Worship of Mammon" (1909).

However, prosperity doctrine often in-cludes distortions that tend to get people out of balance in their faith. This is not the place to do a thorough critique of the prosperity message. But there are three underlying problems that I'd like to comment on:

1. The assertion that poverty is the curse Christ frees us from.
2. The danger of greed being a prima-ry motivation for giving.
3. The related danger of pride when one flaunts one's wealth.

I'll be concise, though there is much to be said on these subjects.

1. Poverty

First, proponents of the prosperity message claim that poverty is a curse. This arises from the statement in Malachi that we discussed in connection with 2 Corinthians 9:6.

"You are under a curse – the whole nation of you – because you are robbing me." (Mala-chi 3:9)

Cursed are those who fail to obey the law (Deuteronomy 27:26). The curses or penalties for disobedience (such as not tithing) include poverty, famine, war, and natural disaster (Deuteronomy 28:15-68). Since Jesus has redeemed us from the curse of the law (Galatians 3:13-14), goes the argument, therefore, we don't need to be poor or suffer financial setbacks – or be sick, for that matter. These, they say, are "the curse" that Christ has freed us from.

Being rich, say prosperity teachers, is evidence of God's blessing; being poor is evidence of a lack of faith, of not entering into all that God has for you. It is God's will for his people to be financially wealthy so they can bless others. Jesus became a wealthy man, they claim, from the gifts of the Magi, rich enough to have an accountant, Judas.

Frankly, this view is entirely too simplistic and relies upon falsehoods. As mentioned in my exposition of 2 Corinthians 8:9, any careful reading of the Gospels reveals that Jesus was not wealthy, but a working carpenter prior to his three-year ministry, during which he was supported by friends (Luke 8:1-3). Judas managed the money given to support Jesus and the Twelve in their mission (John 12:6; 13:29). Jesus' gospel was not centered on prosperity or financial gain. He warned against it. Rather, his focus was on the poor who were receptive to his message. You don't get prosperity doctrine out of Jesus' teaching without serious twisting of the facts and of his words.

Jim Bakker, a prominent televangelist who preached the prosperity doctrine, was sent to prison for accounting fraud in 1989. Later, he wrote in his autobiography how God began to change his mind in prison.

> "The more I studied the Bible ... I had to admit that the prosperity message did not line up with the tenor of Scripture. My heart was crushed to think that I led so many people astray. I was appalled that I could have been so wrong, and I was deeply grateful that God had not struck me dead as a false prophet."[1]

In the passage about Jesus freeing us from the curse of the Law (Galatians 3:13-14), nowhere in the context does it remotely suggest that material wealth and prosperity are the result of Jesus' death on the cross. Rather, we are freed from sin, since Christ fulfilled the penalty of the law for our sins.

Is poverty a curse? Yes, in a sense. It is the result of a condition we experience in this world since God cursed the earth following Adam and Eve sinning.

> "Cursed is the ground because of you;
> through painful toil you will eat of it all the days of your life.
> It will produce thorns and thistles for you,
> and you will eat the plants of the field.
> By the sweat of your brow you will eat your food
> until you return to the ground...." (Genesis 3:17b-19a)

Because of your sin, the Garden of Eden that you enjoyed is closed to you. Life will be hard from now on.

Though Christ died for your sins, the poverty and the struggle of life will not be fully

---

[1] Jim Bakker, *I Was Wrong*. Nashville, Tennessee: Thomas Nelson, 1996), p. 535.

conquered until Christ's coming brings about the new heavens and the new earth in his Kingdom.

Until then, poverty on this earth will continue to result from a variety of causes, including natural disasters, famines, drought, lack of jobs, economic depressions, exploitation by others, imperialism, war, ignorance, lack of a good education, laziness, illness, divorce, death of a spouse or parent, and a host of social problems. It's a long list.

Having said that, I sincerely believe that being a Christian brings with it financial blessings. When you stop wasting money on drinking, drugs, gambling, and racking up credit card debt by purchasing more than you can afford, and begin to take seriously your role of caring for your family to the best of your ability, your economic picture can't help but improve significantly. The Book of Proverbs has much to say about how common sense living helps you prosper. Will every Christian get rich? No. But most will be able to improve their financial situation to some degree. Moreover, there are clear financial promises attached to giving that I discussed in my exposition of 2 Corinthians 9:6-11.

Yes, God will prosper some Christians so they become wealthy. Praise God for that. Wealth is nothing to be ashamed of, but is a responsibility to be used under God.

The promises of scripture are not given to make us fabulously wealthy ourselves, but to enable us to have enough so we can give further to bless others (2 Corinthians 9:11). When we twist the promises to make poverty a sign of lack of faith and riches a sign of God's blessing, however, we seriously misunderstand the intent of God's Word.

2. Greed

The second problem I see in the prosperity message is the danger of giving in order to get more. If giving to God will result in greater blessing to me (as I believe it does), then I'm tempted to give more in order to increase that blessing. It's subtle, but greed can begin to replace godly motivations for giving: love for God, obedience, compassion for the poor, etc.

When I hear some televangelists raise money, they promise that those who give will receive even more in return. Financial gain is used as a primary motivation in their appeal. Even though there may be some truth to their assertions, this appeal to greed corrupts the giving so that what should have been worship is now about us rather than about God.

The New Testament is clear about the dangers of desiring wealth. Here are just three passages that warn us. There are many others.